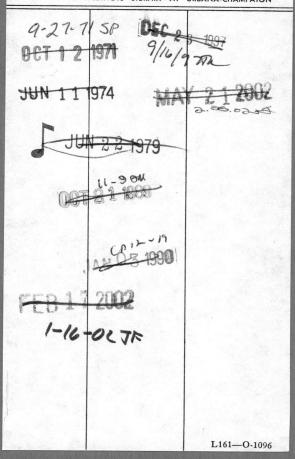

SAMUEL COLERIDGE-TAYLOR

Samuel Coleridge-Taylor

SAMUEL COLERIDGE-TAYLOR ✦ MUSICIAN

His Life and Letters

BY

W. C. BERWICK SAYERS

WITH EIGHT ILLUSTRATIONS

Foreword by Blyden Jackson

AFRO-AM PRESS

DIVISION OF AFRO-AM BOOKS, INC.

CHICAGO

1969

Music

FOREWORD

American Negroes who were born in the earlier years of this century grew up in black communities where the name of Samuel Coleridge-Taylor was as well-known then as now are such names as Martin Luther King, Jr. and Malcolm X.

Of course, the situation was not everywhere the same. Nevertheless a good idea of how it was may be gained from a passing glance at Louisville, in Kentucky, and the shape of some pervasive influences on the Negro mind as they existed there in the span of time between the era of the Republican Roosevelt and the coming of the Great Change under his Democratic cousin. In keeping with its location on the **southern** bank of the Ohio River, the town maintained a dual system of public education — and — metropolis of its region though it was, it was not so populous that Negroes, young and old alike, did not know well all of the Negro schools. The one Negro secondary school, a four-year institution, bore the uncommunicative official title "Central High." But the grade schools, as popular local parlance denominated the several strategically scattered buildings-cum-playgrounds which catered to younger scholars, affected an interest in Negro racial pride. One was named after Lincoln, who, after all, had been both the Great Emancipator and a son of Kentucky. Two others were named, with fine impartiality, after Booker T. Washington and Frederick Douglass. One more, the Dunbar School, celebrated Negro poetry and another, named for Benjamin Banneker, recognized a Negro of a scientific turn of mind. In the densest pocket of the Negro west end, not far from Central High — and no one considered it out of place — stood, as black Louisvillians spoke when they conversed at ease with each other, "S. Coleridge-Taylor."

Negro Louisville was far from alone in its awareness of Samuel Coleridge-Taylor or in the high rank it accorded him in its Pantheon of Negroes worthy of esteem. His face was one that many Negroes, high and low, could easily recognize. Pictures of him, like the pictures of Douglass, Dunbar, Washington, and DuBois, were much in evidence in Negro homes and in establishments that were supported by Negro patronage. His music was performed with frequency, if not with regularity. Prominent American Negroes when abroad, unless they did not go near London, expected to spend some time with him. In **Black Manhattan,** for example, James Weldon Johnson refers to the big night when his brother, J. Rosamond, and their joint partner, Bob Cole, opened as headliners at the fabled Palace Theater in London. "We had," says Johnson, "only two guests that night, Samuel Coleridge-Taylor, the colored English composer, and his wife; they sat with me." And Coleridge-Taylor himself,. before his tragically early death, visited America three times, appearing on each occasion in several cities along the Atlantic seaboard and going also westward — once, indeed, as far as Chicago.

The plain fact is that no truly extensive recovery of the American Negro's Negro past is possible without some recognition of Samuel Coleridge-Taylor. True, Coleridge-Taylor is not legally entitled to such deference. His father was an African from Sierra Leone; his mother, whom he knew much better than her mate, an English girl who spent her entire life in London and its environs. That, too, is where Samuel was born, and where he lived and died, a very English boy with very English ways. But he felt, and sought, ties with the American Negro. There was no reluctance on his part to become a part of a tradition which could be shared by black men and women in both the old world and the new. Indeed, as a matter of constantly expressed emotion, he was proud of his adoption, and the honors paid him, by black America. He loved his music. The titles of his compositions occupy nine full pages of the Appendix to **Samuel Coleridge-Taylor, Musician: His Life and Letters.** He loved his English wife. He loved his two children by her, and he loved the conducting and composing and teaching in which he eagerly spent his busy hours. Life for him was not a thing to be scorned or taken lightly. On his death bed he cried out: "I am too young to die; I am only thirty-seven!" And undoubtedly among the things that must have made him utter his lament was his association with America, particularly with its Negroes, who had shown him such a welcome measure of respect, and to whom we know he had planned to return as often as he could, if he had only continued to live.

To browse, then, in **Samuel Coleridge-Taylor, Musician: His Life and Letters** is to make a valuable excursion into the American Negro's past. As we have already noted, the excursion is admittedly in a very English setting. Even the manner of W. C. Berwick Sayers bespeaks an English scene. How different Samuel Coleridge-Taylor was, for instance, from a Johnny Coltrane need no lengthy demonstration. But, for his day, to the Negro consciousness he was equally important.

Coleridge-Taylor is no mean object of contemplation for himself alone, for the charm and the humanity and the talent of his own person. Beyond that, however, is his importance as a symbol and as an instrument. He stands for the meeting of disparate minds, for the convergence of every twain, and he shows too, how such a convergence may be accomplished. Gentle as he was in manner, refined as was his calling, he was still a fierce apostle of human liberty and a crusader for the rights of man. He was a parable for the black consciousness of his day. He need be no less for the black, or any, consciousness of our present time.

BLYDEN JACKSON
Chapel Hill
1969

THIS WORK IS DEDICATED TO

COLONEL HERBERT A. WALTERS, V.D.

TO WHOM THE WORLD OWES THE DISCOVERY OF COLERIDGE-TAYLOR

AND TO THE

WIFE AND SON AND DAUGHTER

OF THE

MUSICIAN

SAMUEL COLERIDGE-TAYLOR

I

Farewell ! The soft mists of the sunset-sky
   Slowly enfold his fading birch-canoe !
Farewell ! His dark, his desolate forests cry,
   Moved to their vast, their sorrowful depths anew.

II

Fading ! Nay, lifted thro' a heaven of light,
   His proud sails, brightening thro' that crimson flame,
Leaving us lonely on the shores of night,
   Home to Ponemah take his deathless fame.

III

Generous as a child, so wholly free
   From all base pride, that fools forgot his crown,
He adored Beauty, in pure ecstasy,
   And waived the mere rewards of his renown.

IV

The spark that falls from heaven, not oft on earth,
   To human hearts this vital splendour gives ;
His was the simple, true, immortal birth !
   Scholars compose ; but THIS MAN'S MUSIC LIVES !

V

Greater than England or than Earth discerned,
   He never paltered with his art for gain,
When many a vaunted crown to dust is turned,
   This uncrowned king shall take his throne and reign.

VI

Nations unborn shall hear his forests moan ;
  Ages unscanned shall hear his winds lament,
Hear the strange grief that deepened through his own,
  The vast cry of a buried continent.

VII

Through him, his race a moment lifted up
  Forests of hands to Beauty as in prayer ;
Touched through his lips the Sacramental Cup,
  And then sank back—benumbed in our bleak air.

VIII

Through him, through him, a lost world hailed the light !
  The tragedy of that triumph none can tell—
So great, so brief, so quickly snatched from sight ;
  And yet,—O, hail, great comrade, not farewell !

ALFRED NOYES.

PREFACE

GOOD excuse indeed must he have who seeks to draw aside the veil that every man places between the world and the sanctuary of his personal life. Particularly is this the case where such men as Coleridge-Taylor are concerned. When one remembers his disposition, his dislike of public adulation, his unwillingness to discuss his work or himself; when one remembers him in the artistes' room, waving aside with a word of smiling thanks the compliments which were very often showered upon him, and turning the conversation immediately to other and impersonal channels; when one remembers, after his first great work had been received with unqualified enthusiasm by a large audience, that he crept away unnoticed from the hall of the Royal College of Music in order to escape congratulation—the need for excuse seems more pronounced than ever. Fame he could not be said to have despised—he had the natural and right-minded desire of every worker for a sound public appreciation of his work—but its direct expression from the lips of others he always avoided. Wrapped as he was in his art, there was never a man less self-centred.

On the other hand, the ethics of biography are somewhat tangled; and there are those who argue that if great men are given for lights of the world, if they are the product and expression of their time and environment, then is the world the better for a knowledge—so far as it may be gained—of the processes in the growth of such men. Some have gone so far as to declare that a great man is the property not of himself or his family, but of the world which his genius has enriched. But I have a more simple excuse than this in writing the story contained in these pages. A few months after that sunny September afternoon when I stood amongst the crowd of mourners in the beautiful and secluded Bandon Hill Cemetery and watched all that was mortal of the man I had known and loved lowered into his last resting-place, his wife asked me to write the life of her husband. I had known him intimately for many years, as a personal friend admired and valued more than words can express; and the wish of his wife I regarded as a command too sacred to be disregarded. We have talked over the whole of his career since; and many of these pages are largely the result of those conversations. Frail and unworthy I know they are, but their writing has been a labour of love, pursued diligently and with reverence.

The keynote is in major. The whole of his life, from its inauspicious beginning until the end, was one of joyous striving, cheery optimism, ever-growing enthusiasm. Only in its brevity, in the sudden unexpected finale, is there the note of tragedy. Nor is the story wholly devoid of incident. It is nevertheless one presenting real difficulties to the biographer. There are no startling catastrophes, no sudden dramatic moments to give a writer the opportunity of clever description. In many ways it was an even course. Still, the life of such a man, told with candour and without adulation, cannot be wholly devoid of interest. Those who loved him, and they were many, will be the best judges of what I have written. I can only say that I have tried to draw the man as I knew him.

My chapter on his relation to his race has seemed to me desirable on account of a definite attitude of his mind definitely stated. Although certain of his friends whose opinions I value have counselled avoidance of his racial qualities, Coleridge-Taylor never forgot them, never feared to defend them, and his music is so fraught with their characteristics that to ignore them, had it been possible, would in my opinion have been a deliberate misinterpreting of my subject.

Although my work is not a very lengthy one, it has been difficult to write, because Coleridge-Taylor did not keep diaries or correspondence in any systematic manner; and although few men have received greater attention, sympathetic and otherwise, from the critics, the mass of periodical literature which I have thought it my duty to read through carefully has increased my labour without adding materially to my book. To this general remark there are exceptions, as, for example, the articles contributed by Mr. A. T. Johnson to *The Norwood News,* those by "Lancelot" to *The Referee,* and the excellent accounts of the composer published in *The Musical Times.* My principal sources of information, however, have been his masters, friends, and fellow musicians, who have helped me willingly by drawing upon their memories in conversation. Without failing to appreciate the information given me by many others, and without implicating these in any general views expressed in the following chapters, I ought to mention Colonel Herbert A. Walters, his early patron; Sir Charles Villiers Stanford, who taught him composition; Mr. Algernon Ashton, who taught him the pianoforte; his earliest schoolmates, the Messrs. Warner, of Croydon, who have supplied me with the bulk of my information regarding his schooldays; his friends and colleagues, Mr. William J. Read, Mr. Howard B. Humphery, Mr. Julien Henry, Mr. Adolf Schmid, Mr. Henry W. Down, Mrs. Auguste J. Jaeger, Miss E. M. Prosser, Miss F. Montgomery, Miss Kathleen Easmon, and Miss Goldie Baker. I am under a special debt of gratitude to my kindly American correspondents, Mr. Carl Stoeckel, of Norfolk, Connecticut, a most generous patron of Coleridge-Taylor; Mr. A. F. Hilyer, the honorary treasurer of the Samuel Coleridge-Taylor Choral Society at Washington, and Miss Genevieve Lee, of Boston; to the owners of the various letters which are included; to the Editors of *The Norwood News, Great Thoughts,* and *The African Times* for permission to make free use of their columns, and to the Editor of *The Étude* for the use of the article at the end of Chapter XI.; to Mr. Alfred Noyes for permission to include his beautiful elegy; to Mr. J. H. Smither Jackson not only for the list of works in the Appendix, but also for continuous ungrudging assistance; and, if there are others who should have been mentioned here, I trust that they will forgive the omission in accepting a word of general thanks.

W. C. BERWICK SAYERS.

Croydon, 1915.

CONTENTS

CONTENTS

LIST OF ILLUSTRATIONS

SAMUEL COLERIDGE-TAYLOR

CHAPTER I

BIRTH, AND CHILDHOOD

IN the late 'sixties a West African negro lad left the Grammar School at Freetown, in Sierra Leone, and came to England in order to continue his schooling at Taunton College in Somerset, whence eventually he passed the entrance examination of University College, London, as a medical student. Daniel Hughes Taylor had a fair record ere coming to England; he was in person short, and neat almost to dandyness, was remarkably fastidious in his tastes and appearance, and was the possessor of considerable charm of manner which won acceptance for him with his professors and amongst his fellow students. Moreover, he was gifted with an acute, rapidly-working mind, and unusual powers of assimilation. Had these estimable qualities been backed by ordinary tenacity of purpose and a reasonable amount of backbone, he might have achieved distinction in the medical profession. Unfortunately, as the sequel showed, these qualities were not marked in his character. At college his career was in every way satisfactory, was even brilliant; and in less time than is usual he became a member of the Royal College of Surgeons and a licentiate of the Royal College of Physicians soon after he had entered his twenty-second year. Little more can be recalled of the young student, except the joyousness of his disposition, in which he continued the tradition of his race, and his buoyant good nature.

B

'Among the houses he visited was one in which a young girl lived in the capacity of lady's companion. This young girl was Alice Hare, a near connection of the celebrated family of the same name, and her relation to the family in which she lived was not that of servant, but rather that of friend. Daniel Taylor first saw her when she was skipping, a pastime from which her age may be estimated; she was, in fact, in her seventeenth year. The pretty young girl was an object of considerable interest to the student, and interest rapidly became something more tangible. The physical repulsion for the swarthy skin which is commonly thought to be natural to English girls, seems in her case to have been entirely absent. The attraction was mutual, and a secret marriage was arranged.

This boy and girl union was sufficiently improvident, for the means at Taylor's disposal were merely a student's allowance of the most meagre description. They settled with a working-class family of the name of Holman, at 15, Theobald's Road, Red Lion Square, in Holborn, and there on August 15, 1875, a son was born to them. His birth was registered on September 27, when the child received the name of Samuel Coleridge Taylor. This inversion of the name of a great English poet in latter years gave rise to the suspicion that the musician had assumed or invented his forenames. It may be as well, therefore, to say that Coleridge-Taylor himself told me that he was deliberately named after the poet Samuel Taylor Coleridge, and apart from this unimpeachable testimony—he was a man of absolute truth—the Holborn registrar's certificate disposes of any contrary supposition.*

In appearance the baby carried full evidence of his mixed origin. Quite early photographs show him to have been the possessor of a mop of thick, short-curling black

---

* I have used the hyphened form of Coleridge-Taylor's name throughout, as in later years he invariably preferred it, although his earlier works sometimes show it without the hyphen. He was known familiarly as Taylor, as will be seen from some of the letters.

uair, and the prognathous skull characteristic of the negro. His skin was of a dark, golden tint, not black, and the brown hands had white palms in common with all West African children.

Soon after the birth of his son, Taylor secured employment as assistant to a Croydon medical man; and, as an assistant, he was successful. Working under the direction of an esteemed doctor, his patients appreciated and liked the black doctor, attracted, we are told, by his manners and his gaiety. His work in Croydon and the continued straitened means involved the separation of the mother and father, and this, unfortunately, was to be permanent.

When the child was a year old, the Holmans, with whom Mrs. Taylor was living, removed from Theobald's Road to Croydon. The girl-mother accompanied them, and thereafter for many years they supported her, as the unstable side of the physician's character soon became evident, and his contributions to the mother and child ceased entirely. Coleridge-Taylor remembered little or nothing of his father personally, and, as he scarcely enters further into our story, we may add what we know of him here and dismiss him. The success he gained as assistant physician came to a period at the removal of his principal from Croydon. Taylor struggled to continue the practice, but to his astonishment found himself faced with the objection of his colour. As an assistant, he was received, was welcomed. There was, we suppose, the knowledge that he was acting under the instruction of a white man to whom appeal was always possible. As an independent doctor he was mistrusted. The patients fell away rapidly, Taylor's means were soon exhausted, and the young man realised that he was on the verge of ruin. With no further career open to him in England, he turned his face towards West Africa, and disappeared thitherwards suddenly. The rest of his life is the tragically monotonous story of the failure of all that his early life had promised. He held one or two appointments, including that of Acting-

Assistant-Colonial-Surgeon and Acting-Civil-Commandant of British Sherbro, a position he resigned to commence private practice in Sierra Leone. In Sierra Leone he was apparently no more successful in building up a practice than he had been in England. The last letter he wrote to England, addressed to Colonel H. A. Walters, bewails his inability. Later, he was appointed to supervise the health of soldiers invalided from the West Indies, an appointment he held for about four months. The little Coleridge-Taylor was taught by his mother to write regularly to his father; but the latter never contributed a farthing to the maintenance of his family; and the West African papers record his death at Bathurst, Gambia, some years later. Although of sufficient importance to merit paragraphing in this manner, he seems to have been overcome in later life by disappointment and indolence. "There are a few," remarked *The Sierra Leone Weekly News* significantly, "who will remember how he allowed himself to be worried about nothing, and took life in a very easy way."

Meanwhile the Holmans had taken rooms for themselves and the mother and baby at Elys David's lodging-houses, Croydon. They had only three rooms there for both families. Holman was an honest, hardworking man, who was employed as a farrier in the older part of Croydon, and was in receipt of fair but necessarily modest wages. A short time only was spent at Elys David Road; in slightly favouring circumstances the families moved to Waddon Road, Croydon, where again they had to content themselves with three rooms. In the humble conditions accompanying such a home Coleridge-Taylor passed through babyhood to childhood, and there is no doubt whatever that his childhood was as carelessly happy as that of the average child. He was fortunate in his mother, who was a young woman not only devoted to her child, but also possessed of natural ability and artistic inclination. Perhaps the commonest characteristic of children whose lives pass in lowly circumstances is their inability to express themselves correctly in their native tongue, and its lack is only overcome completely in later years by unceasing vigilance. Where the mother possesses sufficient education this is not so as a rule; and I do not hesitate to affirm that the ease and exactness, even beauty, of Coleridge-Taylor's conversation in later years were in their elements to be found in his mother's home. Of his earliest companionships and games I have no record, and he declared after his marriage that he never played the ordinary games of childhood. Perhaps he had forgotten the fact, but Mr. Joseph Beckwith, his music teacher, declares that when he first saw him the boy was on his hands and knees on the pavement playing marbles. We do know that the elder Holman, who had a great affection for the child, bought him, when he was about five years of age, a child's violin. This marvellous toy proved an intense joy to the child, and "Grandfather," as the boy here and always afterwards called Holman, taught him the various elementary positions on the instrument. It was in this way that Coleridge-Taylor received his first music lessons. They were of the most rudimentary type, but through them he learned to play well enough to attract attention. He did not use a large violin until he became a student at the Royal College of Music.

Not many months after he received this present his mother married again, this time with a working-man named Evans. The material conditions of life did not change greatly for the boy, but the marriage gave him and his mother a new home, apart from the Holmans, at Waddon New Road, and here Coleridge-Taylor lived until 1894. One day Mr. Joseph Beckwith, who was then the conductor of the orchestra at the Croydon Theatre and of a local orchestral society, and was in general a prominent figure in the musical life of Croydon, chanced to be giving some lessons at a house in Waddon New Road. Glancing out of the window, he was attracted by the appearance of a "well-dressed, curly-headed, dark little boy" who was playing marbles, "holding a very small-sized violin in one hand and his marbles in the other." The musician was so struck with the appearance of the child that he went out and coaxed him into the house. Here he placed some simple violin duets before him, and was gratified and surprised to find that the little fellow was able to play some of them in perfect time and tune. His interest was thoroughly aroused, and learning the circumstances of the boy's life, he undertook to teach him the violin and music generally. Musical study now began in earnest for Coleridge-Taylor; and for the next seven years he was under the direction of Mr. Beckwith. The teaching was careful and good, and within a year or two he had so far developed the mastery of his little violin that he was able to appear at soirées, "at homes," and similar affairs as a soloist. The pieces selected were modest solos, but they were played with the natural skill of the born musician. His size at this time may be judged from a remark of Mr. Beckwith's: "At one of my pupils' concerts he was so small that I had to stand him on some boxes that he might be seen by the audience above the ferns." Mr. Beckwith's concluding words in describing this part of Coleridge-Taylor's life bring out the characteristic gratitude of the latter, of which we shall have other occasion to speak. "Mr. Coleridge-Taylor has never forgotten me, and we are now very great friends. He taught my son—A. R. C. Beckwith, an ex-scholar of the Royal College of Music—harmony for two years, and he has made him leader of the Handel Society Orchestra, of which Coleridge-Taylor is the conductor."

CHAPTER II

BOYHOOD

PROBABLY the most fortunate circumstance in the career of the boy was his entrance as a pupil at the old British School in Tamworth Road, Croydon. It was one of those now superseded elementary schools which made a fortuitous subsistence from inadequate grants from the Government, the subscriptions of the charitably minded, and a few pence paid weekly by the children. The headmaster, however, the late John Drage, a typical dominie of the elementary schools in many respects, a devoted student of local politics and church affairs, was also a man of considerable perception, who welcomed the shy coloured boy, and was not long in recognising in him the possession of unusual characteristics. This recognition was also accorded him by the boys in the school. It is almost proverbial that men of genius pass through a time of acute misery at school, but no word of this frame of mind has come down to us in connection with Coleridge-Taylor. His golden-coloured skin made him conspicuous among his fellows, it is true, but we hear nothing of the persecutions to which boys of unusual appearance are too often subjected by their fellows. Sometimes a curious schoolmate sitting behind him would run his fingers through the silken mop of hair of the boy in front, but this rarely provoked more than a good-humoured smile from Coleridge-Taylor. They knew that "Coaly," as they affectionately nicknamed him, was an incipient musician, who, even then, seemed marked out for some distinct achievement. He was, as his behaviour just remarked would imply, a lad of even and sunny temper, who, in spite of circumstances, lived on the bright side

7

of things. But he was always a recluse in these days; a lad who walked alone, and who, unlike almost every other boy, had few, if any, definite or intimate friends.

So far as the restricted opportunities of his school permitted, his masters wisely encouraged him in the prosecution of his musical studies, and doubtless something of his later development must be accredited to those who gave him sympathy in those growing, impressionable days. His class-master, a Mr. Forman, was a devoted student of the art himself, and one who created enthusiasm for the weekly singing lessons. At these Coleridge-Taylor would be required to stand upon a table in front of his class and to lead the singing with his violin. A more significant matter was what is probably Coleridge-Taylor's earliest venture into musical composition. At Mr. Forman's request he wrote an original setting for "God Save the Queen." This he did overnight, and next day, standing upon the table, he played it to his class. The boys were required to learn and sing the new tune, and his classmates tell of their amusement at their master's impatience with their surely not surprising difficulties in singing the new air correctly without considerable practice. One can quite imagine that the singing of the words of the National Anthem to any but the tune consecrated by centuries of use must have presented difficulties to the average schoolboy of ten years of age. I have attempted vainly to get his schoolmates who are still living to recall the tune. Possibly, as Coleridge-Taylor was but nine years old, it would not present much of his later creative faculty, but it would have been interesting as the first of his vocal works to be sung by others.

On every special occasion, as when visitors came to the school, Coleridge-Taylor was called forward to exhibit his skill as a violinist. It is pleasant to know that this singling out of the boy from his fellows had no ill-effect upon his character. Undue notice converts children into prigs as a rule, but no such result occurred here. He appreciated being asked to do things other boys were thought less capable of doing; flattery of the sort could not well be ignored. It made, however, not the slightest differe ce in his behaviour to his schoolmates, as the affect   . in which they still hold the memory of the school-boy witnesses; and we are told that after a time he deprecated being placed upon exhibition. However that may be, it is certain that in later life he looked with small enthusiasm upon the public appearance of his own little son, who, like himself, showed in early childhood distinct musical gifts. Nor did he at any time approve of the public enthusiasm for musical child prodigies, holding, as every wise observer must, that it is an interest in the performance of the child rather than of the musician. For the rest, Coleridge-Taylor was, as I have said, of a quick, nervous, shy and lovable, but, as a child, always lonely, temperament. Not only was he seldom seen with a companion; he showed no interest whatever in school games, and no one remembers him as ever having taken part in them. The whole of his leisure seems to have been concentrated upon his music as one predestined and devoted.

So far I have not mentioned the fact that Coleridge-Taylor was more than a violinist. He was a singer possessing a treble voice, which was not large in compass, but remarkably true and sweet. To this fact rather than to his violin must be attributed the happy opportunity which was soon to come to him. As part of his duties as headmaster, Mr. John Drage collected the subscriptions which formed a substantial part of the maintenance of the British School; and amongst those upon whom he was wont to call for this purpose was Mr. (now Colonel) Herbert A. Walters. Mr. Walters was at that time honorary choirmaster of the St. George's Presbyterian Church, Croydon, of which his brother, Mr. Stanley A. Walters, was organist. As is the case with most choir-masters, he was constantly on the watch for boys with useful voices, and was wont to draw a number from the boys attending the British School. In reply to Mr. Walters' habitual question as to whether he had any probable choristers in his classes, Mr. Drage one day mentioned that he had a little coloured boy, who, to use his own phrase, "took to music as a fish to water"; "but," he repeated, "he is a *coloured* boy." Mr. Walters thought his colour of small consequence, and asked that the boy might be sent to his house. Coleridge-Taylor came, and, as was to be expected, was rather shy at the interview, but his bearing and disposition were attractive to the choirmaster. Moreover, Mr. Walters found his voice to be of sweet and pure quality, and certainly that of a desirable recruit for his choir. He therefore entered Coleridge-Taylor's name for the next vacancy. A little later a school competition in singing for prizes offered by Mr. Walters was held, for which twenty singers entered. In this I am told by Mr. F. L. Warner, a classmate and the winner of the second prize, Coleridge-Taylor " won easily." The song the competitor had to present was " Cherry Ripe." Soon after the boy entered St. George's choir.

"Thereafter," Mr. Walters says, "I took him under my especial care, and used to have him up to my house in order to teach him some simple theory of music, voice production, and solo singing. He was a most delightful pupil, quick, eager, and with a wonderful ear. I then practically became his guardian, and looked after him until he came of age. He developed a beautiful voice, and became solo boy of the choir."

In these few words is explained one of the happiest encounters in the history of British music. It is difficult, and perhaps idle, to say what Coleridge-Taylor might or might not have become without the help of Colonel Walters. Genius is dynamic, and cannot be frustrated permanently; but appreciation lags in these competitive days, and a life which in its entirety spanned only thirty-seven years was in any circumstances a short one in which to establish its fame. But when the limitations that poverty imposes, and the consequent lack of every facility for higher education, are remembered, then one must rejoice that so valuable a friend took the little lad in hand; and Coleridge-Taylor's biographer would be failing in one of the most sacred of his duties if he did not recognise the enormous influence of Colonel Walters as the protector and director of the young musician. Certain it is that Coleridge-Taylor himself recognised it gratefully in his most successful days; and for many years after the composer was an acknowledged master of his art he would appeal to the Colonel's opinion in matters requiring such insight and judgment as his choice of libretti, musical effects, and other intimate matters.

The choir days brought the boy his first public appearances. Mr. Walters arranged annually a concert in aid of the funds of St. George's choir. The first of these of which we have any record in connection with Coleridge-Taylor was given on April 16, 1888, at the Public Hall, Croydon, a building which he was greatly to distinguish in after years. At this concert "Master" Coleridge-Taylor played Dancla's *Air Varie* with considerable success to a large audience. Thereafter he constantly appeared at similar concerts, at the earlier ones as violinist, later as vocalist. His second concert seems to have been at Carshalton, where, to quote the local papers, "a violin solo, *Fantasie Pastorale,* by Master Coleridge-Taylor, one of the choir boys, and a pupil of Mr. J. Beckwith, fairly brought down the house. The young violinist responded by repeating the last movement." The last sentence is the earliest example of the practical application of a theory held by Coleridge-Taylor, that an encore is not a request for another example of the artiste's playing or singing, but for a repetition of the work which he has just rendered. It is a debatable point as to whether or not an appreciative audience requires a work a second time, and I fear that the average encore is called for with a view to hearing the artiste give "something else"; but Coleridge-Taylor certainly maintained that artiste and composition were equal partners in producing a public effect, and equally entitled to reappear.

Coleridge-Taylor speedily became the solo singer in the choir, and his voice was soon in request at other churches. Mr. Walters would take the boys on visits to special services at other churches, and to concerts in various parts of London. The most prominent of these was a Presbyterian meeting at Exeter Hall on June 18, 1888, when the singing of Gounod's "There is a Green Hill Far Away " by Coleridge-Taylor, standing small and half-scared upon the platform before a great audience, invoked extraordinary applause. It was upon one of these excursions that an incident occurred which would seem to contradict our description of his relations with other boys. A party of his mischievous fellows set fire to his hair "to see if it would burn." Fortunately the results were not very serious, and the vigorous disapproval of Mr. Walters saved his ward from any repetition of these unpleasant, although probably not malicious attentions.

All this time Coleridge-Taylor continued his violin lessons with Mr. Joseph Beckwith; and when he was twelve years old he is described as being able to play brilliantly. His inborn tendency towards composition, already shown in his version of the National Anthem, developed with his skill as a violinist. Its earliest fruits were a set of hymn tunes, remarkable for their melody and suitability for singing; and in 1890 he produced a *Te Deum,* which he presented to Colonel Walters. "Although," says the recipient of the gift, "the *Te Deum* naturally contains several mistakes in harmony, and has a tendency towards the sentimental—is in fact what musicians call 'sugary'—the setting is admirably conceived, and might, with some little editing, become immensely popular if published."

In 1889 Colonel Walters left St. George's Church in

order to attend the Church of St. Mary Magdalene, at Addiscombe. Here Mr. J. H. Wallis was choirmaster, and Colonel Walters was asked to undertake the training of the boys' voices. As Addiscombe is not far distant from St. George's, it was natural that some of his old boys should beg to accompany their popular choirmaster. Among those who made the request was Coleridge-Taylor, and this was arranged. Thereafter he became soloist in St. Mary's, a position which he held until his voice broke; and until 1900, when his increasing engagements made regular attendance at the church practices and services an impossibility, he sang alto as a member of the choir. At St. Mary's, as at St. George's, he was very popular with the other boys.

CHAPTER III

COLLEGE DAYS AND WORKS

THE interest of Colonel Walters in his boy choristers did not cease when the few brief years for which a treble voice lasts came to an end. As far as it was possible, Colonel Walters endeavoured to secure for each of the boys such a start in the larger business of life as his particular gifts warranted. Several, by the aid of City friends, were placed in offices, or in other cases were apprenticed; and many a man now leading an honourable and useful life recognises gladly the initial help afforded him by his whilom choirmaster. In 1890 the time came when Coleridge-Taylor's case should receive consideration and a career be chosen for him. The circumstances caused the Colonel many moments of perplexity. One difficulty was obvious—the boy was unsuited by temperament for a stool in a City office; and, indeed, his mixed blood did not make him a promising candidate for such a position. Other means were considered. A Croydon firm of pianoforte makers, in perfect good faith and believing they were acting magnanimously, offered to apprentice him to the pianoforte tuning trade. One remembers the remark that to set an intellect of the fine culture of Matthew Arnold's to the work of examining elementary school children was like using a razor to chop firewood; but, if this were so, how much greater would have been the misuse of the instrument had the sensitive and delicately balanced intellect of Coleridge-Taylor been compelled to follow the worthy but uninspiring task of correcting faulty piano strings. Fortunately, however, Colonel Walters gauged the possibilities of the developing mind of the child too accurately to allow it to be employed in this

14

way.   After much thought he determined to offer
Coleridge-Taylor a higher musical education, and secured
both his and his mother's acceptance of this generosity.
In the eyes of friends the experiment was a hazardous
one.   It was true that the boy had possessed a charming
soprano voice, played the violin with more than ordinary
skill and taste, and undoubtedly possessed great musical
perception.   He was, nevertheless, not conspicuous in
that brilliance, too often transient, which has been common
in child prodigies in more recent years; and, indeed, many
a boy who has not achieved any artistic distinction in
mature life has, to superficial sight, shown similar capacity
in his early teens.   Sweeping generalisations were bestowed upon the Colonel in plenty by people possessed
of that itch for prophecy which is one of the commonest
attributes of human nature.   First, the biological reason
was posed.   Children of negro blood or of negro derivation usually showed early and brilliant promise which
always suffered absolute arrest before they reached manhood.   Social reasons followed.   It was removing a citizen
who might conceivably be useful in a humbler capacity
from that state of life to which it had pleased God to
call him; and the want of harmony with the circumstances
of his life which would follow would be intensified by
his mixed blood, and the result would be failure and
resentment.   Moreover, his antecedents and achievements
were not such as would justify the undertaking.   Colonel
Walters considered these things; they were worthy of
consideration for the material reason that a decision in
favour of Coleridge-Taylor's training involved certain
sacrifices on the part of a benefactor who admits that
"I was never a wealthy man"; but he followed his own
counsel.

The careful deliberation with which Colonel Walters
reached his decision to provide Coleridge-Taylor with
a musical education he carried into the choice of the
college at which it was to take place.   He visited and

compared all the colleges of London before he determined that the atmosphere of the Royal College of Music, which, it is said, imparts a certain distinction to students, appealed to him as the most suitable for his protégé. The college was then housed in the old buildings which are now the home of the Royal College of Organists. An interview with the principal, the great scholar and humanist, Sir George Grove, followed. For a moment Grove hesitated over Coleridge-Taylor's colour, rather in relation to its probable effect upon other students than from any distinct objection to it; but the hesitation was brief. "After all," he remarked to Colonel Walters, "his musical gift, and not his colour, is the important thing."

So Coleridge-Taylor was duly enrolled a student at the Royal College of Music, and commenced his study there at the Christmas Term, 1890. The late Mr. Hayles, the then chief clerk of the college, left a record of the boy's earliest days there. His shyness and reticence amounted almost to terror, and more than once Mr. Hayles caught him creeping quietly up the stairs and shrinking into corners to avoid encountering his fellows. A few kindly words and a promise of help in difficulty did much to relieve this painful apprehension. It explains, how-ever, a fact noticeable in these earliest years—Coleridge-Taylor made few friends at first. The violin, naturally, was the principal study to which his time was devoted, and in this subject his professor was Mr. Henry Holmes. As second study he took the pianoforte under Mr. Algernon Ashton; and his days were completed by harmony lessons from Dr. Charles Wood, and attendance at the music class conducted by Sir Walter Parratt. College reports during his first two years show a regular and punctual attendance to the work of his course, and considerable progress, except in the music class, to which, for some reason, he showed a marked antipathy from the first, insomuch that in the course of two years Sir Walter

Coleridge-Taylor's Mother

Parratt's comments descended from "fair" through "irregular" and "very irregular" to "bad." This is the more curious in that the boy's loyalty to the college was almost of a religious character, and the word of his teachers irrefragable law. His progress with the violin was continuous until 1892, when it was abandoned altogether as a college subject. Perhaps the most interesting subject at this time was his second study. Prior to his entrance Coleridge-Taylor had never played a note upon the piano, and not until he was several years older did he possess an instrument of his own. Even his violin, we may remark parenthetically, was a loan from his guardian; he never owned a full-sized one himself. He now devoted great attention to the piano. His teacher describes him as a shy, awkward boy, delicately sensitive to all impressions of music, and regular to assiduity in the pursuit of his studies. At first, however, he showed no more than ordinary aptitude for the study; and Mr. Ashton tells us that it was impossible to predict the brilliant future of his pupil from his earliest impressions of him. However this may be, others speedily recognised the unusual character in the college. Mr. Hayles, shortly after Coleridge-Taylor's first term, warned Mrs. Hayles to watch the career of a young coloured student who had recently entered. " His will be a great name some day," said he. Students are probably in too close proximity in a college to see one another in exact or reasonable perspective; but a few months convinced Coleridge-Taylor's fellows that his gifts were not of the commonplace order.

At first his aptitude for the violin seemed to indicate the future of his genius. He progressed continuously, completely satisfying his teachers, and showing a growing mastery over his instrument. Later he was able to play certain of his own violin works, in particular his *Two Gypsy Movements,* and these demand a technical ability of no mean order. It was, therefore, thought that

c

he would become a reputable violinist. All this time, however, the boy was more or less surreptitiously devoted to composition. We have already mentioned the *Te Deum* written in the year in which his college course began. This he followed up by a series of anthems, which he sent for the approval of Colonel Walters. Amongst them was *In Thee, O Lord,* a careful setting of the words, with broad, suave passages, a promising appreciation of voice values, and a certain amount of tone colour. It is characteristic that this little work already shows, what was conspicuous in all Coleridge-Taylor's succeeding writing, that he gave considerable attention to the right accentuation of the words, and would sacrifice his melody to correct interpretation rather than torture the words to fit a preconceived melody, as less conscientious composers have sometimes done.

With this anthem he first reached the dignity of publication through Messrs. Novello and Co., who issued it in 1891. A reading of these anthems convinced Colonel Walters that they were worthy of attention at the college. He brought them to the notice of Sir George Grove, asking if Coleridge-Taylor were to be encouraged in his composition. A conference resulted, and a few days later Grove wrote as follows:

KENSINGTON GORE,
LONDON, S.W.

October 4, 1892.

DEAR MR. WALTERS,—I have arranged with Dr. Stanford to take Taylor with composition as his first study. Both Dr. Gladstone and Dr. Stanford were much pleased with the anthems, which I think show a great deal of feeling and aptness for that style of work. I have talked the matter over with Mr. Holmes—and he thinks it will be really best for him to drop the violin and take piano for second study, and to work rather harder at it than he does at present. I do not myself see what the violin is to lead to, whereas the piano is all important for a composer.

I enclose the new time sheet in which I hope your wishes

have been met. You will see that for this term I have excused him the music class.—Yours very truly,

G. GROVE

(*Director*).

With the Michaelmas Term in 1892, Coleridge-Taylor came under the beneficent influence of Dr. (now Sir) Charles Villiers Stanford. Rarely has a student shown greater devotion to a master; privately, and as a teacher, Coleridge-Taylor's admiration was only on the saner side of idolatry. Stanford's fine musicianship, great learning, and rigid practicality were themes of real meaning to him as long as he lived. "If," said he, "Stanford's activities had not been displayed over so many and various fields, he would have been as great as Beethoven." Higher praise no man has received from a pupil. At this time Coleridge-Taylor was eighteen years of age. In appearance he was undersized, and very thin, but did not give the impression of delicate health; had rather long arms, and a disproportionately large head, covered with thick, short, curly, silken hair. His forehead was without lines, broad, sloping backwards markedly, the brows protruding over the eyes somewhat; the eyes were large, of a light brown, and intensely bright and vivacious; the nostrils were broad, and assisted his hair in revealing his African origin, as did the lips, which were broader than those of the Caucasian. On the whole, it was a face showing intellect, intensity, seriousness, but essentially a good-natured face.

It was about this time that he made the acquaintance of W. Y. Hurlstone, who was a fellow pupil under Sir Charles Stanford. Their friendship was founded on mutual good fellowship and appreciation, and ended only with the all too early death of Hurlstone. During their studentship they were often together at rehearsals and concerts, and Coleridge-Taylor remembered their mutual *obiter dicta* upon music as a real influence in his life.

Composition now being open to him legitimately,

Coleridge-Taylor applied himself to it with the remarkable assiduity which characterised all his work at the college. His fertility was unusual, his quickness of work extraordinary. Moreover, he had the prodigality of genius; he would destroy unhesitatingly any of his writings which did not meet with the complete approval of his professor. On one occasion a fellow student remonstrated, with the remark that So-and-so (naming a well-known composer) preserved in pigeon-holes all his musical writing, however trivial and unsatisfactory, to be recovered and used when better inspiration flagged. Coleridge-Taylor replied laughingly that the best place for unsatisfactory compositions was the fire, and acted upon his belief. "In those early years," said Mr. W. J. Read, his friend and fellow student, "he must have destroyed much and very beautiful music."

Already, however, Coleridge-Taylor had set his face towards the best in his art, and he had the unshakable faith of the genius in his own fertility. In 1892 four more anthems, *O ye that Love the Lord, The Lord is My Strength, Lift up Your Heads,* and *Break Forth into Joy,* the last-named of which is dedicated "to Herbert A. Walters, Esq., with respect and affection, by his former pupil," were published by Messrs. Novello and Co. These showed bold harmonies and firm phrasing, and confirmed the impression of power already given.

A term with Sir Charles Stanford, in which the professor proved a critic of most wholesome restraining power, shearing and pruning the redundancies of his pupil, sufficed to bring him into prominence. In March, 1893, he entered for one of the nine open scholarships at the college, and was successful as a composition student. "Now you are a scholar," wrote Sir George Grove, "I shall look for a very great advance (not necessarily *show*). You are now *before the world.*" In turning over the college reports, the biographer cannot help being impressed by the felicity of Grove's notes in relation to their purpose. He never hesitated to praise where praise was deserved, and whenever he blamed, the admonition was tempered by some remark calculated to fire the student with enthusiasm to overcome the weakness indicated. So far as Coleridge-Taylor was concerned, his first remark consisted of the somewhat ambiguous but doubtless veracious words, "a beginning"; in the next term he commends him in both first and second studies; for his second year he expresses the hope that Coleridge-Taylor "will be much higher this day twelve months"; but at the end of the Christmas Term he is emphatically asking, "Why this irregularity at the music class? Please let me never have to complain again"; but he softens the rebuke with, "The rest is very gratifying." The next two reports are good, except that "your fingering on the piano seems to want your attention." Thereafter the successive reports are congratulatory notes, concluding in 1894, shortly before the writer's death, with "Excellent boy! I am more than pleased with your hard work and enthusiasm."

All through his college career, Coleridge-Taylor showed the industry commended in this last note. He held throughout life strong opinions as to the value and reality of inspiration, as all great creators have done, but he was without illusions as to the probability of success except through intensity and purpose in work. He was always occupied, always engrossed, and seemed to have no time for the social amenities which usually form part of student days. His avoidance of company was due partly to the shyness I have already emphasised, a shyness based upon his natural temperament, and accentuated by his knowledge of his colour and perhaps of his humble home circumstances. There is no element of the snobbish in this last feeling; a social life at a college often involves home intercourse between its participants; and in the early years Coleridge-Taylor must have regarded this as difficult. He would enter the students' room where the fellows were grouped around the fire, would put down his books without remark, and leave at once. If detained by one of the others, he would answer smilingly and without hesitation, but he left upon the minds of his fellow students the impression that life was a serious and a pressing business.

Sir Charles Stanford has favoured me with some remarks upon his pupil at that period. As a student he was exemplary in his industry, and his disposition was naturally cheerful, and he showed unaffected gratitude for all that was done for him. He had many and brilliant ideas, but he seemed to lack the power of sustaining them, with the result that there was much repetition in his work. His principal defect was largely racial, and was most apparent in his timidity, which was accompanied by want of independence, and made self-criticism difficult; so much so that it seemed best for him to work under direction. He had a keen sense of the dramatic, which was a distinct tribute to his negro origin. The most remarkable matter was that Coleridge-Taylor showed to no disadvantage in the matter of general culture. His education had been that of an elementary school, but he was a diligent reader, and so quick was his wit, so great his powers of assimilation, so retentive his memory, that he was soon able to hold his own with students far more expensively educated. In later life, too, he conveyed the impression of possessing a well-furnished, highly trained mind, able to range with ease over all ordinary topics and over many extraordinary ones.

It was in 1892 that Coleridge-Taylor first appeared at one of the college concerts as a pianist, taking for his subject the first number of Grieg's Opus 18. His reception was enthusiastic, and has been ascribed to the fact that he was already distinctive as a composer rather than to the intrinsic merit of his playing. This, indeed, may have accounted for his triple recall on this particular occasion; but the incident illustrates Mr. Ashton's statement that by careful industry he achieved some skill with the instrument; that he was somewhat slow, but was sure; and later, as an accompanist he had few superiors. His piano playing was a source of wit to Coleridge-Taylor as long as he lived. Sir Hubert Parry has said of him that he was naturally unadapted to the instrument on account of the unsuitable shape of his hands. Later, too, Coleridge-Taylor was wont to joke at himself as an accompanist. Writing to Mr. W. J. Read six weeks before his death, he says of the piano part of his *Violin Concerto*, " Of course I can't play a note of it." Again, we have his own statement that he was no pianist, and at his concert in 1910 he laughingly objected to the services of Miss Myrtle Meggy, the distinguished young Australian pianist, who volunteered to "turn over" for him, because " she will make faces at my fingering." Putting these opinions together, it would seem that Coleridge-Taylor himself was largely responsible for the small estimation in which his pianoforte playing was held. Mr. William J. Read's reminiscences are worth setting against them. He says :

"As a young impressionable student I came to the Royal College in 1894, and it was when I went up to Mr. Algernon Ashton's room for my first piano lesson that I first saw Coleridge-Taylor. He was then seated at the piano playing Schumann's *Carnival*. The piece is not a concert piece such as is played by the great executants, but it is of quite average difficulty, and demands some skill on the part of the player. Coleridge-Taylor played it in an engrossed manner, with a complete absence of self-consciousness. I remember vividly the slender figure and the large dark head of the young musician as he sat there, playing with accuracy and mastery, and with a serious intensity which then seemed to me remarkable. What particularly impressed me was the absence of any of the bodily contortions or excitement which so often mark fine players. He held his body quite still, and, throughout, his playing, even in the more florid passages, which he played easily, seemed to be mental rather than merely emotional.   Emotion, however, was there undoubtedly, and he brought a complete *understanding* to bear upon the matter before him.   In fact, I remember distinctly thinking that it was the manner in which a great composer would play, directing one's attention to the beauty of the tones he was producing, and distracting it entirely from himself.   Mr. Ashton seemed to feel somewhat the same, for we exchanged glances of surprised appreciation. Since that day I have played many times with Coleridge-Taylor, and always with the conviction that he was a perfect accompanist, with unusual powers of interpretation.   The distinction between this and virtuoso piano playing is obvious.   Coleridge-Taylor always played as a composer who understood the mental processes of the musician he was interpreting; and when great men such as Sir Hubert Parry say Coleridge-Taylor was not a pianist, the opinion is relative; they probably have in mind the marvellous technique of a Paderewski or a Dohnanyi, and naturally by comparison Coleridge-Taylor was not a great pianist; but it is well to bear in mind the relativity of ideas.'' .

The rapidity with which he developed as a composer is well illustrated by the principal event of his twentieth year.   On October 9, 1893, he obtained permission of the principal of the Royal College to make his first independent public appearance.   This took the form of a concert of chamber music at the Small Public Hall, Croydon. The programme is sufficiently interesting to be reproduced :

Clarinet Quintet in A	.	.	.	.	.	.	MOZART

Song   .   .   .   " Solitude "   .   S. COLERIDGE-TAYLOR
" To sit on rocks, to muse o'er flood and fell, etc."
MISS ETHEL WINN

Violin Solo   .   .   " Notturno " .   .   .   HANS SITT

Clarinet Sonata in F minor . . S. COLERIDGE-TAYLOR
  1. Allegro moderato. 2. Lento alla marcia. 3. Allegro giga.

Songs   *a.* " The Broken Oar " . S. COLERIDGE-TAYLOR
       b. " The Arrow and the Song "
       MISS ETHEL WINN

Pianoforte Quintet in G minor . . . S. COLERIDGE-TAYLOR
  1. Allegro ma non troppo.   3. Scherzo allegro molto.
  2. Larghetto.   4. Allegro con furia.

The executants were fellow pupils from the Royal College : violins, Miss Jessie Grimson and Mr. William Boxall; viola, Mr. C. L. Jacoby; violoncello, Miss Alice Elieson; and the clarinet, Mr. Charles Draper. Miss Ethel Winn was the vocalist, and Coleridge-Taylor himself took the pianoforte.

Rarely, we suppose, has a lad of nineteen come before the public with a more daring programme. Not only were four out of the six items of his own composition, and two of them works of no inconsiderable character, but the inclusion of one of the two other items was in the nature of an ingenuous challenge to comparison with his own works. The programme was varied on the evening by the substitution of the Minuet and Trio from another of his works, a *Sonata in C minor,* for the first and last movements of his *Clarinet Sonata.* The records preserved of the concert in the Croydon newspapers are eulogistic. Says the reporter : "Mr. Coleridge-Taylor astonished the audience (some of whom had not the privilege of knowing his abilities since a mere child) by his beautiful manipulation of the pianoforte. The audience seemed already gratified with Mr. Taylor's ability, but were astonished when his *Pianoforte Quintet in G minor* was presented," and much else which probably is not to be taken seriously as musical criticism, but conveys the impression received by the audience that they were listening to the work of an original and inspired creator.

On July 5, 1895, Coleridge-Taylor figured upon the programme of the students' concert as a composer, with a

Nonet, the initial key of which was F minor. This composition, which remains unpublished, is scored for pianoforte, violin, viola, violoncello, double bass, clarinet, horn and bassoon, a combination, with the exception of the pianoforte, very similar to that employed by Beethoven in his *Septuor in E flat.* The movements were four in number, in F minor and major, with an *Andante in A flat.* It attracted the audience from the first bar. Sir George Grove was sitting beside Colonel Walters in the audience, and expressed continuous appreciation for the work as it proceeded, with noddings and little *sotto voce* ejaculations such as "Good!" and "This is very promising," until the Andante came. This appeared to be too florid and too quick. Grove turned to Colonel Walters, saying, "He will never write a good slow movement until he has been in love. No one can who has not been in love." At the conclusion of the piece the applause was very great, and there were demands for the composer. He, however, was not forthcoming, and, the applause continuing, Sir George himself went in search of Coleridge-Taylor. He reappeared shortly, bringing the student with him, and more or less compelling him to come forward to bow his acknowledgments. Although he had found courage to face an audience in his own town, at college so great had been his dread of this public ordeal, that he had fled upstairs and had hidden himself in the organ room, whence Grove dragged him forth.

The defect in Coleridge-Taylor's experiences remarked by Sir George Grove he shortly afterwards remedied by conceiving a romantic and exalted passion for one of his fellow students. The details are shadowy to-day; and as the love-affair was an extremely youthful, evanescent business, it is perhaps undesirable to do more than refer to it.

In general the colour-line was not a source of discomfort to the young composer. He was acutely sensitive concerning it in his teens, and one of the rare occasions when he encountered it gave Stanford the opportunity of a kindly word which Coleridge-Taylor remembered with gratitude until his death. A fellow student made some disparaging remark to the lad, in which the contemptuous epithet "nigger" figured. The professor, unknown to them, happened to be in the next room, and overheard the speech. Later he called Coleridge-Taylor to him, and begged him to ignore such vulgarisms, adding that the coloured student's talents were far beyond even the aspirations of his critic. No doubt Sir Charles Stanford would regard a reference to such services as this as an over-emphasis of the trivial; but the writer has been able to realise its effect on Coleridge-Taylor, and knows that the veneration in which he held his professor was due not only to his great powers, but also to such human sympathies.

The performance of the *Nonet* focused the eyes of the musical critics upon the composer, with the natural result that he became keenly interested in current musical criticism. He travelled to and from West Croydon daily, and his train reading was invariably *The Musical Times,* or some other musical journal. So far as he was personally concerned, he was, until about his twenty-fifth year, extremely sensitive to criticism, weighing and perhaps worrying over any disparagement of his work. In after-life a saner attitude prevailed, and the average critical estimate merely amused him. Although he read and thought much in other directions, his devotion to music was the single purpose of his life; it formed the subject of his thoughts and his conversations, and much of the frugal leisure he allowed himself during his college days was spent at the London concerts. A couple of years at college redeemed him from his shy taciturnity somewhat, and he went about occasionally in company with Hurl-stone. He was scarcely more than seventeen when he first became possessed of a complete devotion to the works of Antonin Dvořák, a devotion which if anything increased with the years. It was at one of the concerts I have mentioned that Coleridge-Taylor and Hurlstone conceived the aphorism that "Dvořák was sometimes commonplace but never dull, while Brahms was sometimes dull but never commonplace." In this criticism, which has the dangerous nature of all generalisations, the two young composers were entirely agreed. Some critics have regarded this admiration of Dvořák as an unwholesome influence in Coleridge-Taylor's life, accentuating and aggravating certain natural faults they have discovered in his work. Be that as it may, he took infinite pleasure not only in the study of the Bohemian composer, but found constant amusement in the anecdotes of his life, never allowing even the most crude of them to detract from his reverence for the composer as distinct from the man.

Of the interior life of Coleridge-Taylor our records at this time are clear-cut, but too scanty for much comment. His home at Waddon Road was humble, but one where real affection existed. Coleridge-Taylor was devoted to his mother, and stories exist of his coming into the kitchen, where she was occupied with domestic duties, to sing over to her this or that tune which he had written. His talents were gradually becoming known in Croydon and brought him friends, but they may be said to have been found for him by Colonel Walters and others, rather than to have been of his own seeking. He kept within his home circle tenaciously. "He was always cheerful and affectionate," his mother says, "and until his marriage I was his only companion." He was addicted to long, solitary walks, and read enormously, mostly out of doors. The quality of the reading may be gathered from the songs he set; the English poets were his constant companions at this time, and his knowledge of them was a discerning, if somewhat original, one. As is usual with all young people for whom poetry has any attraction at all, he fell early under the influence of Longfellow, who is the acknowledged poet of youth, and the introduction to all other poets. Two of his poems he had already set for his first public concert, and he was to set many more.

One result of his reading was an acquaintance with Lockhart's *Spanish Ballads,* and he had the courage to set " Zara's Ear-rings." The words have one characteristic which always appealed strongly to Coleridge-Taylor, the queer-sounding names, Musa and Albuharez; otherwise the clumsy lyric is a curious choice :

"My ear-rings ! My ear-rings ! They've dropped into the well,
And what to say to Musa, I cannot, cannot tell."
'Twas thus, Granada's fountain by, spoke Albuharez's
    daughter :
"The well is deep, far down they be, beneath the cold blue
    water.
To me did Musa give them, when he spake his sad farewell,
And what to say when he comes back, alas ! I cannot tell."

It has a certain passionate value, but hardly appeals to one as suitable for musical treatment. Those who hold that the creative genius depends upon externals only for suggestions which precede inspirations, if they are not creating a confusion of terms, may point to this song as a justification; but Coleridge-Taylor held and acted upon the principle that the business of the song writer was to illuminate and interpret his libretto. In this case, the song was one of the finest of his earlier works. It is written for soprano and orchestra, and was first performed at the college concert on February 7, 1895, the voice part being sung by Miss Clementine M. Pierpoint. It is unconventional and skilful in phrasing, and for the first time exhibited the quality of orchestral colouring which was to become the distinctive feature of his work.

This same year Coleridge-Taylor added to his growing list of academic triumphs the winning of the Lesley Alexander prize for composition, a success which he was to repeat in the following year. Almost every college concert hereafter gave a hearing to a composition from his pen, and to each the public press gave encouraging commendation. No doubt the criticism of students' concerts is written according to other standards than those by which the work of the finished musician is judged; but it gives some indication of impressions made, and on other grounds there is much to be said for it. It is a matter for debate whether or not the greatest need of the student is unlimited encouragement. Criticism appropriate to more mature years is usually harmful, and in the case of the creative student, nearly always destructive in its results. Usually, too, the young student is sufficiently quick-witted to realise that a certain indulgence prompts kindly criticism, and estimates it accordingly; but the student who has sufficient ardour to withstand the east wind of adverse criticism is rarer than is sometimes supposed. The concert on March 13 heard his *Fantasiestücke*, a work in five movements, consisting of a *Prelude in E minor*, a *Serenade in G*, a *Humoureske in A minor*, a *Minuet in G*, and a *Dance in G*, written for a string quartet. The *Serenade* and the *Dance* are perhaps the best movements, as they were certainly the most successful with the audience at their first rendering. Originality and individuality were, however, shown in every movement, and comments in particular were made upon the "oriental style and colouring of the work."

At this concert was played Brahms's *Quintet for Clarinet and Strings*, Opus 115, a work which led up to Coleridge-Taylor's next composition. During the rehearsal of this work an eminent musician at the college declared that no modern composer could write for the combination of instruments employed by Brahms without showing his influence. The saw that "fools rush in where angels fear to tread" might well be interpreted into "youth fails to recognise its supposed limitations." To a young composer of unlimited ambition and untried capacity the statement would naturally create the desire for experiment. For the next few weeks Coleridge-Taylor became engrossed in the matter, and the result was his own *Quintet for Clarinet and Strings*. If the fact that another man has used a similar combination of instruments, and so challenged its use by succeeding composers, is in itself an inspiration—and some justly hold that to an extent this is so—then Coleridge-Taylor's *Quintet* is indebted to Brahms. Otherwise a comparative reading of the score fails to reveal the slightest trace of Brahms from beginning to end—as the eminent musician gladly admitted. It was his own, and here, as ever, Coleridge-Taylor was as unique in music as Swinburne was in poetry. The new work was produced on July 11, 1895, and was afterwards published as Opus 10.

It is curious to note that the critics, while commending the various movements as being "as original as they are skilful in workmanship," and expatiating justly upon the beauty of the slow romance movement, found an accidental quotation from *A Midsummer Night's Dream* in the first movement. An elementary acquaintance with the expressive arts has brought poets, musicians and painters alike into contact with the problem of likeness in the expression of like ideas. Generally it may be assumed that this is the outcome of subconscious memory; and I remember a story which Coleridge-Taylor told of his awaking early one morning inspired by a most beautiful melody. He committed it to paper and returned to bed, and it was only in the consciousness of the full day that he discovered his beautiful melody to be an exact reproduction of a melody by Sullivan. Original as he was indisputably, the tenacious character of his memory for music was apt to become inconvenient, insomuch that later in life he avoided concerts as much as was possible to escape the tendency to reproduce whole phrases without recognising them, which he declared always affected him. While this is true, the fact still remains that phrases in his works have occasionally been reminiscent of composers he had never heard. For example, on hearing a work of

Weber's for the first time, he was astounded to discover that several bars in it were identical with an expression in his Overture to *Hiawatha*.

A similar but converse circumstance was his discovery that in the *Welsh Rhapsody* Edward German had a phrase which had an earlier exact replica also in his *Hiawatha* Overture. When his wife confirmed this fact, Coleridge-Taylor vigorously denied any idea of plagiarism. "It just happens so," he remarked. Any such parallel opens one of the most interesting, as it is one of the most elusive, questions in the psychology of art. It will be remembered that Tennyson suffered annoyance by being told that he had imitated a poem of Shelley's which he did not remember that he had read, and men such as the late J. Churton Collins—critics of assured ability—have spent much study in proving similarities of expression between Shakespeare and the Bible, Tennyson and the classical writers, and so on without limit. Influence there must be in all men's work, for a self-contained generation untouched by the heritage of the race is unthinkable, and an academic training in the humanities and the arts necessarily brings about a more or less complete impact between the mind of the present and the past. So much so, indeed, that people who long for originality in expression deprecate any form of college training as having a tendency to crib, cabin and confine the expanding individuality of the young genius within moulds which are traditional and subversive of personal expression. Prolonged too far and too logically, academic training may have some such results; but the general charge is sufficiently rebutted by the simple fact that the most isolated individualist cannot escape the past, is never unique. Superb powers always manifest themselves in the long run, and lesser capabilities are none the worse for following in some degree the highways of art which the experience of the world has found to be good. There has never been an age in the history of the arts when this philosophy seemed so necessary as

Aged 13 years

Aged 3 years

Aged 16 years

Early Portraits of Coleridge-Taylor

now; from journalism to the highest form of the expressive arts the little minds of the age are proving their littleness by trying to throw off what they conceive to be the shackles of the ages, and are making a great many noisy discordances in the name of originality. Memory, it would seem, plays a part in the expression of all men, and is not necessarily plagiarism. Anything that a man has heard or read which he has modulated into his own spiritual life, and which he reproduces and embellishes spontaneously, he has some right to regard as his own; and any study, however scanty, of the history of the arts proves that this doctrine has been held, tacitly perhaps, but invariably, by all great creators. Accepting this truth, it would still appear, where it can be proved that a writer reproduces phrases he cannot possibly have heard, that some more subtle agency than ordinary memory is at work. There may be a racial memory which has no relation to the personal, physical experience of the writer.

I have wandered somewhat from the *Quintet* in discussing this point of apparent copying, because I believe it is too often overlooked that other reasons may be urged for likeness than mere imitation. I do not in any way dispute the assertion that in this particular first movement simple memory may have produced the likeness upon which the critic comments.

So far only the musical journals had commented much upon Coleridge-Taylor's work. With the *Quintet* the wider public press began to take cognisance of the young composer. *The Standard* gave the students' concert at which it was produced the first place under "Yesterday's Concerts," and occupied itself with an analysis of the work in a manner flattering to its writer. *The Daily Telegraph* described it as "a work of very great promise, and something more. The composer's possession of a vivid and poetic imagination has before now been demonstrated, but not as strikingly as in this new work, which, moreover, shows the plainest traces of thorough musical

D

training and the command of his resources." The notice goes on to say that, in his fondness of unusual rhythms, Coleridge-Taylor showed affinity with Dvořák. Dr. Stanford, with whom, of course, the work had been written as a college exercise, found it interesting enough to put it in his portmanteau when about to pay a visit to Berlin shortly afterwards. Here he brought it to the notice of Joachim at the latter's house, and the veteran composer and quartet leader was attracted by the young student's work sufficiently to rehearse it with his quartet in his dining-room. It was recognised as the work of a young writer, but the members of the quartet, used as they were to playing only the greatest music, found the work thoroughly interesting and promising. This eminent opinion Coleridge-Taylor valued greatly.

From some points of view it is unfortunate that so few personal records remain of this period of Coleridge-Taylor's life. In every academic career there are incidents which in retrospect give atmosphere to a man's life. Such must have occurred to Coleridge-Taylor; but he did not keep a diary, and his college mates are unable to recall anything very specific, beyond his extraordinary strenuousness and rapidity. His capacity for work was enormous, his reluctance to waste time, for a student, phenomenal. My account of his compositions to this point is sufficient evidence of these facts in itself, but I am able to mention only such as were considered by the critical judgment of the professor to merit public performance. Songs, quartets, instrumental pieces of various kinds were written all through this period. Some survive, but the majority succumbed to the composer's rigid self-judgment. We get a very occasional story from these days, not without a rough kind of humour. For instance, a new professor had been appointed who was unknown to the students, and Coleridge-Taylor and a fellow student were members of a class which he was to conduct. The two lads went to the room and found no one there but an insignificant spectacled young fellow, apparently a mere student, who was seated engrossed in a book. A wait ensued.

"I wonder when that fool of a —— is coming up!" exclaimed Coleridge-Taylor's companion impatiently.

The young "student" closed his book and rose quietly.

"I am Dr. ——," said he.

Such a story is in itself a trifle, but the fact that Coleridge-Taylor found it intensely amusing illustrates the great simplicity of his character. He saw humour in everything, and a dramatic episode even of this minor sort made strong appeal to him. It shows a child-like and not necessarily childish simplicity of mind. At the same time, it must be said that the story as written lacks the vocal and facial gestures which were vital to some of Coleridge-Taylor's stories, and which made them exquisitely humorous to his listeners.

In 1894 the Evans family, and with them Coleridge-Taylor, left Waddon Road and took a house in Holmesdale Road, South Norwood. I am indebted to Mr. John Warner for an account of his home circumstances which prevailed for the two years during which they remained there. "I used to visit the house," writes Mr. Warner, "as a playmate of Coleridge's half-brother, and was then a child of about nine years of age. The home was a poor one, in which there was little in excess of the common necessaries of life. Coleridge's step-father was referred to by his own son as an 'oily man,' and, as far as I can recollect, was employed in an oil factory of some sort, or in some employment which produced oil-saturated garments. In any case, he seemed to earn only moderate wages, and certainly not an income that would warrant his keeping a step-son at the Royal College of Music. What his relations with Coleridge-Taylor were I cannot say, but Mrs. Evans was wont to tell her neighbours that the expenses connected with him kept the family very poor. I understand that Colonel Walters met most of the expenses of his training, but it certainly seemed that some sacrifices were required of his family. Certainly, too, they regarded him as an entirely superior being. As an instance, Mr. Evans used whimsically to refer to him as ' My Lord.' The poorly-furnished drawing-room was sacred to his use, and in it stood a piano, a veritable ' box of strings,' which had some long time before seen better days, and by its side his violin stand. I remember being told on several occasions, ' We never hear Coleridge play the piano; he always plays the violin.' I saw Coleridge-Taylor very frequently, and he then presented much the same appearance as in later years; facially, he scarcely changed to the day of his death, but perhaps his figure matured somewhat, though very slightly. He was invariably dressed in black, and wore a black broad-rimmed felt hat, after the style of those worn by clergymen, with a hat-guard. He walked with a quick, nervous, swinging step, always carried a walking-stick, and was always in a hurry. He spoke very rapidly, and with the air of one accustomed to authority and to the giving of orders. In personal appearance he was very neat, but his dress gave one the impression of a struggle against poverty; and I remember that a large circular patch on his trousers particularly attracted my attention as a youngster. Scrupulously polite, even to such a child as I was then, he always raised his hat, and with a good-natured smile wished me ' good-day ' whenever I encountered him in the street.''

At the first college concert in 1896 two violin pieces from Coleridge-Taylor's pen figure on the programme. These were entitled respectively, *Dance in F sharp* and *Lament in A*. The former is undoubtedly brilliant, and the latter has the force and piteousness required by the title, and both are as strikingly original in theme and treatment as any works which had yet come from the student's pen. The principal work of 1896, however, was a Symphony. The first movements of this ambitious work were of such character as to justify Stanford in holding out the hope that he would recommend it for public performance by the Manchester Symphony Orchestra, conducted by Richter. Unfortunately the last movement, which some others thought quite good, failed to satisfy the high standard set by Sir Charles, and after a first rehearsal of it by the college orchestral class, it was condemned, and Coleridge-Taylor was advised to try again. He composed, scored, and copied a new final movement within a week, a remarkable physical performance apart from the artistic merits of the work. This was tried and in turn rejected. Nothing daunted, Coleridge-Taylor set to work again, and within a week more produced and scored an entirely new movement, but still without satisfying his professor. He tried yet a third time, completing his work in a similar period. The verdict was the same as upon the previous attempts; it was good in its way, but by comparison inadequate. This time the young composer seems to have lost courage. Immediately after the trial he found his way to the organ room, where Mr. W. J. Read happened to be.

" Look at this," remarked Coleridge-Taylor, "Stanford says it is no good," and without hesitation he tore the score across and flung it into the fireplace.

"But you are not going to destroy your work in that fashion?" asked Read in astonishment.

" Certainly," he replied with a laugh of dismissal, and turned from the room.

Mr. Read recovered the rejected manuscript from the fireplace, and preserved it for many years. It has disappeared now, and the Symphony of which it formed part was finished later and differently again. Years after Coleridge-Taylor recalled the theme of the version Mr. Read had fished out of the grate, and reproduced it in the modified form of a *Melody in F* for the organ. The earlier movements were, indeed, performed later by the Richter orchestra, but were not regarded favourably by its famous conductor. Although it is highly improbable that a lad of twenty should write a symphony—a work requiring sustained inspiration of the highest order—worthy to be compared with those of the masters, it was the general opinion that the music even of the rejected parts was of real quality; and its fate is worth recording merely as evidence of the young composer's fertility and manual industry. To have produced and scored three symphonic movements in three successive weeks is a fact worthy of the attention of those who imagine that the composer reached fame by a few fortunate leaps. His rapidity in work was extraordinary. In reading he resembled Macaulay in the quickness with which he took in the pages of books, reading them as fast almost as he could turn them over; nor was it perfunctory skipping. His memory could reproduce readily the substance of books read in this manner. Similarly, in writing music, he put his ideas on paper almost as quickly as they were conceived. His manuscript was delicate in the extreme, the fine pinhead notes being almost microscopic, but when once the sight is accustomed to them they are quite clear and easy to read. This characteristic was mental; in every movement Coleridge-Taylor was nervously quick, in thinking, in walking, in gestures; insomuch that his manner was sometimes liable to misinterpretation. On one occasion this was made manifest. He was directed to conduct an orchestral class of which the leader was a charming young lady rather aware of her charms, and expectant of attention in consequence of them. Without regarding her in any particular manner, Coleridge-Taylor went to the conductor's desk, rapped the players to attention, and commenced the rehearsal quite unaware that he had severely piqued the young lady in question. She complained to Dr. Stanford that Coleridge-Taylor had "been very rude to her." Without advising Coleridge-Taylor of the fact, Dr. Stanford asked all the members of the class to write to him individually on the matter, and was gratified to receive independently the assurance from each of surprise at the charge, and that the conductor had been perfectly courteous.

Allowing for the evidence of the class, it is still possible that Coleridge-Taylor—who never at any time did an unkind action or said an unkind thing—was a little brusque from sheer nervousness. Nervous people often convey the impression of want of consideration from an excess of it. The single-minded directness exhibited in this incident is responsible for a characteristic which his biographer cannot but regret. Coleridge-Taylor's mental processes were so acute and concentrated that he reduced all matters to their essentials naturally. Insomuch that when he took pen in hand to write personal letters, he dashed off at great speed the bare message which occasioned his writing. He wrote many letters, and I have examined a large number of them with care; but those which it is desirable to publish are very few. Only occasionally do they contain opinions of life, art, music, or current events. They are usually notes making appointments or similar severely practical missives. That he could write he proved by an occasional letter to the press, a brief tribute to Hurlstone's memory, and by other writings that we shall have cause to mention later; but except in his love-letters, which were buried with him, and which remain in the memory of her who received them, few letters such as eminent men have had the habit of writing, came from his hand.

In deference to the unfavourable opinion expressed upon it, Coleridge-Taylor never published the *Symphony*. The first three movements received a hearing at the Royal College concert on March 7, 1896, when the critics agreed that it was the most interesting composition he had yet produced, that its largo movement entitled *A Lament* showed a command of emotional power remarkable in one so young, and foretold that if he continued to develop as heretofore a high place among English composers was assured for him. At this same concert, it is interesting to record, was performed a *Pianoforte Concerto* by Hurlstone, which also received great commendation from audience and critics. It is pleasant to remember that the two young

composers rejoiced each in the genius of the other.   In
his short life Hurlstone never made the great fame which
came to his fellow student, but in these college days his
promise was remarkable; and so sane a critic as Sir Charles
Stanford considered him to be "deeper down," to use his
own phrase, than his better known colleague.   The
authentic fire never descended from heaven more surely
than into the frail body of Hurlstone.   My recollections of
him date from five years later, when I was wont to meet
him in the streets of South Norwood; a pale, bent, slender
figure, carelessly dressed, often with his necktie awry, too
fragile it seemed to withstand the winter winds, and
obviously the victim of the fell disease which was to
destroy him at thirty years of age.   But it was a figure
pathetic only in its physical appeal.   Spiritually and
mentally Hurlstone enjoyed an excellent outlook; always
when I met him he was cheerful, with a ready smile and
a still readier joke at the need which made it necessary
for him to spend the hours which should have been devoted to the development of his own golden talents to the
comparatively barren business of pianoforte teaching, the
arranging of the work of men infinitely inferior to himself in musical genius, and in accompanying at concerts.
I well remember the indignant protest of Coleridge-Taylor
against the hard fate which compelled his friend to such
tasks for the sake of the frugal livelihood they brought
him; but rarely, I believe, was such complaint heard from
Hurlstone.   His modesty was excessive, and only from
his intimate friends could one learn how real and rare were
his gifts.   Occasionally he brightened Croydon or Norwood with a recital, which brought him the infinitesim-
ally small money recompense which such concerts usually
yield; but he never achieved wide recognition or at
any time was in circumstances which by the widest
latitude of phrase could be called easy.   Only since his
death and through the instrumentality of his friend, Mr.
Tom Sutton, has he received a modest shrine in the temple

of musical fame; but we believe it will be more frequented as time passes, for his works have the beauty which makes for life. I lamented to Sir Charles Stanford that Hurlstone was unable to achieve all his greatness owing to the shortness of his life, and received a well-deserved rebuke in his answer: "Yes; in the sense of the words on Schubert's tomb:

> "*Die Tonkunst begrub hier einen reichen Besitz aber noch viel schoenere Hoffnungen.*"*

In later years circumstances threw the friends together less frequently than either would have wished; but their friendship endured, and it was a dream of Hurlstone in 1912 that Coleridge-Taylor regarded as a premonition of his own death.

This period was one of brilliance in the annals of the Royal College. Amongst the students were the composers Hurlstone, Dunhill, Vaughan-Williams, and Fritz Hart; the pianists Herbert Fryer, Howard Jones, and Willy Scott; and the vocalists included several names now famous: Muriel and Hilda Foster, Clara Butt, Agnes Nicholls, Kirkby Lunn, and Harry Dearth are a few of them. Coleridge-Taylor's temperament was such that he came into intimate relations with but few of them, but where he did the relations were cordial, and Coleridge-Taylor possessed the divine gift of an unlimited capacity for appreciation.

The college days were now drawing to a close. Until the last two terms Coleridge-Taylor's punctuality and industry had been invariable; it fluctuated during the last two terms from increasing outside pressure upon his time. In 1894 he was declared to have learned all the counterpoint that his professor could teach him, and the organ replaced it in his curriculum. Upon these organ lessons he received excellent reports from his professor, Dr.

* " Music has here entombed a rich treasure, but much fairer hopes."

Walter Alcock, but he only pursued them for two terms. He had a natural antipathy to the instrument. "I can't think organ," he told his pupil, Mr. E. Beck-Slinn, in 1904, "it is far too mechanical and soulless." He overcame this sufficiently to write small organ works, which are good, but their fewness betrays something of his lack of sympathy. It may be said that his college studies were all in the direction of composition, and, as became a good student, all his intellectual activities were subservient to his main purpose.

Reviewing the whole six years of his college career, and considering the man at the close of them, we cannot help remarking the immeasurable value of the opportunities they had afforded him. In them he discovered at the happy age of sixteen the central purpose of his life, and was encouraged to develop, to prune, to perfect himself for it. His redundancies were the glorious carelessness of genius which has always much to throw away from its great store of gifts. At twenty years of age he had already drawn upon himself the eyes of all who were farseeing in British music, and the list of his compositions contained nearly thirty works, vocal and instrumental, daringly new in rhythm, varied in style, and showing a promise in their colouring and a mastery of the material of the voice and the orchestra alike which had not been witnessed for a long time in an academic course. And these days had developed his social qualities, had subdued his painful timidity to a more practical modesty, had given him personal certainty. At twenty he was not only a young musical Titan; he was an educated, kindly, and polished gentleman. He left the Royal College at the end of the Easter Term, 1897, not without regrets on his own side and on the side of the college.

CHAPTER IV

FAME—THE "BALLADE IN A MINOR"

THE lower part of Holmesdale Road, South Norwood, in which Coleridge-Taylor lived in 1896, is singularly uninspiring. Respectable dwellings of artisans and modest business men occupy either side of the street in a dismal regularity. It has one recommendation to-day—that it is a comparatively quiet street, well removed from the main lines of traffic between Norwood and Croydon. In 1896 only the south side was built, but the fields on the other side, which until then had lightened and given even a sylvan appearance to the place, were in the hands of the builder, and the clink of trowel on brick which came therefrom all- day affected the composer greatly. Then, as ever, he was intensely sensitive to noise—a fact which is brought into relief by an incident which occurred two years later, but which for convenience may be recorded here. Coleridge-Taylor was engaged on a long work requiring complete concentration, and he was tormented intolerably by a street organ which would take up a station about two houses away from his and grind forth ditties which completely precluded any work during the performance. One day, unable to endure it any longer, he threw down his pen, sallied forth and asked the itinerant musician to go away. Whereupon a neighbour rushed out and asked : "Why are you sending this man away?" Coleridge-Taylor explained patiently. "I am a composer of music, and I am engaged on a long and important work, and the interruption caused by this organ is serious for me." "Well," rejoined the other, "my children like the organ as much as you dislike it, and we have as much right to have it as you have to send it away; and as for your piano, it is a good thing that it is interrupted, for there is too much of it." At this moment a policeman came in sight, and the organ-grinder made off; and so, for the time being, Coleridge-Taylor secured quiet. He learned later that the organ-man had been tipped by his neighbour to come and play outside the house for the amusement of a sick child. This gave quite another complexion to the affair, since Coleridge-Taylor was a great lover of children; and when the organ-man came again he consulted him in order to avoid work during his performances. It amused Coleridge-Taylor greatly when the itinerant musician drew out an engagement book and showed his questioner his series of appointments. Beyond this, out of consideration for the child, Coleridge-Taylor refrained from touching his piano during the night hours —no small sacrifice on his part. I have told this not only to illustrate his objection to noises, but also to show the disadvantages under which the poor artist labours. No doubt the sources of experience and inspiration are sometimes found in the vortex of modern town life, in the streets, in trams, in motor vehicles—and I have heard Coleridge-Taylor affirm that the swaying of a motor-bus or the rythmical motion of the Underground Railway were a constant source of suggestion; but for the actual realisation and production of his work the creative artist requires imperatively a certain amount of quiet leisure. Where these are unobtainable and the artist perseveres in his production, the work may not suffer as greatly as may be supposed, but the physical strain on the worker is immeasurably increased. Leisure, except at rare and never prolonged intervals, Coleridge-Taylor seldom possessed, and quiet he managed to secure in a measure only by living in the side streets of Norwood; but the complete seclusion of the house set in the midst of fields or gardens, for which almost every artist longs, was never his.

To return to Holmesdale Road. The noise of the building became an irritant so detrimental to his work that late in 1896 a move was determined upon, and the Evanses and he took up their abode at 9 Fernham Road, Thornton Heath, less than a mile from the old home, and close to the charming public park of Grange Wood.

When not physically composing, Coleridge-Taylor followed his old habit of walking and of reading as he walked. His favourite walk was up and down the Canham Road, which runs along the South Norwood Hill close to the crest of the hill on which Grange Wood Park rests. It still has rural touches, but at the time of which I write it was especially delectable. The fields beneath had scarcely been built upon, and the eye travelled over South Norwood, lying in the valley, to the heather-clad hills of Shirley and Addington on the south, and over Croydon, which from here has a strange and deceptive leafiness, to the Banstead Hills on the west. The view below was almost amphitheatrical, and behind him were the large wooded gardens of fine residences and fields edged with poplars. In these inspiring surroundings he read much, and in particular the Brownings. His admiration for both poet and poetess was intense. Without being aware of his history, he felt curious racial affinities with the former, and held a theory that the expressed sympathy of the poet with the darker races was the outcome of actual blood relationship with them. The explanation of Browning's sympathy is to be found, as Browning students are aware, in the fact that Browning's grandmother was a Creole, and that his father gave up a West Indian inheritance because his religious opinions abhorred the slave system upon which it had been built, and this view of the slave was the natural inheritance of the poet. Coleridge-Taylor's view is worth recording as an evidence of his ceaseless preoccupation with the question of his race. So far he had been, and for a few years was still to be, painfully sensitive to the implications of inferiority which his negro derivation implied, but later saner and happier reasonings prevailed, and the timid, apologetic attitude was replaced by the spirit of the apostle and champion, with an infinite faith in the possibilities of the darker sons of earth.   Results of his readings in the Brownings were settings of "Earth fades, Heaven breaks on me"—the last speech of Strafford in the drama of that name—and of certain of Elizabeth Barrett Browning's sonnets.   The sympathetic beauty of the latter was enhanced for him by the fact that he had now irrevocably fallen in love; and it has been given to few poets to express human affection with the convincing sincerity which lives in the sonnets of our greatest woman poet. Of her exquisite "Substitution" he writes on the manuscript copy of his setting which he sent to his future wife : "The more I read these words the more I am convinced of their magnificence."   He adds a significant and characteristic note : "You'll be clever indeed if you are able to understand this writing.   It is not that I don't take the trouble, but it is nearly one (a.m.) and I am tired."   Already it would seem that he was working at a pressure almost reprehensible; a consuming need to work at every available hour seems to have possessed him always.

For, although Coleridge-Taylor had now no longer to follow his college routine, he was by no means without occupation.   His few published compositions brought him some money return, albeit a very small one—certainly insufficient to procure bread and cheese.   A more stable addition to his modest budget had come in the shape of teaching work.   In the Lent Term, 1895, the director of the Croydon Conservatoire of Music found himself in need of a teacher to give evening lessons in violin playing. This work he offered to Coleridge-Taylor, who, of course, was still a student at the Royal College.   Although it was two years since he had ceased to follow the study of the violin at the college as his principal subject, he had maintained his practice, as may be inferred from the remarks of Mr. Warner given in the previous chapter, and he entered upon the work of teaching with the enthusiasm and the thoroughness which were a passion with him. He taught both preliminary and advanced pupils, but Mr. Howard B. Humphery, the director of the Conservatoire, tells me that he greatly preferred pupils of the latter type, or those who had at least a foundation in technique; that, as a matter of fact, he did not care to give elementary lessons, but was exceptionally successful in imparting a style to those who had overcome the rudimentary difficulties of their art. In the course of this work he had occasionally to contend with the racial difficulty. The musician was not without honour elsewhere, but in Croydon people remembered him as a small coloured boy of negligible social antecedents in whom Colonel Walters had taken an interest; and although musical men living in Croydon, such as Mr. Henry Keatley Moore and the late Henry Lahee, as well as others of social and musical consideration, were interested in and expected much of him, it may be said that the townsfolk in general regarded him as an uncanny youngster with rather inexplicable gifts. The fact that he not only met but triumphed completely over these prejudices is proven by a case recalled by Mr. Humphery. A girl student had made excellent progress under other masters, and required finishing lessons. Mr. Humphery suggested to her mother that she should receive them from Coleridge-Taylor. "She looked at me," said Mr. Humphery, "as if I had suggested something extraordinary, and asked for time to consider the unusual proposal." Eventually she was induced to permit the extraordinary thing, and the daughter studied with Coleridge-Taylor. A term or two with him not only swept away the prejudice, but gave rise to a friendship between Coleridge-Taylor and the girl's family which ended only with his life. His relations with his pupils were fortunate almost invariably. Not only had he the power of imparting knowledge; he inspired his pupils with immense enthusiasm for their art and for their teacher.

At the Conservatoire there existed a small orchestral class, confined to strings, which met weekly. In 1896 its conductor was absent through illness, and Coleridge-Taylor was invited to conduct in his stead. His imagination was stirred at the invitation. Somehow he had conceived the idea that the orchestral class was a full orchestra, and he had visions of performing the orchestral masterpieces of the world. He was much disappointed to find that the class was of strings only, but he proved himself worthy in his disappointment. His management of the class was a revelation to his colleagues; his command over the possibilities of the instruments and his intuitive understanding of every type of work which came before the class was seen to be unusual. Shortly after, the conductor of the class retired, and Coleridge-Taylor was appointed to his position. He remained as conductor until 1907, and it was his work with the Conservatoire String Orchestra which first developed his latent powers as a conductor. He increased its numbers, rehearsed it with thoroughness; and his letters to Mr. Humphery are witness to the scrupulous care with which he chose the works for its study.

A significant friendship came about at this time with Paul Lawrence Dunbar, the American negro poet. Coleridge-Taylor's fame had already been heard of in America in 1896, and the eyes of the cultured men of the negro race were turned upon him with curious anticipation. Dunbar was amongst those who were attracted, and when in 1896 he paid a visit to England for the purpose of giving public readings of his poems, he early sought the acquaintance of the musician. Poor Dunbar was four years Coleridge-Taylor's senior, and his short life of thirty-three years as lift-boy, journalist, library assistant and poet is as pathetic a story as exists in the annals of literature. He sang as naturally and as simply as the lark, and although his place in the hierarchy of poets is a modest one, he had the authentic voice; and lovers of poetry may well learn more of the author of "When Malindy Sings" and "Candle Lighting Time," as well as of the last beautiful lines, in which he summed up his own bitter destiny :

> *Because I had loved so deeply,*
> *Because I had loved so long,*
> *God in His great compassion*
> *Gave me the gift of song.*

> *Because I have loved so vainly,*
> *And sung with such faltering breath,*
> *The Master in infinite mercy*
> *Offers the boon of Death.*

The immediate result of the meeting was a joint recital at the Salle Erard, which was to be in some way a reflection of negro effort in the sister arts. Coleridge-Taylor's contributions were entirely of his own composition, and consisted of no fewer than nine new songs, five *Fantasiestücke* for string quartet, his first venture into the Hiawatha legend in his *Hiawatha Sketches for Violin and Pianoforte,* and settings of various lyrics by the negro poet, the *Corn Song* amongst them. It was remarked that the appearance of Dunbar was somewhat repulsive, but that when he rose to read, the beauty of his voice and the dramatic reality of his delivery quickly cancelled the earlier impression, and left only the impression of the naturally noble soul working behind the unattractive features. Speaking of him in connection with another of his readings, Brand Whitlock writes : "That evening he recited—oh ! what a voice he had !—his 'Ships that Pass in the Night.' I can hear him now, and see the expression on his fine face as he said ' Passing ! Passing ! ' It was prophetic."

This recital was repeated at Croydon in January, 1897, where the successes made at the Salle Erard were sub-

E

scribed to by a large and enthusiastic audience. The performance brought out in particular Coleridge-Taylor's position as an inspired and original writer of songs which have retained until now their place in the programmes of the best English singers. In the writing of songs he was unusually facile. When he had completely grasped the implications of the poem he was setting, the melody and accompaniment came spontaneously and were committed to manuscript with a rapidity which astonished his friends.

During this year he was engaged upon the writing of his *Hiawatha's Wedding Feast,* which, however, was not to see light until the following year. In the late summer we find him taking part in a local controversy on the relative values of abstract and operatic music, in which the opener had averred that operatic was of greater emotional value. Coleridge-Taylor's letter, which appeared in *The Croydon Advertiser* of August 12, 1897, may be subjoined as his first public utterance upon his art. It has a further interest in the fact that one of the cardinal ambitions of his life was to write operatic works, as I shall have reason to show.

TO THE EDITOR OF THE "ADVERTISER"

DEAR SIR,—I was surprised to read your correspondent's letter *re* operatic music.

The writer would evidently have us believe that such music has a greater emotional worth than what is called "absolute" music!

Surely such compositions as the Meyerbeer type—charming though they may be—are not to be compared with those of Beethoven, Schumann, Brahms, Dvořák, etc., from an emotional point of view!

Again, so many things go to make up the opera—libretto, scenery, acting, and a thousand other little realities and artifices—that *music* can only be reckoned as being a fraction of the whole—a most important one, I grant.

Wagner's music dramas are the great exception. He was

his own poet, and his music as far removed from Meyerbeer as the East from the West.

Symphonic music, etc., however, has none of these auxiliaries to assist it in sustaining interest; it is a case of music *only*.

Which, therefore, is the greater—the operatic composer, who is only, after all, *part* creator, or the symphonic composer, who is *sole* creator?

I have yet to be convinced of the existence of "legions who can sing sentimental songs and perform classical music," and am absolutely sure that really first-rate concert-artistes are as scarce as operatic artistes.

Good taste and good sense both forbid operatic excerpts being introduced at concerts. Music originally written for the stage invariably falls flat when divested of its necessary "dressings," and as so much legitimate concert-music has been written I fail to see why dished-up pieces of opera should be advised in its stead.

By all means let us honour operatic composers and their works, but not by taking the music from its proper sphere and thus robbing it of much of its effect.—Sincerely yours,

S. COLERIDGE-TAYLOR.

THORNTON HEATH, *August 9,* 1897.

Early in the next year, 1898, came his great opportunity, and it found Coleridge-Taylor prepared and sufficient. He owed it to the discerning generosity of Sir Edward Elgar, who exemplifies in an eminent degree the truth that a really great artist does not feel jealousy of the younger one, but reaches out to him a welcoming hand. Amongst modern musicians jealousy and envy rage horribly, as any dispassionate observer must have noticed, and this example of the contrary attitude is one to be remembered with gratitude. The vehicle of the kindness was an emphatic postcard written by Sir Edward to Dr. Herbert Brewer, of the Committee of the Three Choirs Festival :

I have received a request from the secretary to write a short orchestral thing for the evening concert. I am sorry I am too busy to do so. I wish, wish, wish you would ask Coleridge-Taylor to do it. He still wants recognition, and he is far and away the cleverest fellow going amongst the young men. Please don't let your committee throw away the chance of doing a good act.—EDWARD ELGAR.

The card had the desired result, and Coleridge was overjoyed to receive the commission. Every young composer aspires to a festival commission. It provides him with an arena in which to display his powers, a huge audience to appraise them, and the almost certain publication of his work. The invitation is in itself a public recognition of his gifts, and if his work be good, or popular, the path of life becomes clearer for him in consequence. For all these purposes there are few English festivals more desirable than that of the Three Choirs, the oldest of the great English musical gatherings. Coleridge-Taylor set to work upon his *Ballade in A minor*. I have been told that he said his inspiration came from listening to the monotonous sounds of the piano-tuner; and perhaps the quick, brief theme which pervades it had this origin. The story, however, has the sound of many similar stories in musical history. Be that as it may, the work, which occupies twenty pages of the ordinary short score, and takes about fifteen minutes in the playing, is a remarkable performance. Its cardinal characteristic is its immense rhythmical vigour, which is apparent in the opening subject, a well-marked haunting theme in six-eight time of rather more than eight bars, proceeding mainly in semi-tones, and not exceeding the limits of a major third. This theme is kept constantly in view throughout the work, which is remarkable for the severe economy of material displayed, and there is an under strain of a curious and characteristic barbaric quality. A melodious song-like theme in two-four time is the second distinguishing movement, which leads through sonorous passages to a repetition two octaves higher of the initial subject in its original time. This subject, with consider able variation in the treatment and keys, recurs again and again, and the work progresses with almost every variety of light and shade, and ends with a whirling *sforzando* passage. Apart from its rhythm, which some few critics said reminded them of Dvořák, the barbaric strain we have noted, and the orchestral colouring, are the most prominently marked features of the *Ballade*.

The commission for the *Ballade* involved Coleridge-Taylor's presence at Gloucester to conduct it. The London orchestral rehearsals for the festival were held at the Queen's Hall, and on a summer afternoon, when the temperature of the concert room was 92 degrees in the shade, Coleridge-Taylor took the baton. Apparently ignoring the great heat, he rehearsed the band vigorously for half an hour. A number of distinguished listeners were present, and when he left the conductor's desk amidst much applause from these and the players, he was delighted to receive a warm handshake and approving felicitations both from Sir Arthur Sullivan and from his former principal, Sir Hubert Parry. With this happy augury Coleridge went to Gloucester. The concert at which his work was produced was given on the evening of September 12, 1898, at the Shire Hall, after a day of exhausting rehearsals. The hall was crowded, and the temperature was only a little lower than that of the rehearsal afternoon. The item preceding the *Ballade* was a melodious but undistinguished choral work, which received a sympathetic hearing, and during its performance Coleridge-Taylor was making great efforts to summon up sufficient courage for what was to him the very real ordeal of facing the audience. At the rehearsals during the day he had been singled out again for cordial treatment by the chorus and orchestra, and had acquitted himself well. The concert itself was a more serious matter. The audience knew that the young new composer was an Anglo-African, and we have the word of a South African who was present that the general impression and expectation was that Coleridge-Taylor would prove to be a white colonist.   There was a general pause of astonishment at the entry of a short, swarthy, quick-moving and entirely conscious young man, whose enormous head, with its long thick hair, broad nostrils, and flashing white teeth betrayed at once the race from which he came.   The pause was momentary only; then a storm of applause "literally stunning" broke from the audience.   Indeed, rarely has a young artist received so enthusiastic a welcome; and this is attributable in no small degree to his coloured blood.   Such was the mind of the audience that any young composer upon whom the Committee of the Three Choirs Festival had set the sign of its approval would have been warmly received; but the unexpected has its appeal to Englishmen, and the sense of fair play, the spontaneous desire to "give the man a chance," which is characteristic of our race as a whole in its relations with the backward races, gave a special vigour to the reception.   The following fifteen minutes justified the applause.   The arresting character of the opening theme, the ingenious economy of material throughout, the unexpected transitions, the barbaric strain informing it, and the mastery of material shown in the richness and balance of the orchestration, made quite clear that here was not merely novelty, but the force and inspiration of genius as well.   Coleridge-Taylor conducted with dignity and becoming reserve, and concluded the performance in a storm of applause.   Three times he was compelled to come forward to acknowledge the ovation, and the festival concluded with the conviction in the mind of every listener that its laurels lay with the young composer.   A worse ordeal for him than this public appearance followed. People crowded round to congratulate him, and many social invitations were offered.   These, in general, he modestly declined.   Lionising of this type frightened him, and the sense of being on exhibition was dreadful.

His success at Gloucester gave a new complexion to his prospects.   Next day the London papers rang with praises of his work, his career and antecedents were chronicled, interviewers made his acquaintance, and reproduced with embellishments his modest account of himself. Few men have received so much public attention as the result of one comparatively short work; none has preserved his mental balance better in such an ordeal. Timidity is characteristic of his race, and in certain business crises of his life it was Coleridge-Taylor's greatest misfortune, but it had the human virtue of giving him a juster view of his talents than might have been his had there been no such restraining quality. Be that as it may, the lad of promise who went to Gloucester on September 12, returned a day later a recognised master of his art, to whom in the course of natural development the highest achievements of music might be open.

CHAPTER V

" HIAWATHA'S WEDDING FEAST "

AS a consequence of his success at Gloucester, Coleridge-Taylor was invited to conduct the *Ballade* at the Crystal Palace on November 4. The fact is interesting, because no institution in England has been more definitely associated with the renaissance of English music in the last forty years of the nineteenth century than the Crystal Palace; and although the platform had lost some of the prestige it enjoyed in the days when the young Parry and Stanford had proved their prowess there, it was still a place worthy of musical consideration. Moreover, the concert marks a beginning in Coleridge-Taylor's relations with the Crystal Palace, in the school of which he was to be professor of music during his last years, and in the concert room of which he was to appear frequently.

In connection with the *Ballade* Coleridge-Taylor scored a point against the critics too good to be forgotten. A worthy doctor of music, a composer of no mean ability so far as church music was concerned, but a novice at orchestration, had written a *Te Deum*. This he persuaded Coleridge-Taylor to orchestrate, supplying certain bass indications which puzzled him until their creator admitted that he scarcely knew what they meant himself, and allowed their rejection. The orchestration was completed, and the *Te Deum* was produced with the *Ballade*. Next day a critic came out with an interesting disparagement of the orchestration of the *Ballade*, and the advice to Coleridge-Taylor that if he would understand well-balanced orchestration he should study that of the *Te Deum*.

In every way the year 1898 was to be crucial for Coleridge-Taylor. As already stated, he was at work on Longfellow's poem "Hiawatha"; in fact, it was a college composition in the first place; and it owes something to the suggestions and criticisms of Sir Charles Stanford, a debt which may be readily admitted, as it detracts not in the least from the individuality of the completed work. At first sight it would seem to have been a remarkable choice of subject for musical setting, in spite of the fact that earlier musicians had essayed to deal with the very sections which Coleridge-Taylor was now attempting. The staccato trochaic measure, borrowed by Longfellow from the Danish *Kalevala*, with its inevitable feminine endings and endless repetition, promises an effect of monotony which would be fatal if translated into music. But difficulties such as these were a challenge which Coleridge-Taylor would accept with joyous confidence. If the youth was not daunted by the wooden phrasing of the lyric, "Zara's Ear-rings," the young man was not likely to pause at the "Hiawatha" metre. He always said that the curious names, Pau-Puk-Keewis, Iagoo, Chibiabos, Nokomis, and so on, which he would roll out with intense appreciation of their sound values, were the first cause of his affection for the poem. More intimate acquaintance gave him an intenser appreciation of the beauty of the poetry itself.

"The essential beauty of the poem," he told Mr. Walter Hayson, "is its naive simplicity, its unaffected expression, its unforced idealism," and the primitive character of the story made a natural appeal to the primitive elements in his own character. Of most of this he was doubtless unaware at the time; theories usually follow practice; and what seems to be the plain fact is that he had found a certain body of verse which struck his fancy. His first scheme was for an unambitious cantata with the canto "The Wedding Feast" for libretto. His copy of Longfellow, a cheap, vilely printed edition, such as ten years ago were common in drapery stores, is scored with underlinings and suggestions which show that the plan of the cantata was completed in his mind before composition began. He then, as was his wont, committed the poem to memory, and lived with the words until they became a part of himself. "I take it," he further told Mr. Hayson, "to be an artistic crime in the musical treatment of a poem to make it subordinate to orchestral effect. The music is only justified if it speaks in the language of the poem." The actual writing of the work was accomplished with extraordinary rapidity, but the task of revision was undergone again and again.

The finished work was rehearsed during the autumn by the choir and orchestra of the Royal College of Music, under Sir Charles Stanford. The performers rejoiced greatly in the composition, and much excitement was felt as the time drew near the college concert on November 11, at which it was to be produced. By some means, although there was a more or less tacit agreement amongst the students that secrecy was to be observed concerning the work, the excitement leaked out, and music-loving people in touch with the college gained the impression that something unusual would appear at the concert. Messrs. Novello and Co. had undertaken the publication of the work. On the morning of the performance Coleridge-Taylor called at the publishers, and while he was there Sullivan entered in order to obtain a copy of the work. He was then in the advanced stages of the cruel ill-health which clouded his life, but he met Coleridge-Taylor with enthusiasm. "I'm always an ill man now, my boy," said he, "but I will come to this concert, even if I have to be carried into the room." When Sullivan arrived in the evening he found the old hall of the Royal College buzzing with a crowded, expectant audience. Every seat was occupied, and people were sitting on the steps of the platform and standing in the passages. A chair was brought in for Sullivan and placed well in front of the hall.

The orchestra, which was led by Coleridge-Taylor's friend, Mr. Willie J. Read, was suffering apparently from nervousness, and the chorus lacked balance. A perfect performance was not forthcoming; but when Sir Charles Stanford took the baton and the trumpets gave out the severely simple but arresting opening subject, the interest of the audience was secured, and it increased as the curious rhythmic plan of the work was unfolded. Rarely before had music made the domestic details of a wedding festival so entertaining. The unusual melodic design, the rapid transitions from rhythm to rhythm and from key to key; the unexpected orchestral effects, the descriptive effect of the writing, and the entire singableness of the whole were realised even in the weakest parts of the rendering. The broad suavity of the appeal to Chibiabos intensified expectations which were realised fully when the audience heard for the first time the tenor solo "Onaway, 'Awake," perhaps the most perfect tenor aria of the last generation. It is good to be present at the birth of an immortal thing, and the song was recognised at once at its real worth. When the last strains of the orchestra died away the demonstration of the audience was memorable. Coleridge-Taylor was recalled again and again. The laurels won at Gloucester were now clearly of no meretricious withering type, the one fortunate happening of a career artistically commonplace. Here were more sustained power, a larger canvas, and even richer detail. After the concert was over, a student tells me that as she was going home she saw the successful composer dodging into doorways to get out of the sight of members of the audience who were passing. Literally here, as always up to this time, Coleridge-Taylor was frightened of his success. Whatever doubts may have existed about his fame after the first performance of his *Ballade*, they were laid now; and next morning he awoke to find himself indeed famous. Every London paper devoted considerable space to *Hiawatha's Wedding Feast*, almost without exception a pæan of joyous appreciation and congratulation, and this was echoed by the newspapers throughout the kingdom.

Again he was biographed, interviewed, his opinions were solicited on all subjects musical, he was attacked by autograph hunters, and indeed was subjected to the various virulent forms of persecution which the successful man has to endure. He bore it meekly and with his invariable good humour, and went back for the time being to his quiet violin teaching at Croydon.

One cannot but reflect, however, in connection with *Hiawatha's Wedding Feast,* upon the necessary fallibility of criticism, a theme common to the creative genius from the first day when an imaginative worker put forth the result of his imagining. The morality of British musical critics is unassailable. No doubt in obscure journals occasionally the friends of mediocre people puff them into a transient celebrity; but the central newspaper press of England is, as regards music, incorruptible. That coteries and cliques do not exist is proved, as Mr. J. A. Fuller Maitland has observed, by those differences of opinion amongst them which provide amusement for the critics of critics. A man is necessarily limited by the extent of his own vision, and the most catholic taste is rarely universal or even approximately so. It is with these implications in mind that one notices the critical accounts of *Hiawatha.* In praising the work as a whole the chorus only differed in the degree of intensity shown; in details opinions differed widely. The solo furnished an example of this. Said the critic of *The Guardian,* after a cautious preamble, in which he protected himself from any possible consequences of overrating the work: "His vocal part-writing, though effective, is the least individual part of the work; the tenor solo, again, though extremely peaceful, might have been written by almost any modern composer." *The Referee,* a paper for the musical pronouncements of which Coleridge-Taylor maintained a high respect, said, on the contrary, that "Onaway, Awake" "is a gem of impassioned melody," with the further remark that "all tenors who are in the throes of courtship should learn it at once." These two absolutely contradictory statements are examples of the criticism that was often levelled at him. Well, too, might he have prayed in these days to be saved from the friends who pronounced him the greatest of living musicians, a new Schubert, a Mozart, another Dvořák, if it were not patent to all but musicians and critics themselves that public opinion is not much or for any length of time influenced by criticism of any kind. The only grave danger of criticism is its effect upon its object, its likelihood of raising hopes that are unrealisable, or of destroying the faith of the worker in himself and his work.

So far as character was concerned, as I have sufficiently emphasised, the almost countless laudations bestowed upon Coleridge-Taylor made little difference in his outlook upon life. He taught his pupils and rehearsed his orchestra with even greater care, if that were possible, as a result of his success. His letters of this year and the next are all characteristic of his whole life. Notes to Mr. Humphery upon his choice of music for the Conservatoire orchestral class, with remarks upon the time each piece will occupy in performance; notes to various members and friends of the class on rehearsals; notes on his smaller compositions—short, simple, cordial notes all of them, modest in tone and rushed off in his tiny, almost undecipherable handwriting. One or two are typical and may be quoted. The first two are to Miss Leila Petherick, a member of a well-known musical family in Croydon :

21 SAXON ROAD,
SOUTH NORWOOD.
January 14, 1898.

DEAR MISS PETHERICK,—Do you play the viola as well as your sister, or have I been wrongly informed?

Kindly let me know. And have you seen my *Fantasiestücke* for two violins, viola, and 'cello, published by Augener?

They are quite short, though intricate in ensemble; but if you would like a copy I'll have one sent you during the week.

With kind regards to Mrs. Petherick and your sister,—
Believe me, yours very sincerely,   S. Coleridge-Taylor.

To the same.

21 Saxon Road,
South Norwood.
January 15, 1898.

Dear Miss Petherick,—Many thanks for your kind reply.
I am sending copy of my Quartet movement by the same post
—an early work, so don't be disappointed!

Will your sister help us with the viola on February 4?
If so, will she come to as many of the full rehearsals as
possible? *I shall be grateful.*

My friend of the Wessely Quartet will be absent, hence my
request.—Yours sincerely,   S. Coleridge-Taylor.

The following is to Mr. Howard B. Humphery, the
director of the Croydon Conservatoire, and concerns his
orchestral class.

30 Dagnall Park.
January 14, 1899.

My dear Mr. Humphery,—I should think that the following
would be a very good arrangement of the Programme :

1. *Serenade.* Fuchs.   (20.)
2. *Nocturne.* Dvořák.   (10.)
   b. Songs. Goetz.   (5.)
   c. *Meditation.* Wilson.   (5.)
   d. ——. Massenet.   (5.)
3. *King Robert.* West.   (15.)
4. *Serenade.* Mozart.   (20.)
   ————
   (80.)
   ————

Possibly a little less time will be taken than that appended.
Enclosed is receipt at last!
Great haste.—From yours very sincerely,
S. Coleridge-Taylor.

Amongst those who were in the habit of attending
the concerts at the Royal College was the late Auguste J.

Jaeger. The German enthusiast, who is already farther from the memory of this generation than he deserves to be, early recognised the expanding powers of the student. He wrote to his future wife: "I have long been looking for a new English composer of real genius, and I believe I have found him." This opinion he accompanied by a manuscript of Coleridge-Taylor's *Ballade for Violin;* and he was soon on intimate terms with his discovery, and became a formative influence of unusual value in his career. In his capacity of principal musical adviser to the firm of Novello, and as critic to *The Musical Times,* Jaeger brought to bear an attitude which may fitly be called critical enthusiasm. He had, in spite of his Continental derivation, an intense sympathy with English music. One of his closest friends wrote: "I think Jaeger's secret was his unfailing ear for the emotional signs in music. From that point of view alone he could register how much vitality there was in a new work. His defects in judgment arose from the same cause. He believed in a piece if it made him feel like tears. But he did not only bid for emotion. He demanded noble effort and sanity, and sometimes came to hate that which once moved him but subsequently showed its over-emotion. His help to young composers was marvellous. If he gave us over-praise he tempered it with much candid criticism." Intercourse with a man so gifted and with such an attitude could not fail in its effect. Coleridge-Taylor would often visit him at his house in Kensington, where the critic would listen with an evaluating ear to his songs, which were sung to Coleridge-Taylor's accompaniment by Miss Jessie Walmisley. At times he was sufficiently severe, but from the beginning he recognised in the young composer an authentic voice, and this he stimulated with a right good will. The beautiful songs which Coleridge-Taylor published in his early twenties all came under Jaeger's influence, and when the time came for publishing *Hiawatha's Wedding Feast,* it was upon Jaeger's importunity that the publishers issued it, in spite of their own emphatic assertion to the composer that "they did not expect to sell a copy of it."

Coleridge-Taylor would visit the Jaegers several times a week. When he was not trying over and discussing his compositions he seemed quiet, with little conversation; but he was delightfully unaffected and lovable, and the possessor of an irresistible sense of the comedy of things, which caused him to explode with laughter at the least of Jaeger's witticisms. Jaeger had great faith in Coleridge-Taylor's potentialities, but, in common with Stanford, he held that he was entirely deficient in self-criticism. This is the more extraordinary in that Coleridge-Taylor would write and re-write passages again and again before he would be satisfied with them; and such activity would seem to indicate an excess rather than a want of this valuable quality. One other thing Jaeger held was that at this time Coleridge-Taylor was anything but an efficient accompanist. During the composing of *Hiawatha's Wedding Feast* he brought "Onaway, Awake" for his hearing, with this remark: "This is the most beautiful melody I have ever written," and sat down to the piano and played and sang it. The result was to leave the Jaegers in complete mystification. His voice was a very different instrument from the pure, clear treble of the solo boy in Colonel Walters's choir; it was a thin, reedy baritone, with many falsetto notes, and the accompaniment seemed beyond his powers. It was only when Mr. and Mrs. Jaeger came to examine the score quietly after he had gone that they recognised how justly he had appraised the melody. On another occasion, just before the performance of the *Hiawatha* trilogy by the Royal Choral Society, the Jaegers and the Coleridge-Taylors met at the house of Mr. Andrew Black, who was to sing the title character, in order that Jaeger might gain a complete conception of the work. At first Coleridge-Taylor accompanied, although Mrs. Andrew Black, a highly-accomplished pianist, was present. Jaeger, who wished to gauge the effect of air and accompaniment together, soon grew impatient. "Here, Taylor," said he, "give it up, and let Mrs. Black play." Instead of showing annoyance, Coleridge-Taylor jumped up with a laugh, and joined his own request to that of the others.

The publishing of the work has occasioned much controversy, which I am reluctant to revive, seeing that it can serve very little purpose. It is necessary, however, to give the few facts in order to explain why the composer of the most popular cantata ever published in England, a work which has enjoyed enormous public regard from the day of its publication until now, should have had a life-long struggle for a livelihood, literally working himself to death at the age of thirty-seven, and leaving only the slenderest financial provision for his family. The facts are these. Coleridge-Taylor was a new man, of admitted ability, but yet unproven as a writer of saleable compositions. His poverty made it necessary that he should get on in the world, and qualifying everything was the shy timidity of his race. When, therefore, he submitted his work to the publishers—before its performance, it must be remembered—they followed the natural course of business men, and looking for elements of popularity, failed to find them. They would have returned the work to the composer but for the intervention of Jaeger, who assured them of his conviction of its ultimate success. They thereupon, with the prophecy of financial failure, and after some hesitating attempts upon Coleridge-Taylor's part to secure better terms, offered him fifteen guineas for the entire copyright. If this were not acceptable, the negotiations would be at an end. This reply created a panic in the composer's mind. He feared that his work would never be published; he felt that he was young, and that he would write other works that would recompense him better; moreover, his principal, Sir George Grove, had often said that a composer should not care much about the financial return

F

from his work; and here was a chance of making a bid for fame which might be lost if he held out for impossible terms. He capitulated, and I have a letter of his to Jaeger upon which the remark "Accepts £15 15s." is written in the latter's hand. When the work was at the height of its immense popularity the publishers presented him with a second cheque for twenty-five pounds.

We may conclude this account of the *Hiawatha* transactions by a reference to the entire three parts of the *Scenes from the Song of Hiawatha*. *The Wedding Feast* had succeeded beyond his dreams, yet he sold irrecoverably the copyright of both the second and third parts, the total money he received being two hundred and fifty pounds. This is astonishing; but the reason turns upon the extremely simple fact that the composer was in great need of money, and that he lacked the self-confidence and tenacity necessary for sound bargaining. Indeed, he appeared eager to sell the works in this manner. The publishers, it must be repeated, behaved as business men. To them the publication was a speculation; it was not their practice to give royalties to young composers, and as events proved, they made a satisfactory bargain. Occasionally in after years they made small unsolicited gifts to Coleridge-Taylor, who had, however, the chagrin of seeing that his work sold by hundreds of thousands of copies and of knowing that the only benefit to himself was its fame.

The letter referred to above is interesting as showing several of his characteristics :

3 Dagnall Park,
South Norwood.
Sunday.

My dear Mr. Jaeger,—*Of course* I shall be perfectly willing to leave *all* arrangements regarding *Hiawatha* with Mr. Littleton.

Will you tell him this on my behalf—or would it be advisable to write to him personally?

I am really sorry to have overlooked the mistakes you have

pointed out in the 2nd violin part of the *Waltzes*, but I *will* use coloured ink for corrections in future (some I have already done in black, unfortunately).

Very many thanks for Mr. Cowen's *Onaway*. Some of it I like much; but why has he *missed* one beautiful section out altogether and *repeated* another? Evidently Onaway's lover in Mr. Cowen's conception is a very different—and less senti-mental, less languid—person from mine.

I do not intend committing any very terrible deed *yet*, but soon I shall hold *The Musical Standard* responsible for some-thing extremely horrible. I give the writer of Augener's reviews one more chance! As matters stand, I have decided to overlook the insult (?) and have kindly and graciously sent him a copy of the *Waltzes* addressed to "The Editor of the *Musical Standard*, with kindest regards from one with whom (alas!) ' *melody is not a strong point* '!" But he is already convinced about this very dreadful failing of mine, so I'm afraid any such overtures on my part will be treated with contempt.

Can you tell me the names of the birds that arouse me every morning at about 3.30 a.m. with *this*:

The one at the top is "in the distance " (thank Heaven!); the other two sit in a tree close to my window.

I love birds, but at 3.30 am. *my love cools just a little*, I'm afraid.

I will return *Onaway* to-morrow or Sunday—for which I thank you very much.—Yours ever sincerely,

S. COLERIDGE-TAYLOR.

CHAPTER VI

WE must retrace our steps a little way. Unknown to Coleridge-Taylor, there was at the Royal College contemporaneously with himself, a young Croydon girl, a Miss Jessie S. Fleetwood Walmisley. One evening her family gave a party, for which some of the music was supplied by a few paid musicians from the town. Among these Coleridge-Taylor served as violinist. Towards the end of the evening, when he had played all that was required of him officially, he timidly approached Miss Walmisley and asked her if she would accompany him in something of his own. They played "The Legend" from his *Concertstück* together. It was a not unnatural result of this that, when, in 1893, Miss Walmisley was required as a vacation exercise to practise some violin and piano duets, and was casting around for someone with whom to practise them, it should occur to her that the clever coloured lad, who lived somewhere in Croydon, might be induced to help her. She wrote to the college for his address, but was wrongly directed to another student whose name was Coleridge. She was already somewhat nervous, and this encounter with another man than the one she sought did not decrease the feeling; and it was with some trepidation that she knocked at the right door that of the modest house in Waddon Road. It was opened by the young composer's mother. "I will ask him if he can see you," she replied to Miss Walmisley's inquiry.

About two minutes later Coleridge-Taylor appeared smiling, but shaking his head energetically.

"Can't do it now; can't possibly do it now," said he "I am writing a quartet."

"I am sorry to have troubled you," she said, turning away.

"Wait a moment," he suggested.

"I could not think of bothering you now," she answered. But Coleridge-Taylor was insistent. He repeated his suggestion, and without waiting further answer, dived back into the house. He was absent for a few minutes, in which he probably set down his notions regarding his quartet. He then reappeared with his characteristic smile, and threw the door wide.

"I can give you an hour," said he.

They practised; and from this day the central fact in the happiness of our composer began to take being. The first practice naturally led to others, and the mutual interest in music developed into something more personal. Not an unnatural result, surely. In person Miss Walmisley was dark, attractive, and vivid, the possessor of a beautiful voice both for speaking and singing, a quality which had great attraction for Coleridge-Taylor at all times. Mentally and emotionally she was easily the peer of the lad, and her sympathy and wit were quick and complete. Musically, she was of good derivation; her uncle was Thomas Attwood Walmisley, who was professor of music at Oxford in the middle of the last century, and one of the first English organists of his day; a man who is best remembered by a few graceful anthems and services and his madrigal *Sweete Flowers*. A few years passed in pleasant acquaintance before their relation became more definite. There was the shadow upon its bright surface of Coleridge-Taylor's colour. Relatives disapproved emphatically. The negro, they argued, necessarily belonged to a lower stage of development; and in many respects the composer was regarded as an impossible friend and husband by her family. Nor need we blame them for notions which were common to the white race. They were honourable, kindly people, who desired the best for the girl; and with them Coleridge's achievement and promise counted little in face of his derivation. Something must be attributed to the fact that in the nature of things there was more promise than actual achievement. It has been made abundantly clear that at this time he was without any such financial support as would lend an even colourable justification to his taking a wife. For her part, in her schooldays, Miss Walmisley had worked her lessons side by side with coloured girls; nor could she remember at any time having realised that there was a vast gulf socially and morally as men supposed between her and the friends whose complexions were more swarthy. But her own freedom of apprehension was not shared by her people, who prophesied for her social ruin, or at least ostracism if she accepted the musician. Fortunately she possessed a will sufficiently decided to keep her own course; and Coleridge-Taylor worked on incessantly, waiting patiently for the clouds to clear from the horizon.

From his leaving the Royal College until the production of *Hiawatha*, Coleridge-Taylor had identified himself in every way open to him with the musical life of Croydon. At first these opportunities were not great. In the early 'nineties the town could by no means be regarded as a musical centre. Its nearness to London militated then, as it militates now, against the local concert and drama, insomuch that a Croydon musician prefers to give a concert or recital in London and to invite Croydon people thither rather than to court disaster by giving it in his own town. Only an analysis of the suburban mind such as would be out of place here could discover a probable explanation for this fact. Coleridge-Taylor's main work, as I have shown, was teaching the violin at the Conservatoire, and he gave occasional concerts and recitals of his own works when he could afford the monetary risk they involved. The Conservatoire itself gives annual students' concerts, in which the string orchestra figures prominently. When Coleridge-Taylor became its conductor, by the help of Miss Walmisley, Miss Edith Carr, Mr. Henry W. Down, and other musical enthusiasts, he proceeded to work up the orchestra in numbers and in quality, so that it could undertake works of some proportions. Amongst these it is interesting to note that Dvořák constantly appears. During his whole life his devotion to the Bohemian composer never wavered. "I am always a champion of Dvořák," he wrote in the last year of his life.

Amongst the players were the Misses Petherick, who have recalled these days for me. The rehearsals at the Conservatoire were regarded by the members as important weekly events. They took place in the afternoons, and the majority of the members were ladies. The personality of their conductor occupied them much, and they were intensely loyal to him. When once he was referred to as "black," one of the girls retorted indignantly, "Please don't call Mr. Coleridge-Taylor black; he is only black outside." The class had certain signs for foretelling what was to be expected of a rehearsal from the composer's face. When his complexion was dark they prognosticated a good-tempered, suave rehearsal, where everything would go well; when he was pale, it would be fiery, impassioned, nervously irritable. But whatever the shade of temperament thus shown, the conductor was never unpleasant. He would sing the passages *sotto voce*, as he conducted, to give his players the context of more difficult passages. I frequently noticed this peculiarity : he was wont to sing the passages to sounds which may be rendered as "pim, pim, pithery, pim, pim," etc.; and the players seemed always to understand and to like this unobtrusive habit. He had, too, at this time a peculiarity of speech; he was unable to pronounce the consonant "h." His nearest approach to it was "ay" and "ai." This inability he overcame completely in later years. The rehearsals may readily be pictured. "The little dark man with the white stick," as he was called, with his large bushy head and quick smile, beating time to an orchestra which had overflowed the practice room, so that the double passes played in the passage outside taking their tempo through the open door. A boy conductor, scarcely out of his teens, but a vigorous, painstaking one, who insisted on accuracy. Although he had no difficulty in locating faults, and would stop the orchestra to correct them, his correction was never pointedly directed at particular members, but was given in a serious voice, with his glance carefully fixed upon the cornice of the room. They rarely failed to reach the understanding of the delinquent. An amusing variation was his afternoon cup of tea, which was usually brought to him in the practice room. He would drink it, with complete absence of self-consciousness, conducting the while. Such energy would he put into his conducting that it was usually necessary for him to retire and change his collar half way through the rehearsals. The story is told of a playful prank of Mr. Henry Down's, who decorated the large bust of Beethoven in the Conservatoire with Coleridge-Taylor's sombrero. It was a small hat for so large a head, but it helped to show the remarkable likeness that existed between the sovereign composer and the young coloured one. This likeness in brow and the outlines and general expression of face has been remarked in later photographs of Coleridge-Taylor, but our composer never bore on his brow the lines that suffering had graved upon the brow of the master. Throughout, indeed, his face was singularly unmarked by the anxieties of his life.

For a time Miss Walmisley wavered as to which was her path of duty; and, in order to have time to give the matter serious consideration, ceased to meet Coleridge-Taylor. The time was scarcely a happy one for either of the young people, and the separation only confirmed the young lady in her determination to stand by him. They met again at his mother's home in Saxon Road, South Norwood. His room had been newly furnished for him, and rearranged with that regard for neatness and the fitting which always distinguished him. In every vase,

on the table, piano, mantelpiece, were red roses, her
favourite flower. Coleridge-Taylor was an intense lover
of flowers, and he had gathered these from his garden himself, and arranged them for her welcome. The interview
that followed must remain the possession of her who
naturally remembers it as a sacred event in her life.
"What have you been doing of late?" she asked him in
the course of it. "What have you written?" She confesses
to have been a little hurt when he replied, "Some
Humoresques; I'll send you a copy," but thought she deserved the answer. A little reflection, however, will convince that the answer was neither calculated nor mean; the
resilient buoyancy of the artistic temperament of whatever
character would explain his work. The outlook of the
creative genius is almost invariably one of hope, and none
such dwells long in the shadows, especially if he be as
young as Coleridge-Taylor. Further with the interview
we need not go. Suffice it to say that they convinced one
another that their determination to become life-partners
was unalterable.

Coleridge-Taylor immediately followed the honourable
course of calling on her family to ask their consent to the
engagement. Miss Walmisley was then paying a visit
to St. Leonards. On coming down to breakfast at 8.30
one morning she found a telegram from him asking her
to meet him at the railway station. She went immediately,
and found him pacing up and down in front of the station.
The interview, he told her, had failed; his reception had
been distinctly chilly; but what had transpired he, with
characteristic consideration, could never be persuaded to
tell her. "You will now have to act without your family,"
he said; and thereafter this was their attitude towards the
matter. On this same morning Miss Walmisley had to
keep an engagement, and she left Coleridge-Taylor. Returning, she found him chatting merrily with a little girl,
whose mother was sending her to London, and who had
asked him to take care of her as far on the journey as

Croydon. He wrote later that his little charge a quarter of an hour afterwards had climbed upon his knee and was sitting for the remainder of the journey with her arms around his neck. This happy omen shows a characteristic side of his sunny nature. As is the case with most good men, he was a lover of children, entering into their life and play with zest and complete sympathy; a sympathy which is reflected in his musical interpretation of a child's feelings in his *Fairy Ballads*. Children were drawn to him instinctively; and he seems unconsciously to have realised that one of the best possessions of man is the power to inspire confidence and love in the little ones.

Apart from the shadow we have described—perhaps at disproportionate length, but advisedly because of the unusual nature of the case, and because of the prejudices of men—the engagement was calm, sunlit and altogether delightful. Miss Walmisley visited him in the afternoons, where, while he composed she would read through the proofs of his works, sing his new songs, and enter with a trained and affectionate understanding into all his work. They appeared together at concerts on several occasions, the first time at the Conservatoire at a concert given by Miss Lucy Hillier on February 24, 1898, when Miss Walmisley sang from the unpublished manuscripts his four new songs, *You'll Love Me Yet, A Canoe Song, A Blood-red Ring Hung Round the Moon,* and *Sweet Evenings Come and Go, Love*. Another such occasion was on May 24, 1899, at the Salle Erard, London, when Coleridge-Taylor played his own *Romance for Violin*, and Miss Walmisley sang his *Three Rhapsodies for Low Voice and Pianoforte*. If we may judge from the comments of their audience, the singer suffered from a nervousness which outran that of the composer.

The love-letters of Coleridge-Taylor were buried with him. So far as personal intimacies are concerned, this is well; but one regrets that his sketches of his compositions, his notes on the songs of birds he heard in his garden, and his musical views, which he was wont to include in these letters, have vanished, especially as at this time he was engaged upon the *Ballade in A minor*, *Hiawatha*, and the *Characteristic Waltzes*.

One day he and Miss Walmisley were to go together to a concert at Eton. The morning was foggy, and, appreciating the preoccupation which often caused Coleridge-Taylor to overlook such practical details, she sent him a telegram : "Consider the fogs delaying the trains." In a brief time the reply came : "Consider the lilies also." Not brilliant wit perhaps, but characteristic of the sparkle and joyousness of the young man. It was at this Eton concert that the usher announced them as "Mr. and Mrs. Coleridge-Taylor," to their amused embarrassment

During these years his life was of necessity a simple one. His main recreation as heretofore was walking, but now in company with his future wife the walks were further afield. He had a keen eye for the varying aspects of the countryside, especially for flowers, but of scientific botany he never acquired any knowledge. Miss Walmisley, on the contrary, was a keen botanist, and he would remark humorously that half of his leisure hours were spent "sitting on field gates while she poked about in hedges." Her rejoinder that these pauses were responsible for frequent beautiful melodies was not wanting in justice. In other society the only friends whom he visited were the Carrs, the Pethericks, and the Downs, all Croydon families with marked musical inclinations. In these days he would call for tea, or for a quiet evening when he was sure that other company would not be present; and to these friends he would talk of his various designs in music, and ventured his opinions freely. Teaching, well as he performed it, he disliked intensely. "Never teach," he told a woman friend; "it will kill you physically and artistically. Everything you give to your pupil is something taken from yourself." Another characteristic was his scathing criticism of his own violin playing, which lacked the humorous note of his references to his pianoforte playing. After a concert at Wallington, in which he had figured as a violin soloist, he remarked abruptly that "The singing was beautiful, the violin playing rotten," nor would he be persuaded otherwise. It may be that his love for the violin as his personal instrument was failing, and in later years he more and more relaxed his character as player in his concentration upon composition; but I think rather that his love for the instrument was so great and his delight in its perfect manipulation so sincere, that he was unsparing in his criticism of what he regarded as his own deficiencies. I would not put forward the attitude towards his own playing as a commendable quality; on the contrary, it was a weakness, one more outcome of that lack of assurance which was probably racial in its origin.

Besides his teaching at the Conservatoire, Coleridge-Taylor gave private lessons to a few pupils. Amongst these, it may be mentioned, was the mother of Liza Lehmann, the well-known composer of *In a Persian Garden,* and of many songs characterised by delicacy and charm. She was a most interesting and interested pupil. But, remarked the young teacher, "I don't think she really wants the lessons at all. She only takes them in order to help me to an income." At night he still continued his writing, and the strain damaged his eyes seriously, insomuch that for a few weeks in 1898 he was compelled to relinquish all work. It is not a matter for wonder. His manuscripts are clear, but microscopic, and their writing by artificial light must have been unusually trying to the eyes. The pause was timely, however, and although his eyes troubled him in 1906—a trouble the oculist attributed to cigarette smoking—in after-life I do not remember that he ever complained of a recurrence of the trouble; but he was keenly sensitive to any possibility of defect in his sight, and when any reference was made to the deficiencies or diseases of the eyes of others, he would cover his eyes, and a quick, involuntary shiver would run through his whole body.

It was a period of incessant and rapid composition. As early as 1896 he appears on the programme of the Bridlington Musical Festival with an orchestral version of the old English melody *The Three Ravens*. The programme book has this note on the work, "Mr. Coleridge-Taylor, composition scholar of the Royal College, has already won his spurs on the battlefield of orchestral composition. It is more than probable that in many of the first-class programmes of the future his name will be found—like the decimal fraction—' constantly recurring.' " Another work of this period was the *Danse Nègre,* which he afterwards incorporated as the fourth number in his beautiful *African Suite*. It was subjected to an unusual number of re-writings. Originally, he told Mr. Henry Down, it was written as a joke, and a minute copy of the opening twenty-three bars which he wrote in Miss Leila Petherick's autograph album shows his inspiration in a quotation from Paul Lawrence Dunbar, which he had written between the staves,

"Civilised? " "Waal——! " "Sing? " "Waal——! "
"Dance? " "I'll be *cursed* if they can't! "

In this copy it is a work for two violins, viola, 'cello, and bass. The completed version he presented to Mr. Down, and the beauty of the manuscript, which is without visible corrections, is remarkable. The *Danse* was produced very unwillingly at one of the Conservatoire concerts by the composer. He had the greatest dislike of using the concerts as a personal advertisement; and it was only under pressure from Mr. Down and other members of the orchestra that he consented to its figuring in the programme, and their urgency was justified by the warm reception it obtained. His principal compositions of 1897, however, were the *Three Humoresques,* with which he told Miss Walmisley he had filled their days of separation.

I have already made general references to the various songs which appeared in this and the next year. In nothing was he more rapid than in song writing, and he obtained some small income by this means; or, it is truer to say, that whenever he was in need of money, he wrote a song and sold it. This latter contingency was frequent, and his facility made him careless of securing a royalty basis of publication even had he been able to do so. Although admittedly some of these songs were *pièces d'occasion*, it would be unjust to suggest that they did not receive the same loving care that he bestowed upon all his work. On the contrary, one had only to study a few of the songs of these days—such as *As the Moon's Soft Splendour*, with its beautifully appropriate melody, so like and yet so unlike the everyday serenades of inferior composers, and its accompaniment through which runs his authentic phrasing and colour; or his *Sweet Evenings Come and Go, Love*, which has not the same perfection perhaps, but which is still, in melody, accompaniment, transitions and phrasing, as fair an interpretation of the words as even George Eliot could have desired—to realise that, though *pièces d'occasion* in actual physical writing, they were the result of long and affectionate familiarity with the lyrics. The *Six American Lyrics* were composed in a very brief time on a similar urgency. That many of his songs were written for contralto may be explained by the simple fact that Miss Walmisley's voice was of that quality.

The end of 1897 saw the end of his college career, and 1898 was, as earlier pages have shown, the crucial year of his life. Immediately after the success gained by *Hiawatha's Wedding Feast* at the "Tabernacle" of the Royal College, the newspapers had drawn him into the brightest light of publicity, and commissions began to flow in upon him. His most important commission was to provide a choral work for the North Staffordshire Musical Festival to be held at Hanley in the following October. The result was *The Death of Minnehaha*. It was not Coleridge-Taylor's original intention to compose

The Song of Hiawatha as a trilogy as we now have it; *The Wedding Feast* was to have been a complete and individual work. The commission, however, presumed a libretto; and it was natural that he should attempt to exhaust the possibilities of the poetical treasury from which his first great choral success had been gained. Natural as it was, it was a highly dangerous experiment. If the earlier work had in its metrical form presented every prospect of monotony, there were still the variations suggested by the subjects—the narrative, the dance, the love-song, and the boasting. In *The Famine,* which forms the text of *The Death of Minnehaha,* the metre and the substance are an unrelieved and gradually intensifying sorrow. The composer was master of his materials, and the result was the loveliest part of *Hiawatha,* and perhaps the most beautiful choral cantata ever written in this country.

In the intervals of writing this work, other compositions of importance were flowing from his pen. On December 16, 1898, he gave a concert at the Public Hall, Croydon, at which were produced two part-songs, *How They So Softly Rest* and *We Strew These Opiate Flowers.* Another feature of the programme was an operatic romance entitled *Dream Lovers,* the libretto of which had been written by Paul Lawrence Dunbar. It is a brief one-act work, sustained by four characters and a chorus. The story is of a beautiful quadroon lady and a prince of Madagascar, who meet first in dream, afterwards recognise one another in real life, and wed without undue hesitation. The principal rôles were undertaken by Coleridge-Taylor's friends, the chorus parts by a choir of ladies, organised by himself, which bore the name of the Brahms Choir, and his small orchestra was of members of his Conservatoire class and a few friends. The little operetta, with its simple unconventional story and melodious setting, was very acceptable to his audience. The most important work produced at this concert belongs to his highest range of orchestral writing, his *Four Characteristic Waltzes,* at the time his principal purely orchestral work since the *Ballade in A minor.* This same year Coleridge-Taylor published a bright and melodious school cantata for female voices, *The Gitanos,* a work of considerable value in its rather limited class, although the libretto is of no special importance.

He found his Conservatoire class useful occasionally in trying over his new works, although he would not produce them at the public concerts except under pressure. An example of such is shown in connection with the *Characteristic Waltzes,* in the following letter :

30 DAGNALL PARK,
SOUTH NORWOOD.
Monday.

DEAR MISS PETHERICK,—Will you and your sister grant me a very great favour?

If you are disengaged to-morrow afternoon twenty-five minutes before the class commences (not unless) will you kindly play through the published string parts of my *Waltzes?*

They are in the final proof condition, and Novello's principal is nervous about printing two or three thousand copies unless they are perfectly correct.

Knowing I have a string orchestra at my disposal, he asked me to do them, but as the sight-reading of certain members of the class is not *very* wonderful, I'm afraid much time would be wasted—hence my request, which I had much rather you did not grant unless you are QUITE AT LIBERTY.

I also was given to understand that your other sister (Miss Ada) would assist us sometimes, *if she were asked!* I was under the impression that she was always very busy—if this is not so, and she can at any time come, I (and the Director) will be only too pleased to see her.—Yours very sincerely,

S. COLERIDGE-TAYLOR.

P.S.—Kindest regards to Mr. and Mrs. Petherick.

Miss Ada Petherick did become a helper in the Conservatoire class, and the relations between the Petherick

Photograph by Debenham & Gould, Bournemouth.

S. Coleridge-Taylor shortly before his Marriage

family and the composer ended only with his death. As
a constant visitor at their house, who would sit down to
their piano and sing over in his curious voice the melody
he had just written or was writing, as a companion at concerts, a merry, never-ruffled, laughing person, he spent
many memorable nours with them. An interesting little
token of his friendship is the musical conceit turning upon
Miss Ada Petherick's Christian name, which he wrote in
her album,

A-D-A—

August, 1899.

The year 1898 told heavily upon him. The completing
of the *Ballade* and *The Wedding Feast* in itself would
have been no mean achievement, but I have shown that
these were only the chief works of the year. The result
was a brief illness towards the end of December. He had
accepted the invitation of the Gloucester Choral Society to
conduct a performance of his *Ballade* and *The Wedding
Feast*, and was looking forward to his second appearance
in the city in which he had found fame. On the concert
day, however, he was suffering from cold and over-work,
and was compelled to remain in bed. His resilience soon
overcame the illness, and within a week he was busy with
projects for his future; but the cold was to recur frequently.
To all appearance he enjoyed good health, and, in general,

G

appearance and reality coincided, but he had the dread chest weakness which is so common to members of the negro race who live in England; and more than once severe colds prevented him from fulfilling important engagements. Not that he was an invalid or gave way at any time to simple everyday ailments; on the contrary, he fought indisposition as well as any man I have known.

One outcome of the strain of his work was his determination to teach no longer, in the ordinary sense. I have already recorded his opinion of the results of teaching, and the prospect of the relinquishing of lessons must have been a relief. Unfortunately later circumstances made it necessary for him to resume them, although under different conditions.

He had another project. Ever since his Quintet had been played over by Joachim and his Quartet, Coleridge-Taylor had longed to produce his works in Germany. The desire seemed to be near fulfilment early in 1899. He writes concerning his lessons at the Conservatoire and this matter :

30 DAGNALL PARK.
January 2, 1899.

MY DEAR MR. HUMPHERY,—Enclosed is my report and account, which I hope you'll find correct.

As I have so many commissions to complete within the next three years, my friends have strongly advised me to give up my teaching after this next term, more especially as I'm expecting to go to Düsseldorf at Easter for a time.

So will you kindly arrange so that I may have no fresh pupils during this term?

If my visit to Germany is postponed till July, I shall be staying at Gunnersbury, in which case I should like to take the class on Tuesdays as usual. But these arrangements rest with Mr. Jaeger, who is now in Düsseldorf, and I cannot say for certain until I see him again.

Regarding the new scores—I think we shall like :

1. *Serenade.* Goetze, No. 2 in G.
2. *Serenade.* Jensen, Op. 37.

3. *Russian Suite.* Wüerst.
4. *Elegie.* Tschaikowsky.
    Folk Songs. Svenden.

These numbers will fill a performance very well, I think.

I'll have the scores sent you to-morrow.

Trusting you are perfectly well, and with best wishes for a most Happy New Year, both to Mrs. Humphery and yourself,

—Yours very sincerely,

S. COLERIDGE-TAYLOR.

Unluckily for him, the desire was never to be gratified, although Jaeger endeavoured to procure a hearing for him in Germany. Mrs. Jaeger tells me that his work did not find favour with the leading conductors in Düsseldorf; it was not sufficiently philosophical, they contended. Jaeger did not share this opinion, but in consequence of it, although references to possible visits to Germany occur from time to time in Coleridge-Taylor's letters, and although a performance of *Hiawatha* was given later in Berlin, he never entered the country. He, nevertheless, then and always, had the highest admiration for the German people and their music and literature. 'After he was thirty he undertook the study of the language, and in a very brief time mastered it sufficiently to read and write it without difficulty, and one of his warmest friends in later years was Theodore Spiering, the well-known German violinist.

His release from lesson-giving was accompanied by efforts even more strenuous in composition. It was the natural sequel of his success at the Gloucester Festival that he should be invited to write another orchestral work for the following meeting of the Three Choirs Festival. This was held at Worcester on September 13 of this year; and the work he presented was his Opus 40, *A Solemn Rhapsody*. This title did not meet with the approval of his publishers, and at their request he changed it to *A Solemn Prelude*. It is a work with a three-fold theme for full orchestra, with occasionally the organ, and its actual meaning, which the composer wisely left vague, was a source of much speculation. The first theme seems to express dignified complaining, which is met by a second or consolation theme, a haunting melody of much beauty, and the third theme, which is announced only, leads to a suggestion of peace in the closing six bars, which is intensified in a remarkable manner by subdued pedal notes. In the elaboration of the scheme there is genuine thought and earnestness, although it may be admitted that the work is rather more emotional than intellectual, and that the passion that it undoubtedly expresses is more human than spiritual; it has bold arresting harmonies, and a melodic beauty and orchestral richness which show how masterly his control of his medium had become. One critic believed that he discovered in the work the influence of Tschaikowsky. It was dedicated to Mr. Paul Kilburn, of Bishop Auckland, who, as conductor of the Sunderland Choral Society, had directed the first really public performance of *The Wedding Feast,* and who remained Coleridge-Taylor's life-long friend.

Coleridge-Taylor conducted the Worcester performance of the *Prelude* himself, receiving a public reception as notable as had been his a year before at Gloucester, and acquitting himself as a conductor in a manner which showed that a year had enormously increased his power of conveying his ideas to his players. The reference to Tschaikowsky is interesting, as I do not believe that Coleridge-Taylor received any great influence directly from the Russian composer. In 1900 he admitted, as he was always eager to admit, his admiration of, and indebtedness to, Dvořák. Tschaikowsky, however, he talks of in a comparison between that composer and Grieg in a manner which seems to indicate that his admiration for the great Russian, although very real, was hardly that of the disciple. He said, "He is greater than Grieg in some of his works, but far more unequal. His songs are many of them very beautiful, and his *Symphony in B minor* is a

gorgeous conception." And, being asked if he did not
think *The Symphonie Pathétique* the work "of a mind
diseased," he replied, "I don't think there was much the
matter with the mind to which we owe the *Pathétique*. It
is morbid; but then Russian thought in literature and
music is largely morbid. No, no; I regard Tschaikowsky
as a great composer, but a most unequal one."

As I have already said, the principal work of 1899 was
the second part of *Hiawatha, The Death of Minnehaha.*
When he received the commission to write a new work, I
understand that he replied that he would not write an entirely *new* choral work, but would be willing to continue
his already successful cantata. This proving acceptable,
he worked at it, with intervals in which he wrote the
Prelude and various smaller works, through the first seven
months of the year, with his usual extraordinarily rapid
facility, and with his unsparing dissatisfaction with his
results, which led to the usual rewritings. His methods
were interesting. He had the great composer's mental
sense of sound and tone-colour, and could evaluate a
musical work far more easily by reading it through than
by playing it over upon the piano or violin. His ideas
came to him everywhere and almost unaware. Frequently,
after a walk or attendance at a concert or the theatre with
friends, he would walk into the house with them and say
suddenly, "Don't talk to me for a moment." He would
then go to his room and commit his ideas rapidly to paper.
A few minutes later he would return, and with some casual
remark take up the conversation at the point at which it
had been dropped. He invariably composed away from
the piano, but occasionally he would sound a chord or
resolution on that instrument. Erasures or corrections in
his manuscript were intolerable to him. Whenever he
found it necessary to correct, he would cut out a piece of
manuscript paper, and paste it over the offending staves,
and rewrite his passages upon it, or if the corrections
were too many he would paste the rejected sheets together,

and rewrite them as a whole.   As a result his manuscripts
were models of neatness and legibility.

It was during his occupation with *The Death of
Minnehaha* that he decided to make the Hiawatha story
into a trilogy, a decision which was accelerated by an
invitation from the Royal Choral Society.   Coleridge-
Taylor decided that the complete work presupposed an
overture, and he found another inspired interval in which
he wrote the Overture to *The Song of Hiawatha*.   This
work has no pictorial intention, and does not describe
any scene in the Hiawatha story.   It is intended, as
Coleridge-Taylor wrote, to be "an attempt to reproduce,
or, at least, to suggest, the impressions received by the
composer on reading Longfellow's poem."   Although this
was the acknowledged source of his inspiration, his actual
theme was drawn immediately from the music of his own
race.   A little previous to this time the negro choir known
as the Fisk Jubilee Singers had toured England, and,
commenting in connection with them on the inherent
musical character of the negro and its possibilities, the
newspapers had specially emphasised the work of our
composer.   It was not an unnatural thing for him to
use as his theme one of the revivalist hymn tunes which
formed the principal staple of the programme of the
Jubilee Singers.   The hymn chosen :

> " *Nobody knows the trouble I see, Lord,*
> *Nobody knows but Jesus,*"

does not seem an especially appropriate one on which
to build up the introduction to what after all is essentially a pagan story ; but students of music, and especially
of mediæval Church music, will find examples of thematic
adoption far more extraordinary.   The Overture is much
less barbaric in style on the whole than the *Ballade* or
the *Solemn Prelude,* but occasional iterations of detached
and extended chords give the Indian suggestion.   In
form it is more orthodox than its orchestral predecessors,

and consists of a first subject in B minor, a second in E flat, recapitulation and a coda; but there are many modulations, and the resolutions of both main subjects are arresting and original. The opening is a delicate passage for the harp, and the phrasing and orchestration throughout are of commanding freshness and colour.

The Overture was first performed at the Norwich Musical Festival on October 7, under Coleridge-Taylor's own baton. If he had any lingering doubts as to his acceptability to music-lovers, they must have been routed by the warmth of his reception. The work was hailed as one of intense purity and refinement, rich in ideas and devices, melodious and sincere. "It is safe to prophesy," wrote one critic, "that this Overture will henceforward be played at every important performance of the cantata." This prophecy has been curiously unfortunate. Even Coleridge-Taylor himself recognised that the Overture was an independent work; and its connection with the cantata has been regarded generally as nominal, and certainly the beautiful composition is more often than not omitted from important performances of *Hiawatha*. The Overture was succeeded at Norwich by *The Wedding Feast,* in which "Onaway, Awake" was sung by Edward Lloyd. I am told that Edward Lloyd was wont to say, that this air had been written specially for him. However that may be, he was one of the first to include it in his programmes, and it is safe to say that no one has ever interpreted its passionate beauty better than he. His singing of the upper notes, which are all-important in this song, has never been excelled, and I doubt whether his flute-like B flat in the final phrase has ever been equalled.

It was in connection with the Norwich Festival that the veteran critic, Mr. Joseph Bennett, wrote a brief article on Coleridge-Taylor which is worth quoting from, as it shows the position he had made for himself at this time :

Certainly the musical man of the hour is Mr. S. Coleridge-Taylor. He has written, everybody knows, a work called *Hiawatha's Wedding Feast.* Let us see how that stands at the present time. It is to be performed this week at Norwich, and, three weeks later, at the North Staffordshire Festival. It is in the winter programme of the People's Palace Choir, also in that of the Bermondsey Settlement Choir, and in that of the Highbury Philharmonic Society. Two choirs in Birmingham have it on their respective lists. At Manchester the Vocal Society promises it; at Liverpool a similar society has it in hand; and South Shields awaits it. That is pretty well for one work, but the young Anglo-African has written a companion for it, *The Death of Minnehaha,* as yet unpublished and unperformed. This will be heard for the first time at the North Staffordshire Festival, yet already several societies have made ready to take it upon trust, among them the People's Palace Choir and a Sunderland musical institution. Mr. Coleridge-Taylor is now engaged upon a third composition of the same class—*Hiawatha's Departure*—which, with its two fellows, will be given at one of the forthcoming concerts of the Royal Choral Society.

Is not such blazing success enough to turn the young musician's head? The answer depends, of course, upon the strength of the head, and we can only hope for the best. It is, perhaps, more important to look for the qualities which the public approve so quickly and completely, but these had better be discussed a little while hence. I may, nevertheless, mention that in *Minnehaha* the composer works upon the lines which served him so well in *The Wedding Feast,* showing again the remarkable freshness and vigour, the novel features, and the power of picturesque expression that make him the Rudyard Kipling of our younger composers. To the greater intensity of the *Minnehaha* subject, as compared with *The Wedding Feast,* Mr. Coleridge-Taylor easily accommodates himself.

The Death of Minnehaha was produced, together with *The Wedding Feast,* at Hanley, on October 27, the composer conducting. The cantata itself is so familiar that any description I could give of it would be a task of supererogation, and Joseph Bennett has written a technical analysis of it, which demonstrates how skilfully Coleridge-Taylor avoids the almost certain pitfall of monotony, the power with which themes suggested in *The Wedding Feast* are given sequels, and how human is the pathos which pervades it. Drama in choral music has rarely reached the heights of the passages where Minnehaha sees and hears the forms of famine and fever, and shrieks for Hiawatha, and the cry is heard miles away in the forest by her husband. Rarely has a Dead March had more simple emotional intensity than that which accompanies the chorus, "Then they buried Minnehaha," and a more beautiful baritone solo than his "Farewell, he said, Minnehaha" is not to be found in the range of English music. The work is a triumph in itself and in its performance.

Out of the publication of his various works Coleridge-Taylor had now prospect of an income. His fame was secure, commissions to write continued to reach him, and engagements to conduct his own and other works became frequent and promised to be profitable. Moreover, his publishers had, for an annual sum of £100, secured the right of first refusal of all his new works for the next five years. There was also a small income from his work as conductor at Croydon. In sum his earnings were inconsiderable, but the horizon seemed bright. This brightness was intensified by the already noted invitation which he received to complete *Hiawatha* for the Royal Choral Society's performance in the following May; and in November the Birmingham Festival Committee asked him for a new work. *The Daily Telegraph* records the last matter thus:

It is understood that Mr. Edward Elgar and Mr. Coleridge-Taylor have accepted commissions from the Birmingham Festival Committee to prepare new works. Let us hope that these composers will not yield unduly to temptation, and overreach themselves. The inducements are many and great, but beyond a certain point no creative musician can go without risk to both health and reputation.

The advice seems gratuitous, and certainly was unnecessary, as the immediate sequel proved in Coleridge-Taylor's case, but it was some indication that his friends thought he was working too incessantly and too hard. To the end this view prevailed in several quarters, but he met the criticism to some extent in 1906, when writing of the untimely death of his friend, W. Y. Hurlstone :

Like many another highly gifted musician, the late Mr. Hurlstone, whose death we all so deeply deplore, was remarkably prolific in composition. This seems to be one of the surest proofs of an imagination above the ordinary. Truly quantity is not quality, but with the single exception of Chopin, all the famous composers have left a vast amount of work behind them. We have only to think of Schubert and Mendelssohn, both of whom were in the thirties when they died, to realise the truth of this assertion.

With such prospects as we have indicated, Coleridge-Taylor felt justified in taking the most important step of his life. He and Miss Walmisley were married quietly on December 30, 1899, at Holy Trinity Church, South Norwood. Dr. J. W. G. Hathaway, the well-known organist, attended him as groom's man. On the wedding morning the bride received a telegram from her husband that was soon to be :

"I will never leave thee, dearest,
I will take thee to my wigwam."—*Hiawatha*.

Coleridge-Taylor had hoped for a quiet wedding, from which the young married couple could slip away unnoticed to their new life. A letter to Miss Leila Petherick, in which he thanked her for some decorative paintings of his favourite flower, the chrysanthemum, expresses his point of view :

30 DAGNALL PARK,
SOUTH NORWOOD.

Friday.

DEAR MISS PETHERICK,—Please will you and your sister accept our sincerest thanks for your kind remembrance, which I am sure we shall value more than anything else we have received—for artistic reasons. I think I ought to explain that Miss Walmisley and I both wish the ceremony to be kept very *private.* It is so difficult to know exactly where to draw the line without offending anyone—so that practically there will only be ourselves present. So you will understand why you have had no formal invitation—simply because none have been sent out! A small loss, you will say (!), but I thought you would like to know the exact reason, and I'm sure you will think of us as if you were present.

Miss Walmisley will write to you herself.

With kindest regards to all.—Yours very sincerely,

S. COLERIDGE-TAYLOR.

To ensure further privacy he eschewed the orthodox carriage and pair, and ordered a weather-beaten hansom cab from the station rank to await bride and bridgroom outside the church. Somehow, however, the news had leaked out, and the embarrassed young pair found a church filled with people awaiting them.

The service over, they fled by train, and had their wedding breakfast alone at the Grosvenor Hotel, Victoria, proceeding in the afternoon to Shanklin, in the Isle of Wight, where a brief honeymoon of a fortnight was spent. Even during his honeymoon Coleridge-Taylor could not tear himself from his beloved work. The first draft of *Hiawatha's Departure* was now complete, and at Shanklin he was busily engaged in scoring it; and while he worked his wife would read novels to him, in particular the works of Marie Corelli and Marion Crawford. This seems a curious example of a mind able to engage in double exercise; and that it was double exercise is proven by the fact that Coleridge-Taylor would make critical comments on the story without looking up from his score or ceasing to write.

Never was a marriage, disapproved of by well-meaning friends, more triumphantly justified in its results. For Coleridge-Taylor it was the happiest and most successful enterprise of his life. From a domestic standpoint the remaining thirteen years of his short life were sheltered, wisely counselled, entirely happy. "I have been very happy in my surroundings all my life," he told his old friend, Mr. A. T. Johnson, in the last year of it, "first in my mother and then in my marriage. Even without any moderate success I think I should have been one of those rare beings—a happy man. Unlike a great many painters who want to be musicians, musicians who want to be painters, and barristers who want to be journalists, I want to be nothing in the world except what I am—a musician."

CHAPTER VII

AFTER their return from their honeymoon the young couple settled for a few months in lodgings in St. James's Road, Croydon, where Coleridge-Taylor completed *Hiawatha's Departure,* and with it the trilogy. The earliest draft of *The Departure* was a failure in several ways. It seemed that Bennett's advice to Coleridge-Taylor not to over-reach himself was not without justification. Jaeger played over the manuscript, and came near to tears; the choruses were commonplace, the melodies in the setting of the scenes where the Black-Robed Chief appears were little better than mediocre hymn tunes. "This will never do," wrote he frankly to the composer. "The public expects you to progress, to do better work than before; this is your worst." It was not simple advice to offer to a man whose name started out from every important newspaper of England as one of the most remarkable men of his day; but the advice was given, and it is to Coleridge-Taylor's credit that he received it modestly and admitted its truth. At once he recast the whole work, consulting Jaeger at frequent intervals; and the final draft was worthy to be a pendant to *The Wedding Feast* and *The Death of Minnehaha.*

From St. James's Road the Coleridge-Taylors moved back to South Norwood, and for two years they lived at 30 Dagnall Park, a modest house, but convenient to their needs, and well out of the noise of main street traffic, in a road which is leafy and somewhat retired. Here he entered with enthusiasm into the minor domestic details. Mr. Henry Down tells me that he found him on his knees one day merrily laying carpets, and not at all perturbed

in this unmusical occupation by the appearance of his
visitors. His home-life was quiet, regular and contented.
He would rise invariably a little before eight in the morning, and was always at the breakfast table by twenty
minutes past. Punctuality was a virtue which he cultivated in all things. In his personal habits, from his
speech to his well-kept hands, he was exemplary. He
held, and rightly, that the outward appearance is the
index of the mind. His clothing was scrupulously neat,
and the least speck of dust irritated him as much as a
bad note of music. This was no pose for occasions; it
was the expression of the refinement which pervaded the
whole life of the man. For his thought was as clean as
his appearance. He was undoubtedly the best *raconteur*
I have ever known; his fund of amusing stories seemed
to be inexhaustible; but in a very real and long-standing
intimacy with him, alone in his drawing-room, in his
"music shed" at "Aldwick," on top of omnibuses or in
restaurants, I never once heard him utter a sentence which
could ruffle the serenity of the most sensitive mind. He
had a pretty theory, which I am afraid is only a theory,
that people who played beautifully were always beautiful
people. Perhaps in a moral sense this is so, but one
can vary the phrase justly, and say that in his case,
although the Miltonian assertion that high art can only
be found in conjunction with personal purity is a question-
able one, he wrote beautifully because his own mind
was itself beautiful. Ten years after the time of which
I am writing he was asked if he did not believe that an
artist could not produce anything better in moral influence
than he was himself. He demurred at first, but then
admitted its possible truth, "Because," said he, "what a
man is often means so much more than we think. 'At
the moment when the artist composed his sublime idea
in music there must have been something in him to corre-
spond to it, although perhaps only a sub-consciousness.
I remember studying the work of a composer of an ex-

ceptionally tender and dreamy type, and what was my surprise when I shook hands with a swarthy giant as the composer." This is an explanation to be considered; but he was, in any case, a standing contradiction of a too popular notion that the artistic mind is, or need be, decadent in any way.

He never lost his natural modesty, his dislike of open adulation or notoriety; and when he was fulfilling engagements in strange places he usually preferred the anonymous solitude of a hotel to private hospitality, because he feared that the latter, however kind, would bring him into contact with the strangers whom his well-meaning hosts would assemble to meet him. It has been asserted frequently that he loved the advertisement of newspaper paragraphs, that he wrote his music with one eye upon his applauding audiences. The best reply to the criticism is a knowledge of this true reticence, this physical shrinking from satisfying the desire to lionise which seems to dominate some people when they meet an eminent man. It is true that his would-be admirers were often fulsome to his face in their outspoken praises. A simple man, such as Coleridge-Taylor was, who had his own natural and just consciousness of his peculiar powers, is apt to weary of being told that he is "a great genius"; and I have heard him receive such speeches in his own drawing-room; and, what is more, I have seen him laugh them away and turn the conversation rapidly to other matters. He would in later years discuss his music with only a very few of his intimate friends, and he had a peculiar objection, almost amounting to a superstition, to allowing anyone to look over his works while they were in process of composition.

Strong as was this retiring disposition, to a fairly large circle of friends his home became open house. Hospitality of an exaggerated kind he never professed to dispense; but to those of us who cared to come in on Sunday evenings for coffee, cigarettes and conversation, he offered an unaffected welcome. He had a great fondness for all

three things. His most characteristic attitude, as I see it
in retrospect, was a standing one on the hearthrug with
his back to the fire and his elbows on the mantelpiece,
and his face and eyes vividly eloquent with the experience
or story he was telling. I seem rarely to have seen him
sitting in his own house. Experiences seemed to throng
his existence, and he had the imagination which trans-
forms quite simple occurrences into significant happenings.
He would smoke many cigarettes and drink innumerable
cups of coffee; he never drank intoxicants of any kind.

It was on evenings like this that we gathered and
treasured scraps of his conversation. Most of it has been
forgotten; much of it he would no doubt wish to remain
unrecalled, as he did not always confine himself in the
nature of the case to deliberately considered opinions.
What strikes one most is the continuous development of
his opinions on most things. Early in life he favoured
absolute music as compared with vocal or operatic music,
but he gradually progressed towards operatic music. *A
Tale of Old Japan* is essentially operatic in its method,
and is as dramatic as a purely lyrical libretto will permit.
"I always enjoy writing for the stage," he told me once;
and I remember that his first request to me was that I
should endeavour to provide him with the libretto of a
grand opera. To write such an opera was always one of
his ardent desires. One day we fell to discussing the
modern musical play, the technique and melodies of
which he quite ungrudgingly admitted to be often excellent; and on my rather obvious suggestion that the
writers of such trivial music rarely, if ever, rose to musical
excellence, he pointed out that Sullivan had accomplished
much; "but," he added, "it is not fair that a musician
should be able to write in both kinds." Devotion to light
music, he thought, destroyed one's higher inspiration,
and admitted, too, the converse of the proposition. This
view he modified greatly in his last years, and he would
have undertaken a light opera had he been fortunate

enough to secure a libretto. "I am full of tunes such as that," he exclaimed to Mr. J. H. Smither Jackson after they had listened to the performance of a musical play of the most gossamer character. Another instance of the fluidity of his opinions refers to poetry. The thing which appealed to him last was almost invariably "the best I know." His first loves were the Brownings, as I have amply made evident; then followed Longfellow; but he surprised me one day by saying that he had just been reading the greatest poet he had ever read, who proved to be Lady Florence Dixie. I pressed the question a little in dissent, and found a deeper chord than usually appeared on the surface of his nature. There was in Lady Dixie's poems a mystical other-worldliness which appealed to his religious sense. He impressed me often quite unconsciously with a suggestion of his sense of the infinite which I could not define or express; a something that still remains a mystery to me. Of his religious opinions I am unable to say much that is definite. We have seen that as a youngster he was a chorister first at a Presbyterian and later at an Anglican church. He rarely discussed his belief, but he had a sure instinct for the Hereafter, and his life was essentially a religious one. "I do not know what his creed was," Mr. Henry Down tells me, "but at the back of everything he did—even his minor works—lay a strong religious feeling."

His relations with the clergy were limited. Once a clergyman came to tea with him, and had the unlucky inspiration to be surprised at the likeness in habits which Coleridge-Taylor, a man of negro extraction, showed to an English gentleman. "Do you actually drink tea and eat bread-and-butter like other people " he asked in real astonishment. Mrs. Coleridge-Taylor came to her husband's rescue, and the gentleman was not invited to the house again; but it is just one more instance of the isolation in which he stood so frequently.

Coleridge-Taylor rarely set his opinions upon paper,

H

but he was frequently interviewed, and some of his views given out by both means are worth recording here. One must start with Dvořák, with whom he had affinities both artistic and racial, and from whom his allegiance never wavered. Writing of W. Y. Hurlstone, he says : "In our student days we each had a musical god. His was Brahms, mine was the lesser-known Dvořák." In 1900, he said, "I have been greatly influenced by Dvořák—a bad choice you will probably say, for Dvořák's influence on English music generally has not been great. I think his *Symphony in G minor* one of the finest compositions of modern times. Please remember that I do not advance this view as a criticism. It is simply my personal predilection, and is possibly largely temperamental. His *Piano Quintet in A* is another splendid work, while his *Stabat Mater* is, in my opinion, unsurpassable. It is undoubtedly his finest composition." And, in 1911, writing to Mr. A. T. Johnson about *Stabat Mater,* "I wonder what you think of Dvořák—personally it impresses me more than any religious work I know, and I think that the last number stands by itself as a really noble inspiration—but, then, I am always champion of Dvořák."

One magazine* drew forth a few of his ideas on the influences on modern music.

Bach, he thought, exercised the first really determinate influence. "There is no doubt that Bach suggested even more than he wrote, but what he wrote is so great and so resourceful that every composer since his time must have found a perfect mine of musical treasure in Bach's works. I do not think he has had any *direct* influence on the composers since his time. On the other hand, his genius is so all-embracing that you can find the foundation of most subsequent methods in his works. What I should say of him is that he presents an encyclopædia of composition which covers, more or less, everything in music, while, in addition, he is a composer of strong

* *The Crystal Palace Magazine,* November, 1900.

individuality, and ranking, as he is worthy to rank, as a master."

He attributed the most direct influence on modern composition to Beethoven, and gave his view with animation. "Beethoven undoubtedly gave to musical expression that wide view, depth, and emotional character which subsequent music has only developed. Beethoven, compared with his predecessors, Bach alone excepted, represents an advance as striking as if one exchanged a spinet for a modern grand piano. Earlier composers were thin, mechanical, and artificial, and had no conception of orchestral use or resource such as Beethoven employed."

He placed Brahms at the head of modern composers. "Brahms has exercised more influence on modern English music than any other composer. It is, however, an influence from which present-day writers are most noticeably freeing themselves, so that the effect has been mainly educational."

"I do not think that Grieg will exercise—indeed, I do not think he *can* exercise—any influence on music generally. His music is essentially individual, just as Chopin's was individual. Like Chopin's it will, I feel sure, live, but will live unique. It is also national music in tone and character, and that is bound to limit its influence. It is solely its beauty which can be universal, not its influence. It is, in a word, music for the public rather than for the schools."

Six years later, in 1907, he said, "I don't think I have any favourite piece, but I am a great admirer of the modern Italian. I think Puccini has done a great deal for modern music. But then, of course, my sympathies are all with the stage and opera." At this time, it may be remarked, he was contemplating his own opera.

"I think Sullivan's *Golden Legend* is the finest cantata that has been written by any British composer," he told his pupil, Mr. E. Beck-Slinn.

In discussing form in music, and its effects upon inspiration, he said, "I confess that my preference is for shorter pieces than symphonies, and on definite themes, dramatic by choice, but I do not think that the last musical word we shall hear, or that will be worth listening to, has been spoken in the old forms. There is a tendency towards freedom in this direction, but even those composers who show it most are to a great extent governed by the set forms, though that form may sometimes appear to be nowhere. I think the tendency will increase, just as in opera and oratorio the composer has been guided by the inspiration of his subject, and broken away from the traditional limitations, but I believe in orchestral composition the process will be one of enlargement rather than a breaking away. The development of the ' symphonic poem ' may perhaps point the way out, but it is a matter on which I should hesitate to be didactic, nor do I think anyone can, at the present stage of music, speak with confidence on the subject."

These views, most of which were uttered in 1900, would doubtless be subject to some modifications had he ever thought of reviewing them; but they are perhaps better as indications of his attitude towards music at this time than any retrospective view coloured by later experience could be.

He had accepted the commission to provide a new work for the Birmingham Festival of 1900; but shortly after the Christmas of 1899 he realised that if he meant to do justice to *Hiawatha* he must concentrate upon that work. He accordingly intimated to the chairman of the Birmingham Festival Committee that he found it impossible to compose a new work of importance at that time, adding, "I will not compose, unless I feel that I have got it in me to compose." The Lord Mayor, in commenting upon his letter, said, "It is a great disappointment, but we must respect a man who makes such an assertion." The committee therefore decided to give the whole of *Hiawatha*, as being completely representative of the composer.

At last *Hiawatha's Departure* was completed, to his own and his critics' satisfaction, and was put in rehearsal by the Royal Albert Choral Society. The performance was dated for March 22, and Coleridge-Taylor was asked to conduct. The occasion was not one to be regarded lightly. Said *The Times*: "It is probably without precedent in the history of music that the first part of a trilogy should be composed while its author was in a state of pupilage, its second commissioned by a provincial festival, and its third brought out by the most conservative society in existence." It was an opportunity, too, that comes rarely to any young composer. To have an entire evening devoted to a single work, by a choir and orchestra of a thousand people, before an enormous audience, and in the largest concert room in the kingdom, are elements well calculated to upset the equilibrium of any young man of twenty-five. But at the same time it was a considerable strain upon him. There is none of the glamour of a festival about the Albert Hall; the huge building overawes, and the audiences are usually remarkable for a refined austerity which indulges in no unnecessary enthusiasms. A man of Coleridge-Taylor's temperament might well shrink from facing it.

The concert evening found the chorus in a state of unpreparedness. The rehearsals had been insufficient, and there was in consequence a deficiency in light and shade, and several ragged entrances in the singing. This was naturally attributed to another cause—the conductor's inexperience; quite unjustifiably, as a clear-sighted critic declares that it was principally due to his clear beat, enthusiasm, and presence of mind that the performance was as good as was the case. In spite of these imperfections, the original beauty of the music found its way to an audience which included many well-known musicians. Old concert-goers could remember only one work that had raised the same tremendous enthusiasm—Sullivan's *Golden Legend*; and by the time the end of *The Death of*

Minnehaha was reached it had risen to great heights. Coleridge-Taylor had been recalled three times, and had disappeared, but the audience remained unsatisfied, and went on applauding for exactly five minutes, until he was found, and came forward to receive an ovation of cheers, "which," says one observer, "astonished no one more than its recipient." Much the same experience met him at the close of *The Departure*.

It was now possible to judge the work as a whole. In the books of words, which contained analyses of the respective sections by Jaeger and Joseph Bennett, Jaeger aptly compared the work to a symphony of which *The Wedding Feast* formed the opening allegro, *The Death of Minnehaha* the slow movement, the first portion of *The Departure* up to the Iagoo scene the scherzo, and the rest of *The Departure* the finale, with the baritone scene, *Hiawatha's Vision,* added as a short fifth movement or intermezzo between the scherzo and finale. The criticisms varied, but in general it was held that from the standpoint of technique the work was a progress, and that each section showed a greater command of the resources of the composer's art than its predecessor. At the same time it was agreed that *The Wedding Feast* still held the pre-eminence in its complete originality; that *The Death of Minnehaha* was the work in which the means to the end were most perfectly conceived and employed; while *The Departure* gave rise to a variety of opinion. It was considered to be worthy of its companions, and its orchestration was almost faultless, but there was a feeling that it was too long, and that the final chorus wanted cutting. Coleridge-Taylor took the hint, and in future printed copies a large possible excision was marked in the chorus indicated. One or two thought that in so long a work the monotony of the metre of Longfellow's poem made itself visible through the music, but this view was by no means general; on the contrary, congratulations were many and openly expressed upon the ingenuity with which he had avoided the pitfall of monotony.

I do not wish to weary the reader by quoting too freely from the newspaper critics, because journalism is for the day only, and in all probability if the writers had contemplated any permanence for their utterances they would have modified them; but it is impossible to realise the position Coleridge-Taylor had attained unless some review of them is made. Every journal of repute devoted a column to the Albert Hall performance, and not a few several columns. The appreciative outpourings were not confined to any particular set of critics, but came from the whole musical world and through the pens of its most reputable writers. *The Standard* said of Coleridge-Taylor that he "promises to contribute to the glory of our music." *The Times* was only a little less restrained : "The success so unusual in the case of an English work is most thoroughly deserved, and in fact the work in its strongly-marked individuality, perfect adaptation of means to ends, and general effectiveness has few rivals among recent compositions." *The Daily News* was most emphatic about *The Death of Minnehaha,* of which it says : "The treatment so often dramatic and never exaggerated, shows the hand of the master; marvellous, indeed, seeing that the composer is so young." *The Globe* declared that "His flow of melody is unfailing, and the brilliancy of his orchestration and the fertility of his imagination are quite astonishing. Not less surprising is his originality; from first to last every page of the score is stamped with the composer's originality. This is, perhaps, one of the most satisfactory features of his talent, but quite as striking is his power of producing big effects by comparatively simple means." One highly esteemed critic is worth quoting, not only in this connection, but also for the ethical value of the parallel included in his remarks. " I can scarcely pay a more sincere tribute to the young composer's genius than the recording of the fact that his *Hiawatha* kept a not inexperienced musical critic out of his bed until the green dawn made the street lamps a deep gold by contrast. Genius is a strong word—it should be the last in the critic's vocabulary. It is like a banknote—worthless unless it represents wealth. For the critic to give it away easily and without being very sure that within his brain are impressions equal in value to that verbal draft is nothing less than dishonest. The word cannot be recalled; the banknote cannot be stopped without damaging the critic's credit. I paid it away in my brief chronicle of Thursday night's performance, for of one thing I was sure at least—Mr. Coleridge-Taylor is a genius. And now, writing some hours after, I find I was more than justified." And he proceeds to devote a thousand words to determining whether Coleridge-Taylor belongs to the sublime class which includes Beethoven, Brahms, and Wagner, or to the less sublime one which includes Dvořák, Chopin, and Tschaikowsky. To this last question the writer in *The Birmingham Post* gives an answer when writing of one of the rehearsals. "He is, in gorgeous imagination, a second Tschaikowsky; in economy of thematic material another Dvořák. . . . I would strongly advise the Festival Choral Society to give the whole work as I heard it this morning. The result would be the greatest musical sensation (in the best sense) experienced for years." But of these comparisons the earlier critic disposes : "The music of *Hiawatha* is not Tschaikowsky or Wagner or Dvořák—there may be passing reflections of these masters, but on the whole the music is Coleridge-Taylor."

These are typical quotations, and sufficient to indicate that Coleridge-Taylor had attained a celebrity such as many great men only reach after a lifetime of effort; and it is well to remember this in view of the often unkind criticisms which were levelled at him in later years. But across my contemplation of these eulogies will flicker the whimsical thought of the little quick-moving man whose face lighted up when one encountered him, with the smiling exclamation, "You! How are you? Why haven't you been round to see us lately?"; who, saying suddenly, "Come and have some coffee," would seize one's arm and pilot one into the nearest café, where, to the accompaniment of the inevitable cigarette, he would pour forth a stream of his experiences as artless and unaffected as if he were entirely oblivious of his claim to any more consideration than the humblest of his friends.

One may say safely that beyond an innocent elation in these appreciative accounts, the praise of his listeners had small effect upon Coleridge-Taylor. In other ways, however, they did him incalculable harm. The generous, warm-hearted Jaeger had burst forth enthusiastically on the publication of *The Wedding Feast*. "Here is a real heaven-sent musician, and we feel inclined to quote Schumann à propos of Chopin: ' Hats off, gentlemen, a genius! ' " Immediately a cautious critic whispered in his ear: "You have forgotten Sullivan"; and later, when he felt even more assured of Coleridge-Taylor's achievement, an eminent musician gave him the cruel suggestion that he should moderate his praise, as people of negro blood did not develop beyond a certain point. Jaeger did nothing to arrest the progress of his young friend, but these opinions were bruited abroad by others; they became canons indeed with many of his critics, and it is necessary to refer plainly to such brutal nonsense as found expression in a phrase overheard by a friend of my own in a publisher's office concerning Coleridge-Taylor at this time: "He's a damned nigger. He'll never do anything more," was the choice observation repeated to me. No other man of genius since the birth of time has had to suffer the horrible, soul-destroying indignity of such an assumption —an assumption which the composer of *The Atonement, Meg Blane, Kubla Khan, A Tale of Old Japan*, to say nothing of *The Violin Concerto* and *The Bamboula*, has falsified in every particular.

On a former page I have asserted that the British musical critic is unassailable, but it is very curious to note that shortly after this a conspiracy of silence seemed to occur. How much of this is imagination I cannot say, but I am not alone in the belief that Coleridge-Taylor's works were consciously or unconsciously ignored by many who profess to shape musical opinion in this country. When they did deign to notice his later works, it was nearly always in the form of a comparison between them and *Hiawatha*. Probably the burning desire for originality which has pervaded not only music, but every form of art during the past ten years, is responsible for the critical attitude which did such despite to Coleridge-Taylor's work. *Hiawatha* was at once his glory and his bane; it had genius and novelty combined; and thereafter the critics demanded novelty of him rather than music. Music he gave them in every way equal to *Hiawatha* in inspiration and technique; they failed to acknowledge it. Without wishing unduly to magnify the opinions of a negligible critic, one instance must be quoted as an example. At Birmingham *Meg Blane* was given in the same programme as Beethoven's *Mass in D*. In a Birmingham journal next day a notice occupying a column appeared, with the caption "Beethoven's *Mass*," and in the last line appeared words to the effect that "Coleridge-Taylor's *Meg Blane* was also sung," without comment either upon the work or the rendering. This was typical. I cannot pretend to explain on any grounds of criticism this attitude towards a really fine choral work, nor the statement of a *Saturday Review* critic that "any day would do to talk about a work of Mr. Coleridge-Taylor." They are the statements of men who seem not to have learned that prejudice and criticism are not convertible terms.

The whole of the spring and early summer of 1900 was a time of strenuous work. On April 30 we find him conducting the final version of his *Symphony in A minor*,

of which I have already written at length, at tne Winter
Gardens, Bournemouth. This was the beginning of an
unbroken connection with the excellent orchestra at
Bournemouth. He often conducted it in later years; and
in many talks with myself he had rejoiced that one muni-
cipality at least in England has been wise enough to
support an orchestra of the highest character. Moreover,
he was loud in his appreciation of the musical director,
Mr. Dan Godfrey, who, without in any way relaxing a
lofty musical standard, has shown a patriotism in the
production of new works by British composers which is
as rare, unfortunately, as it is commendable. At this
concert he also conducted a performance of. *The Wedding
Feast.* On May 3 he was at Worcester, conducting the
Festival Choral Society in *The Wedding Feast* and *The
Death of Minnehaha.* On May 24 he appeared at the
concert of the Philharmonic Society at Queen's Hall to
conduct a new orchestral suite entitled *Scenes from an
Everyday Romance.* What the everyday romance is no
one has been able to discover; and although almost every
critic has propounded it as a conundrum, Coleridge-Taylor
maintained silence upon the point. It may have been a
story of his own fashioning. He certainly had imagination
enough, but I do not remember him exercising it in any
such manner. However that may be, the work was produced under pressure, and at the time of the writing of
the analytical notes for the concert programme the parts
were in the hands of the copyists, and the annotator, Mr.
Joseph Bennett, was unable to do more than give a skele-
ton idea of the movements. These are four: an *Allegro
in E minor* in sonata form, with two themes, one vigorous
and with several variations of key; an *Andante in G major,*
a simple, melodic, straightforward treatment of a single
theme; a *Tempo di Valse* and *Molto Moderato* which together form the third part, the waltz being treated with
considerable grace, and again passing through many
transitions to a Trio in G minor as melodious as the

Andante, and concluding with a coda in the tonic major; and a *Presto in E minor,* in which the leading themes are recalled and worked up to an energetic conclusion. "The work as a whole," remarked the analyst, "may be described, with the aid of some fancy, perhaps, as a symphony in miniature. The changes in key indicated at the head of the various numbers are more apparent than real, and the old principle that a suite should be of one key throughout is in the main loosely preserved by the invariable return after each of the many harmonic changes to the initial key." His hearers were agreed that the work held most of the best elements of his writing—vigour, grace, melodic beauty, and an almost barbaric vigour in the *Presto.* If any criticism can be levelled at the work, it is that too great economy in the use of thematic material is observed, and in consequence there is somewhat too insistent repetition.

It was during 1900 that Coleridge-Taylor began to have really definite relations with America. His works had already gained a considerable vogue in that country, and on March 12 the Cecilia Musical Society of Boston gave a performance of *The Wedding Feast* to a crowded audience, which was repeated on March 14. Coloured Americans, too, had long since discovered him as the rising star of their race in the artistic heavens. So much may be gathered from a *Tribute,* written of this year in 1912 by Mrs. Mamie E. Hilyer, of Washington, the wife of the treasurer of the S. Coleridge-Taylor Choral Society.

Having ended a very delightful visit to Paris and the Exposition, I was preparing to leave for Oberammergau, where I expected to experience the climax of my visit in witnessing that great drama, "The Passion Play," which can be seen only at Oberammergau once in ten years, when I received a letter from my dear friends in England, the Loudins, saying that they would be in London in a few days, and wished me to join them there and meet the now famous coloured composer, Samuel Coleridge-Taylor. Such was the magic of this name, that when I found myself again I was in London, having given up without any mental struggle whatever my long-cherished purpose to see "The Passion Play" at Oberammergau, one of the objects for which I had put three thousand miles of ocean between myself and my loved ones.

Mr. Coleridge-Taylor regarded Mr. Loudin as the best friend he ever had, saying, "He, more than anyone else, helped to make me known to our dear American people." Before going to London I knew something of this talented composer's work, thanks to Mr. Loudin, who had kept us supplied with English papers from time to time containing glowing accounts of this young Anglo-African, and to Mr. Harry Burleigh, who had sent me a copy of *The Wedding Feast* shortly after it had made its triumphal appearance in 1898.

In due time, Mr. and Mrs. Loudin took Dr. and Mrs. Cabaniss and me on the train to the modest suburban house of S. Coleridge-Taylor, who, with his charming wife, gave us a hearty welcome to their home and hospitality. The simple and unaffected manner, the ease and modesty of bearing, the enthusiasm and magnetic personality of this remarkable man, his intense interest in his people in the States, his high musical standing in England, as the musical man of the hour, were qualities calculated not only to awaken our admiration, but unconsciously planted within us those seeds of inspiration, possibility and hope which were destined to grow in virgin soil and to blossom so abundantly, as you have all seen.

I thought it was an unspeakable privilege to have had the opportunity of seeing the world's contributions and triumphs in the arts and sciences as they were so wonderfully portrayed in that great international exhibition at Paris, but when, after my return home, I began to speak of my experiences while in Europe, out of the fullness of my heart my lips would repeat, "Coleridge-Taylor," and very soon in my little world all were acquainted with his fame and name.

Shortly after my return, Miss Lola Johnson hearing that I had been quite ill, sent me word that she was coming round to sing for me and talk "Coleridge-Taylor." Together we dreamed of the possibility of having a choral society here to sing his works. She volunteered to write Mr. Coleridge-

Taylor and ask if he would come over and conduct for us if we should get up a chorus. He wrote her a ready and affirmative reply. This inspiring letter was read to the ladies of " The Treble Clef," a small band of married women music-lovers, who immediately pledged themselves to promote the cause. A meeting of the prominent musical people was called at my home. Then and there was born the S. Coleridge-Taylor Choral Society, whose achievements and triumphs are of such recent history that it is not necessary to mention them in this presence.

The musical society thus foreshadowed was composed entirely of coloured singers, and was named appropriately after the greatest coloured exponent of music. It came into being in 1901.

Second only to the Albert Hall performance of *The Song of Hiawatha* was the performance of the complete work at the Birmingham Festival on October 3. The festival was notable, too, for the début of Elgar's *The Dream of Gerontius*, the only choral work written within its decade which seems in any way to challenge the repute of Coleridge-Taylor's work. This finely inspired work was performed on the same day as *The Song*, occupying the morning, while the latter occupied the evening. The veteran Dr. Hans Richter conducted both, not altogether to the satisfaction of Coleridge-Taylor, who admired the giant conductor greatly, but believed that his sympathies did not centre in choral works.

The results on the audience of the two works were exactly opposed. *The Dream of Gerontius* fell on ears yet unprepared to appreciate its depth and splendour. On the other hand, the huge audience in the Town Hall cheered *The Song of Hiawatha* with an enthusiasm as unrestrained as any audience had yet bestowed upon any section of it, and that in spite of the complaint that the conductor failed to bring out in its actual intensity the pathos of *The Death of Minnehaha*. We have here one of those fine problems of popular criticism which are so difficult of solution. In character, of course, it is impossible to compare *Gerontius* with *Hiawatha;* but both are inspired works on the highest plane of choral art. Perhaps the melodies in the latter are more spontaneous and evident, while the former attains its effects by means much more complex; but, even admitting this, we can only wonder at the failure of any audience to grasp the beauty of the simple orchestral opening of the second part of Elgar's work, the grandeur of "Praise to the Holiest in the Height," and the melodious originality of the interplay of soli and chorus throughout. Elgar's work affirms the theory that the public fails to recognise great music at sight; while Coleridge-Taylor's is its refutation.

I believe that it was at Birmingham that Coleridge-Taylor witnessed what he afterwards said was the most whimsical incident in his life. Some of the principals gathered at a private house after the evening concert, and Richter contributed to the interest of the occasion by playing the overture to *Tannhäuser* on a pianola. The juxtaposition of the greatest orchestral exponent in England of Wagnerian music and the mechanical piano-player struck Coleridge-Taylor as being irresistibly funny.

A great personal happiness came to Coleridge-Taylor during this same month. On October 15, his son Hiawatha was born. In appearance the baby showed something of his father's swarthy complexion, and with the progress of years he has become more and more like him in features. It is not inappropriate to quote from a letter from his mother's pen, written a few weeks later : "Quite apart from a mother's point of view, he is perfect ! He has very small features—a beautiful little head, thickly covered with black, silky hair. A broad, musical forehead. Very tiny ears. Very small mouth. A very sweet nose and a *bridge* ! (Most babies haven't got one !) Perhaps the most perfect points about him are his beautiful expression, in which he exactly resembles his dear father; and his lovely hands ! " Much of this we seem to have heard

before in connection with other babies, but there is no
doubt whatever of the joy the child brought to his parents.
The enthusiastic young couple named him Hiawatha—
tentatively, as his mother explained, and subject to his own
ratification when he should reach years of decision. "Unless I am greatly mistaken by his intelligent little face
now," she added, "I feel sure that he will be proud to be
named 'after father's great work.'" All things considered, this was the happiest period of the life of the
composer. Into his home circle this new and promising
interest had come, his various engagements and compositions brought him modest but still comfortable financial
circumstances, his name came first to the lips of all lovers
of music as the new dynamic force in British music; and,
so far, the shadow of criticism, of faint praise which half
veiled contempt, had not fallen upon him.

In the summer he first received a commission from
Mr. (later Sir) Herbert Beerbohm Tree to provide the
incidental music for his prospective production of Mr.
Stephen Phillips' poetical drama *Herod,* a task which he
hailed with enthusiasm. Dramatic in character we know
all his music to be, and very soon after the appearance of
Hiawatha his mind turned with almost violent longing
towards musical drama in the real sense. This commission seemed to be an approach towards the desired end.
Admittedly this was music written to order, but I venture
to think that finer music of the kind has rarely been
written than is to be found in the incidental music which
he furnished for the four successive poetical dramas of
Stephen Phillips, *Herod, Ulysses, Nero,* and *Faust.* He
threw himself into the task with delight, drawing real inspiration from the beautiful verse of the poet. The *Herod*
music as we now have it consists of four numbers, *Processional, Breeze Scene, Dance,* and *Finale,* and is entirely appropriate, and therefore splendid and dignified,
as becomes the drama, in the straightforward, massively
simple *Processional* and the *Finale,* which are both much

less chromatic than is usual with him; while the *Breeze Scene,* and particularly the *Dance,* are rich and graceful. The last, which is in three-quarter time, occupies five pages of the ordinary pianoforte score, and in this compass has five key transitions, yet one theme pervades it, and the medium is a fairly simple one. In regard to the songs, Coleridge-Taylor may be said to have done well with difficult material. Richness and splendour, and a mellifluous spontaneity, are characteristics of the blank verse of Stephen Phillips; but when he ventures upon lyric poetry he is upon alien ground. Certainly none of his songs sing of themselves as the true lyric must do. But mere suggestions seemed enough for Coleridge-Taylor. "At times," said he, "I could set a butcher's bill to music." There were other times, indeed, when he gazed with a simple wonder at the facile compositions of a young composer friend who seemed to be able to produce music of no mean character at will, and admitted that his inspiration was not a thing which he might call and recall at any moment.

CHAPTER VIII

THE three years, which for considerations of space I group together, have been regarded as a period in which the composer moved as a whole upon a level plane, rarely falling below his acknowledged powers, but again seldom rising above them, and certainly not fulfilling the promise of his early youth. It is still too soon to judge of the justice of these views. I do not accept them without grave qualification, and I am prone to believe that they were not the views of the public, but rather those of the professional musical critic. I have already said enough about the type of prejudged criticism which assailed him; and it is safe to say that it has an infinitesimal effect upon the public—that is to say, directly. It has, however, an immense effect upon those who organise and conduct music; and herein lay the struggle for Coleridge-Taylor. His own attitude towards criticism varied with his years. In early youth, as I have shown, all musical scribblings were of intense interest, but in early manhood, in his twenties, his sensitiveness was little less than painful. Outwardly he bore criticism cheerfully. Once when a friend remarked upon the flagrantly unjust disparagement of a critic, he remarked smilingly, "Oh, they are all very kind; it is quite a kind notice," but secretly he felt these attacks so keenly that his wife persuaded him to cease reading criticisms altogether. We have the amplest evidence that they did not act as an obviously paralysing force, but I know that he would have done better work had a wider understanding and a saner sympathy been extended to him. In his thirties he gained the detachment and independence which made him entirely indifferent to them, and the sense of values which enabled him to gauge the character of his critics and to appraise their work. "In later life," Mr. W. J. Read tells me, "he was superior to criticism, and that in no vulgar sense."

He continued to conduct his orchestral class at the Croydon Conservatoire. His many engagements, however, must have occasioned much trouble on the part of that institution, as nearly every one of his letters to Mr. Humphery in these years is a request either for an alteration in the time of his class, or that one of his friends, Dr. Ernest Fowles or Hurlstone, should be asked to deputise for him. Doubtless, on the other hand, Mr. Humphery, who maintained the happiest relations with him, regarded Coleridge-Taylor's presence in the Conservatoire as a privilege not to be dismissed without thought; and his frequent "please apologise to the ladies for me," did not give rise to the least resentment. It must not be supposed that he neglected his duties. His letters amply prove the contrary. Every piece of music to be played was carefully studied, and the rehearsals were still minute in their care, in spite of the fact that often within an hour of their conclusion he would be on his journey to a distant part of the country to conduct an important concert. In the same way his pupils never doubted the importance he attached to rehearsals. Brief notes, with heavy underlinings of date and hour, he was wont to dispatch to most of them, and it was an unusual pupil who did not succumb to his enthusiasm. How he himself came to regard the pupils this brief note to Miss Edith Carr will indicate :

30 Dagnall Park,
South Norwood.
Saturday.

Dear Miss Carr,—I am more than sorry to hear you are leaving the class.

It is always painful to lose old faces, but as you have belonged to the class ever since I first conducted it (and before,

I believe), it makes the wrench particularly severe, especially as I was unprepared to hear any such thing.

Why did you not tell me—this afternoon at rehearsal, so that I might have bidden you "Good-bye"?

With many thanks for your loyalty and enthusiasm all through, and with kind regards to Mrs. Carr.—Believe me, very sincerely yours,

S. COLERIDGE-TAYLOR.

Immediately before a Conservatoire concert he would have at least two rehearsals weekly, and often more. He would leave nothing to chance. The concerts themselves were unusually good students' concerts, and the audiences which gathered at them were not solely of the parents and relatives of pupils, nor was their applause the encouragement they gave to the efforts of learners out of mere human kindness. Here, as at all concerts at which I saw Coleridge-Taylor conduct, he expected the courtesy of a hearing from his audience. He would stand with his baton raised waiting for absolute stillness for what seemed to at least one member of his audience a painfully long time, and only when the tiniest rustling in the concert room was silenced would the baton descend in its first beat. An incident at one of the concerts deserves record. The strings were playing some very soft music; and throughout this some ill-mannered people at the back of the hall persisted in talking. Coleridge-Taylor stopped the concert, and turning round to the audience, said, "Will those people who want to talk, please go outside." The remark, which was received by the audience with appreciative applause, galvanised the interrupters into attention and reasonable behaviour.

The coloured American friends whose visits are recorded in the previous chapter maintained their correspondence with him, and he received many visits from other friends from over the Atlantic, many of whom pursued him with the well-meaning pertinacity which is characteristic of the American, calling upon him at all hours and even at midnight. Whatever inconvenience these unconventional visits may have caused him he concealed, and he welcomed them with his simple hospitality and conversation. In February, 1901, the Hilyers sent a present for the baby, Hiawatha, on behalf of the Washington musical society, The Treble Clef, which he thus acknowledged:

February 22.

DEAR MRS. HILYER,—It is difficult to express our thanks on paper for the very handsome present received yesterday from the members of "The Treble Clef."

When Baby grows old enough to understand I am sure he will be ever so proud of such a remembrance from his coloured friends of Washington.

Please tender our appreciation to each member of the club on behalf of Hiawatha.

When we come to the States we shall make it our first engagement to visit you all, but it is as yet undecided as to when we can undertake the journey. As for my compositions, I am just at present very busy with my new choral work for Leeds Festival which takes place next October.

A photograph of Hiawatha in his mother's arms and one of myself will reach "The Treble Clef" in a week or two; which I hope you will all accept.

With the kindest regards from us both to you and Mrs. Cabaniss and the other members.—Believe me, very sincerely yours,

S. COLERIDGE-TAYLOR.

This year Coleridge-Taylor became conductor of the annual Westmorland Festival at Kendal, an appointment to which he refers in another letter to the Hilyers, which has, however, a deeper interest.

May 12.

DEAR MR. HILYER,—Many thanks for the kind remembrance.

I was keenly interested in reading your remarkable compilation of the doings of the coloured race. It makes me wish to be out among you doing my share of the great whole; but perhaps, in matters of art, it is better for a coloured individual to live in my country than in America, as we are so dependent on mood; tho' I must say the people I have met from the States have all seemed to be extraordinarily cheerful! Perhaps it is because they are philosophical and I am *not* very much so, I am afraid.

Still I would like to come over to conduct some of my music, especially if a real good coloured chorus were available.

I have been appointed permanent conductor of the West-morland Festival, a huge gathering held in the beautiful Lake District every year. This first one you will be pleased to know was a great success, and the singing (choir was 600 strong) was magnificent.

Moreover, the famous Hallé Band from Manchester was engaged for my benefit, and so we had a really wonderful performance each evening.

I suppose in your States such a thing would be impossible —and yet, why? I cannot but believe that all this real striving and earnest work will do something to leaven the prejudice between black and white; or am I wrong, and is it a fact that it rather tends to increase it, as I was last week informed by a coloured American?

Whichever way it is, it seems certain that substantial footing has at last been gained, and also that that footing will be kept.

I hope you will be kind enough to let me know of anything interesting. I can assure you that I appreciate and value the book very much indeed. It would be so kind of Mrs. Hilyer if she would and could send me a copy of a photograph of the Clef Club. In fact, as I sent a photograph of my wife and boy to these ladies, I think the least they can do is to return one of themselves.

I was surprised to find Dvořák's name in your list. I hope the club is worthy of his name, as indeed I am sure it is. Dvořák was my first musical love, and I have received more from his works than from anyone's, perhaps. I love the "open-air" sound his music always has and the genuine simplicity which our modern music so often lacks.

I am sure you will look on this letter as an imposition,

which, indeed, it is, but as you'll never get another letter quite so long from me (I hope) you'll forgive this one.

Mrs. Taylor wishes me to send her kindest regards to Mrs. Hilyer and Mrs. Cabaniss, and with my own remembrance to you all.—Believe me, very sincerely yours,

S. COLERIDGE-TAYLOR.

It was during the autumn of this year that he accepted his first invitation to officiate as adjudicator at a musical festival. The eisteddfods in Wales in particular made much of him in this capacity, and it is curious to think that he liked the work. He was warned of its exacting, and not always pleasant, character. "My dear fellow," said the late Dr. E. H. Turpin, the principal of Trinity College of Music, when Coleridge-Taylor mentioned the matter to him, "don't you undertake that job at any price! You have no idea what adjudicating at that place is like. Why, I had my hat knocked in and only got safely away with great difficulty." He continued to Mr. A. T. Johnson, to whom he told this story, "I thought at first, after hearing this, of throwing up the job, but second thoughts made me go on with it, and I have never regretted it."

I think he must have enjoyed the spectacular side of these festivals, since it is difficult to believe that the hearing of bands, choirs, or soloists producing the same works a large number of times, with varying degrees of perfection or otherwise, could have appealed to the musician in the man. He admitted himself that "a Chopin Scherzo played continuously by different people from nine in the morning till six in the evening was apt to get tiring"; but he defended these festivals a few years later. "Much is being said at the present time against the competitive idea, especially in music, because of the gambling spirit that may be introduced. But there is none of this kind of vicious excitement; nobody seems excited in the room except the competitors. There is one great thing to be learned from an eisteddfod : you get to know and use your judgment with regard to pieces of music which perhaps you would not otherwise understand."

In his early experiences as an adjudicator he complained of the quality of the music set, and of the narrowing effect which the exclusive study of the test pieces had upon the competitors. "There is no reason," said he, "why people should not read music at sight just as they read words. It is only a little application that is wanted." And in the choice of vocal music he made a plea for modern part music. "You cannot hear it in any other way. For instance, there is one composer, Cornelius, who has written some beautiful part-songs; but you cannot hear them anywhere except in Lancashire."

He derived perennial amusement from the methods adopted by the organisers of these festivals to ensure perfect impartiality on the part of the adjudicators. The story may be told in his own words to Mr. Johnson : "At one place there were three adjudicators, and on arriving at the hall we found three Punch-and-Judy-like erections set on poles. Into these we three poor men climbed by means of ladders, and then curtains were drawn closely round. As each choir finished a man mounted the ladder, poked his arm through the curtains, and took our folded lists of marks, which were added together on the platform.

"But the brass band contest takes the palm. Everybody connected with one seems absolutely unable to trust the judge. I was once adjudicator at a brass band contest, and I had to stay in my room at the hotel, right away from the window, and judge the bands as they played in passing along the street. On another occasion the contest was held in a large field, and a deep hole was dug in the ground in which the adjudicator was placed, and covered over with boards, so that he should not see anything. At another place, I had finished my work, and was passing by the end of a platform on which the bands were competing. It had been raining all day, and the water was standing a foot deep under this platform. There I saw a man with his body hanging over the supports and his feet dangling in the water. I said to the committee-man with me, 'That poor fellow seems very ill. Hadn't we better go and help him?' 'Oh, he's all right,' was the airy reply, 'That's the adjudicator.'"

This, in retrospect, is the lighter side of this work, but Coleridge-Taylor gave severe attention to its serious side. He was scrupulous in his judgments, but modest and genial in his pronouncement of them, and even the failures rarely went empty away. Of the few speeches he made in his life, most of them were made to choirs at such gatherings. In giving judgment on solo work particularly he laid more stress on the emotional interpreting of the composer's intention than on the technical excellence of the performance. "There is a higher thing than technique," he remarked once on the competitive playing of a Chopin nocturne, "and that is understanding."

Part of a letter from a girl competitor at a festival at Leamington may be introduced here as an instance of the effect he made upon the competitors, although the occurrence to which it refers did not take place until the year before he died.

"I am sure," she writes to Mrs. Coleridge-Taylor, "that you will like to know how he is loved and remembered by one who knew him but slightly.

"The first and only time I saw him was at the Leamington Competition Musical Festival last year. I heard him adjudicate the violin competition on Thursday, and looked forward to playing in the pianoforte competition which he was to adjudicate on the following Saturday. Although many of us were very nervous, he did his best to put us at our ease, and in his adjudications there was no competitor to whom he did not say something encouraging. At first he awarded me a second prize, but afterwards he made us equal, and himself made my half-guinea up to a guinea. When the competition was over he called me and spoke most kindly to me. I have always been passionately fond of music, but from that time I have had fresh vigour and interest in it all, and whenever I feel discouraged I think of what he said to me that day. I have thought of him continually since, and I always hoped that some day I might see him again. It was not, of course, that he gave me a prize, but that so great a musician should show kindness, sympathy, and encouragement to a nervous girl of sixteen greatly impressed me. Though it was only for a short time that I met him, you can hardly wonder that his influence entered deeply into my life."

One interesting remark in connection with choral competitions that he made in passing in a conversation was, "I invariably find that choirs of children sing part-songs much better than grown-ups."

Although early in 1900 he had refused reluctantly to provide a new choral work for the Birmingham Festival, no sooner was the *Herod* music off his hands in the later part of the year, than he commenced a choral cantata for the Leeds Festival of 1901. In this and in each of the two following years he was to produce a choral work of considerable dimensions. The cantata of 1901 was *The Blind Girl of Castél Cuillé,* a setting of Longfellow's translation of a Gascon romance of the troubadour kind, by Jasmin, a Gascon poet who presents a few of the characteristics of Burns. Here it is only just to say that in the choice of his words Coleridge-Taylor made the cardinal mistake of his life. His astonishing musical fame had been won by the interpretation of a story which had all the elements of primitive romance, a barbaric twilit background of trackless forests, great rivers and lakes, illimitable skies, and a noble pagan human sentiment which answered elements in his own racial make-up. Here, instead, he had a simple story which has probably been enacted in every village in England. It tells with inartistic circumlocution of Margaret, a betrothed girl, who loses her sight through disease. Her faithless lover is lured into marriage with another girl, Angela. Whereupon the heartbroken Margaret goes into the church where the ceremony is taking place armed with a knife with which to stab herself before the eyes of her lover; but before she is able to carry out this suicidal intention she falls dead at his feet. The scene is a Gascon village landscape flowering under bright March sunlight. In the original the story has probably great charm; but in translation it is dull, slow-moving, and its undoubtedly dramatic final touches are reached through tedious passages describing the weather, the village, and the wedding accessories. Clearly, from the point of view of character, this story has few of the elements of *Hiawatha*, and Coleridge-Taylor, in chosing it, had loaded the dice against himself from the outset.

The musical treatment he gave it resembles *Hiawatha* in so far as it consists of brief orchestral introductions and interludes, a chorus narrative, and more or less dramatic solo numbers. The opening is as sunlit and joyous as the landscape it describes, and in several places the work comes within easy distance of the more excellent parts of *Hiawatha*. Certainly, too, the phraseology, the musical texture of the work, is reminiscent in not a few places; but there are considerable differences in the two works, and a comparison such as this is entirely misleading. His handling of the orchestra is as masterly as anywhere in work written previous to this, and his command of melody in the principal song, Margaret's "He has arrived," and of simple pathos in the interjected explanation of the chorus, "Thus lamented Margaret," show no failure of power, while the final chorus is a sombre counterpart of the opening chorus of undoubted strength. It is rather in the connecting links between the dramatic points that the interest flags; and this is so obviously the fault of the libretto that little more can be said than that the difficulties he overcame in making music of them would have overwhelmed a composer of inferior powers.

It was produced at Leeds under Coleridge-Taylor's own

baton on October 11.   He had excellent principals in
Madame Albani, and in Andrew Black, who sang the
character of the boy, which, with a curious disregard for
actuality, Coleridge-Taylor had given to the baritone.
Both chorus and orchestra found an enjoyment in the
work which appeared in the excellence of their singing and
playing.   The audience received the work with the
warmest approval, and the composer was accorded the
customary vociferous honours at the conclusion of the performance.   From the point of view of popular judgment,
the work was successful; but there were doubters.   Sir
Charles Stanford, who in a retired corner had listened to
its rehearsal, was greatly disappointed in it; insomuch that
he avoided meeting Coleridge-Taylor lest he should be
compelled to hurt his feelings by admitting the unfavourable judgment.   On the whole the professed critics praised
the work, but with reservations.   "Composers seem sometimes guided by an evil genius in the choice of their subjects," said one otherwise enthusiastic critic, "and certainly Mr. Coleridge-Taylor's good angel was slumbering
when he engaged himself to make a cantata out of *The
Blind Girl of Castél Cuillé,*" and the burden of this complaint weighs down every criticism I have encountered.
But while there was much praise, there was also the inevitable comparison with *Hiawatha.*   "Is it an advance on
Hiawatha?" the critics chorus together.   No, they decide
upon a single hearing; and thereafter the question and the
answer become traditional.   One critic who admitted that
he had never heard any of the later works kept up the
answer to the end.   He was typical, and, if there was any
tragedy in Coleridge-Taylor's life, it was this bland acquiescence in the inferiority of his later powers by men
whose profession it was to have known better.

The principal orchestral work of this year is another
evidence of his interest in his father's race.   This is his
Toussaint l'Ouverture.   The career of the greatest negro
before the advent of such modern geniuses as Frederick

Douglass and Booker T. Washington—the slave-born soldier, who rescued Hayti from the invader, and as its President restored order and prosperity, only to be crushed in his last brave stand against slavery by the treacherous cupidity of Napoleon—would naturally appeal to Coleridge-Taylor. The work, which was produced at the Queen's Hall Symphony Concerts on October 26, 1901, and again on December 1 of the same year, illustrates some of the characteristics of this remarkable leader.

The conducting work at the Croydon Conservatoire was not the only work of this character in which Coleridge-Taylor was now engaged in Croydon. The musical life of the town during the 'nineties had sunk low. Coleridge-Taylor's first master, Mr. Joseph Beckwith, had indeed for some years given orchestral concerts, but when he left the town sometime during these ten years, Croydon found itself almost entirely without music of any regular sort. Seeking to remedy this state of affairs, Messrs. Henry W. Down, T. W. Wood Roberts, Sidney Edridge, and other lovers of music, banded together to organise the Croydon Orchestral Society in 1897. At first, Mr. Henry W. Down, who was the leading spirit, depended upon a conductor from London, and the first season ended with the usual deficit. It was soon determined to offer the baton of the society to Coleridge-Taylor, and in the season of 1898-99 he accepted it. From the numerical standpoint the society left nothing to be desired; there were seventy players in all, in proportions such as eighteen first violins, twenty seconds, five violas, seven violoncellos, four double basses, besides wood, wind, and tympani. The quality was not in proportion to the numbers; there were one or two good players in each section, but many were indifferent, as is generally the case where a musical society is composed entirely of amateurs and where social and personal considerations blend with musical in the admitting of players. With this material Coleridge-Taylor occupied himself strenuously, and although in the face of such odds as I have indicated he rarely secured results to his complete satisfaction, the society held together under his direction for nearly six years. The concerts were given in the Pembroke Hall, which is not far out of the centre of Croydon, but quite sufficiently so to make it a doubtful place in which to hold such concerts. The programmes, of which I have a complete file before me as I write, were laid out upon a consistent plan of from eight to ten numbers, one of which was usually a symphony, two were vocal, and one or two were for solo instruments. The concerts were of two hours' duration, and Coleridge-Taylor was scrupulous in keeping them within this limit, inflexibly refusing to allow encores when there was a possibility of exceeding it. He held rightly that longer concerts were an undue tax upon the audience, which must be protected against itself. I have already shown that in encores he preferred to repeat the work encored to performing another work. Moreover, he had the wholesome view that an audience should be reasonable in its demands upon performers, a matter which is not seldom overlooked.

A study of the programmes is disappointing in one respect; the conductor's own compositions occur scarcely at all. One would imagine that he would have used his opportunity to secure performances of his new orchestral works, and there is little doubt that the orchestra would have welcomed them; but only the *Danse Nègre, The Characteristic Waltzes,* and, later, *Ethiopa Saluting the Colours,* seem to have been performed during the whole of the society's existence. An interesting feature was the annotations which he provided for the later programmes. The notes, which are signed "S. C. T.," are so characteristic that I cannot refrain from quoting one or two of them.

Speaking of Grieg's *Concerto in A minor,* he writes :

Grieg has written no Symphony. His one String Quartet is not by any means one of his brilliant achievements, and therefore the Concerto being played this evening may be correctly designated as his most important work in Sonata form.

It is a fine composition from every point of view.

The opening Allegro is one of the most imaginative movements in Musical Literature. There is no preliminary fuss : a very few introductory bars (of which much is made during the progress of the movement) lead to the first subject proper, which is rhythmic rather than melodic in interest.

The characteristic second theme should not pass unnoticed : the short repeated phrases, the ever-varying and highly original harmonies helping to produce a very beautiful and new effect.

Note the Cadenza, too—not a mere flourish of notes to show off the soloist—but a splendid variation of the principal themes, which in its logical elaboration *does,* nevertheless, incidentally give the chance all soloists, not excluding the present one, so ardently long for.

The slow movement calls for few remarks. It is a short, simple little song without words, full of tenderness and pathos.

All the strings are muted, and but a portion of the wind instruments are used.

The Finale is a light, bright, fanciful movement in 2/4 time, quite in the accepted Rondo form, with one important exception.

This is the second subject, a lovely piece of music, heard in the upper register of a solo flute, the strings accompanying *pp* tremolo.

After the usual repetitions, etc., this second subject is broadened and enlarged in a most masterly fashion.

The key suddenly changes to A major (that bright key), the *pp* changes to *ff,* and an astounding climax, which also forms the Coda, is made from the few unoffending notes originally heard as the second subject.

One recognises in this Concerto, more, perhaps, than in any other of Grieg's works, that the author is a poet as well as a musician.

Of Schubert's *Unfinished Symphony in B minor* :

Of this, the most glorious of all Symphonies, so much has been said that only the briefest reference is necessary.

Whether the third and last movements would have equalled the two first (if they had been written) no one can say. Let us, however, be satisfied with those we have, for they never have been (and probably never will be) surpassed, not even by the great Beethoven himself.

The opening Allegro is astonishing in its perfect form, exquisite conception, rich melody, and clever construction.

Probably Schubert spent more time over this music than any other, for, generally speaking, the more spontaneous music *sounds,* the more trouble it has given its writer—a strange and difficult fact for the uninitiated to realise.

Nor need anything be said of the slow movement (E major).

Too poetical, too entrancingly beautiful for words, it speaks for itself in language so clear that the dullest listener can understand and appreciate.

Of Mendelssohn's *Concerto in E minor for Violin and Orchestra* :

There are only three Violin Concertos written by the Great Masters : the Beethoven, the Brahms, and the Mendelssohn— not counting those of Max Bruch and Tschaikowsky. Those by the first-named composers are undoubtedly finer compositions than the Mendelssohn, and yet how is it that this one is still considered (rightly or wrongly) *the* Concerto for Violin and Orchestra? It may be explained in this way perhaps.

That, splendidly written as the others may be for both Orchestra and Solo Instrument, there is nevertheless a feeling that the Orchestra is getting the best of it in many places, and the *strain* on the Soloist is often apparent.

In the Mendelssohn everything seems to be easy and perfectly fitted together. The solo writing is beautifully clear, effective, and grateful to both player and listener.

The opening movement (Allegro molto appassionato, is in quick duple time, and the Solo begins at once, minus any introduction, announcing that first subject of which Mendelssohn makes such splendid use during the course of the movement.

Of Beethoven's *No. 2 Symphony in D* :

The Symphony, No. 2 in D, which is being played this evening, belongs to the earlier or "first period" of Beethoven's compositions.

It was composed in 1802, and is particularly interesting, if only because it seems to mark a dividing epoch in Beethoven's works.

For in this Symphony there are none of those vivid picture-like impressions with which the following Symphonies are charged, and yet what an immense advance we have here on No. 1! True, the influence of Mozart is apparent in many places, but nevertheless the work is entirely Beethoven. Moreover, to the uncultured (musically) listener, this No. 2 is perhaps the most easily followed, the most straightforward, and the most obviously *apparent* of all the nine.

It opens with an introduction of 33 bars on slow 3/4 time, proceeding without a break into the real first movement (Allegro con brio).

This is in quick duple time, and the violas and 'cellos answer the first rhythmical subject, which is soon repeated by the whole orchestra.

After an energetic and almost fiery episode, the second subject appears. It is divided into phrases of four bars each; the first being given to clarinets, bassoons, and horns—*piano,* and immediately repeated by strings, trumpets, and drums—*ff.* Another interesting episode follows before the double bar is reached.

Then comes the development, and who shall write worthily of a Beethoven development?

But, notwithstanding its amazing cleverness and ingenuity, it is clear and comprehensible to the most casual listener. The usual repetition follows, and a fine coda completes the movement.

Of the slow movement (Larghetto) some writer says : "No one has ever written more beautiful, sustained, abstract music than this."

Remarks are therefore superfluous, but the beautiful contrasts between wood and strings will be noticed, as will the more than usually lovely subjects.

J

The following movement is a real Beethoven Scherzo indeed.

What energy! What spirit! What quiet fun pervades the music! And where is there a more charming trio than in this Scherzo? Clear as crystal, simple as you please—but—Beethoven.

The last movement (Allegro molto) is a fine Finale—charged with an abundance of fire and strenuous energy. The strongly marked rhythmical first subject and the quiet legato second subject are conceived with the composer's usual inborn feeling for sudden and effective contrasts.

The movement is full of signs of the "Great Man to be," and is a magnificent example of a Symphonic movement is one tempo, without any interruption from beginning to end.

I do not feel it necessary to apologise for these quotations. That they present little of the prescient phraseology of the professed critic is not their least charm; and they show that simplicity of mind which is a cardinal characteristic of the man who understands from the inside and loves because he understands.

During 1901 the Samuel Coleridge-Taylor Choral Society came into being at Washington, largely with the purpose of producing Coleridge-Taylor's work. Naturally he felt the keenest interest in this organisation of musical coloured people, and not a little pride in the appreciation that its existence implied. The close of the year brought him an invitation from the society :

> 2302 SIXTH STREET,
> WASHINGTON, D.C.
> *December* 17, 1901.

MR. S. COLERIDGE-TAYLOR,
LONDON, ENGLAND.

DEAR SIR,—An organisation known as the S. Coleridge-Taylor Choral Society of the District of Columbia has recently been perfected in this city. Its specific object is the presentation of your *Hiawatha;* its general purpose the inculcation of higher musical ideals through a better understanding and appreciation of standard musical compositions. This society has been organised partly in response to a long dormant desire for a fuller development along musical lines, but the direct incentive and prime inspiration of the present movement was the stimulus awakened by your prospective visit to America and our own city. The society has, agreeable to the conditions suggested by yourself, organised a chorus under the leadership of Prof. John T. Layton, for many years Instructor of Vocal Music in the public schools of this city, and Director of one of the largest and most proficient choirs in the city. His co-workers and associate officers include most of the coloured musicians and prominent citizens, so that competent leadership is assured.

The work is being enthusiastically received by the public at large, the sentiment in its favour is growing, and only the definite assurance of your coming to America remains to crystallise that sentiment into practical results.

We are directed by the Board of Managers to convey formally the earnest desire of the society that you visit our city at such time as will be convenient to yourself to conduct the presentation of *Hiawatha,* and to extend to you a cordial invitation to be the guest of the society during such portion of your visit to America as may be spent in Washington, and to assure you that the organising and drilling of a competent chorus and the procuring of a suitable orchestra are gladly accepted by us as conditions precedent to the arrangement of final details as to the time of your coming.—Very truly yours,

ARTHUR S. GRAY
(*President*).
JOHN F. COOK
(*Secretary*).

Circumstances prevented his acceptance of the invitation for a year or two, but the prospect appealed to him, and an American tour became a fixed purpose.

The success of the incidental music to *Herod* brought him a commission to provide music for Stephen Phillips' *Ulysses,* which Mr. Tree contemplated producing in January, 1902. I am sure that he was never more happy than when engaged upon work for His Majesty's Theatre. He would return in the evenings after the rehearsals of the play, with long whimsical accounts of the readings, the effects of particular passages, and would mimic the peculiarities of the actors with vivid good nature. He had much admiration for Mr. Tree and his remarkable fertility in ideas; and he formed a warm friendship with the talented conductor of the theatre orchestra, Mr. Adolf Schmid, which was to be permanent. Characteristically he believed and affirmed that the blank verse of *Ulysses* was "the greatest he had ever heard"; and in a conversation on this point he made the side remark that "the verse of Shakespeare does not appeal to me except when it is read aloud; then it has real grandeur." The music to *Ulysses* consists of an overture, interludes, and entr'actes, the fine song, "O Set the Sails," and a remarkably dramatic and effective storm scene. Unfortunately, all Coleridge - Taylor's attempts to induce a publisher to produce this music, or as was usual with his incidental music, an orchestral suite from it, resulted in failure. The theatre retains the score, but the world has not heard the music, except the song, which was published later, since the run of the play ceased.

Mr. Schmid tells me that Coleridge-Taylor was almost an ideal composer for the theatre. His quickness in assimilating the ideas of the drama upon which he was working was unusual. Mr. Tree would give him some such suggestion to interpret as "the moon rising over an ivied wall," and he would assimilate it immediately into his music. Nor did he place ridiculous values upon the music that he wrote for the theatre; he welcomed, accepted, and was most grateful for all suggestions.

The year 1902 opened badly for Coleridge-Taylor; towards the end of the month he was incapacitated by a brief illness. He wrote to Miss Edith Carr:

11 DAGMAR ROAD,
SOUTH NORWOOD, S.E.
February 6, 1902.

DEAR MISS CARR,—Many apologies for not answering your kind letter before.

This has been a week of disappointments for me—among other things I was to have conducted the first performance of *Ulysses* at His Majesty's and the Scottish Orchestra at Glasgow, but for once King Influenza has reigned supreme. Now you know why I have not been able to write.

I am really glad you and Mrs. Carr were able to sit through *The Blind Girl,* and thank you most heartily for your appreciative letter.

Regarding Violin pieces—you are a little too early I am afraid. Miss Ethel Barns will produce these new pieces of mine early in March, and the only advance copy there is ready she of course must have, or I would with pleasure send the music on to you. I'll send you a copy as soon as they are published—neither of them is particularly difficult, though perhaps the tempo of the last will prevent it being called easy.

I hope you and Mrs. Carr will go to see *Ulysses*—nothing has ever been seen on the stage to equal it—and I think you'll like my music, though it is not Grecian and therefore not ugly enough for certain critics! Our united kind regards to you and Mrs. Carr.—Yours sincerely,

S. COLERIDGE-TAYLOR.

Coleridge-Taylor spent a few weeks at the seaside every year, making that his only holiday as a rule. Work was incessant with him, and, as the wind of the spirit bloweth whither it listeth, much of the time which he spent in supposed idleness was fruitful in ideas and in actual composition. It was at Hastings that the germinal idea of *Meg Blane* came to him. He was standing in the upper room of a boarding-house on the parade watching the sea; one of those huge storm-tormented seas whose great waves burst over the sea-wall of the esplanade, and spent themselves in white cataracts against the windows of the houses opposite, when :

> Hither and thither, thick with foam and drift,
>   Did the deep waters shift,
> Swinging with iron clash on stone and sand.

Robert Buchanan's powerful and sombre rhapsodic poem had been in his thoughts for some time, and in his fascinated watching of the waves he found the inspiration of its setting. A work was commissioned for the Sheffield Musical Festival, and he went about this setting with his usual ardour. It is a briefer work than *The Blind Girl*, and its text is incomparably finer; indeed, tragic grandeur and drama are rarely so combined and concentrated as in the brief poem which describes some fisher-folk who stare through a howling storm at a wreck which has been flung upon a reef, and watch a woman, Meg Blane, and a few other heroic souls, launch a boat to the rescue, only to be overwhelmed by a great wave, which hurls both their boat and the wreck to one and the same destruction.* The work consists of a lyric prologue, which is repeated as an epilogue, and an irregular lyric narrative, in which the form of the verse echoes its sense. Its fault, if any, as a subject for musical treatment is its unrelieved sombreness; there are no light and shade, except the starlit descriptive passage in which a momentary lull in the storm is described. This, however, is at unity in feeling with the intensest part of the lyric. Coleridge-Taylor laid the work out for mezzo-soprano solo, chorus, and orchestra. The opening is a poignant passionate appeal, "Lord, hearken to me! Save all poor souls at sea," for the mezzo-soprano, in which drama is aimed at by both voice and accompaniment rather than melody, with a drum pedal in the accompaniment which extends over seventy-six bars. A brief interlude intervenes between this and the descriptive choral opening of the cantata proper, "Black was the oozy lift, Black were the sea and land," which is immensely realistic. Throughout, the music is pervaded by the sup-

---

* This is the *dénouement* implied by the libretto. Buchanan's poem, however, has a sequel, which is not hinted at in the cantata.

plicatory motto theme which is heard in the opening solo, and which receives variant treatment in the prayer, "Ah God, put out Thy hand." The launching of the boat and its progress renew the dramatic realism, and in this strain the work continues until the tragic close of the narrative. The epilogue is a repetition of the prologue, but as an eight-part chorus of satisfying beauty and appropriateness.

At the performance at Sheffield on October 4 the quality of the work was abundantly recognised. The soloist was Madame Kirkby Lunn, who did ample justice to her part, and the chorus, we are told, "revelled in the fine descriptive music." Judging by its reception, the public and critics were equally convinced that here was one of the very finest of the composer's works. Drama, descriptive writing, colour and melody, and powerfully rich and resonant orchestration were all present. The after-neglect of the work is altogether inexplicable; but it is safe to affirm that the future will give it its rightful place.

References occur in several of the letters of 1902 to his *Novelletten,* a brief and most original suite for orchestra. One such letter may come here :'

11 DAGMAR ROAD,
September 5, 1902.

MY DEAR MR. HUMPHERY,—We have just returned from Bexhill, and have had a most enjoyable time, thank you.

Regarding music; the *Serenade* of Dvořák has never been played in its entirety at a Conservatoire concert, so I should think it might be reserved for the first meeting. Novello's have my *Novelletten,* but I have correct MS. parts of the first two numbers to go on with; through my alterations the parts differ of numbers 3, 4 and 5, but I hope to have correct printed copies of the whole set in a few weeks.

I shall be quite ready for the nineteenth.

With kind regards,—Believe me, yours sincerely,

S. COLERIDGE-TAYLOR.

P.S.—You'll be surprised to hear that my American trip is "off" (!), at any rate for this year. What with bargaining about terms, and the fact that I should have to give up my new

Rochester Society and the Kendal Festival, not only for one season but for always, I thought it better wait till another month than April could be selected—for the English societies all seem to finish up immediately after Easter with a big concert!

The societies mentioned in the postscript were recently-added activities. Coleridge-Taylor became conductor of the Rochester Choral Society in 1902, and occupied this position until 1907. His connection with the Kendal Festival was more brief,* but he greatly enjoyed his work with the fine choir in Westmorland, and a photograph of the concert hall at Kendal was one of the features of his drawing-room.

His home-life was further enhanced by the birth, on March 8, 1903, of his daughter, a fair, pretty baby, who was to become, in a very special sense, his companion. His admiring friends asked somewhat twittingly if she would not be named Minnehaha; but counsels, which I think were wiser, prevailed, and the welcome little maiden was called Gwendolen.

By far the most ambitious work of the three years under consideration was an oratorio, or as Coleridge-Taylor chose to call it, a sacred cantata, *The Atonement*, the composition of which occupied much of 1902 and 1903, and which was produced at the Three Choirs Festival, this time at Hereford, on September 10 of the latter year. In seeking to set the last phases of the World's Tragedy, Coleridge-Taylor remarked, in spite of the difficulty of securing an adequate libretto, he preferred to set original verses rather than to select Scriptural texts which might convey them. He secured a libretto to his satisfaction from the pen of a member of the Three Choirs, Mrs. Alice Parsons, the wife of a Cheltenham journalist and newspaper proprietor. Its framework is dramatic; its intention largely lyrical. The book does not fall below the literary level, but is undistinguished, and is, I think, inadequate.

* Owing to the custom of appointing conductors for periods of three years only.

It may be that the author made the very common error of librettists of writing with the attention focused upon the composer rather than upon the stupendous poetical potentialities of the theme. Coleridge-Taylor, indeed, may have suggested certain rhythmical pecularities; but this seems improbable. In the result there are many short staccato lines of prose in the more dramatic scenes, and some of the more pathetic are reflected inappropriately in imitation *Hiawatha* verse. At the same time the theme is a difficult one for any poet on a lower level of inspiration than a Milton, and allowance for that fact is readily made; and, indeed, in certain parts there is a freshness of feeling and treatment which may be acknowledged as readily. The four situations chosen for interpretation are : the agony and betrayal in Gethsemane; an interlude in the shape of an intercessory prayer of the Holy Women and Apostles; the scene before Pilate; and the final tragedy on Calvary which culminates in a triumphant chorus, "It is finished." An analysis of the musical elements of *The Atonement* would not convey the real character of the work. The treatment, according to the composer, is "partly dramatic and partly descriptive," but drama predominates, although there is a recurring reflective atmosphere. All the solo voices are employed in the scheme, the prominent characters having a modern distribution as follows : Christ (baritone), Pilate (tenor), Pilate's wife (soprano), Mary, the mother of Christ (soprano), Mary Magdalene (contralto), Mary, the wife of Cleophas (mezzo-soprano). A prelude of one hundred and sixty-eight bars foreshadows the principal themes. This is an impressive example of his bold massive chords, his rhythmical resource and transitions, and daring bass passages led up to a stately march theme, *grandioso* which swells to *triple forte* and dies away on a high quavering *pianissimo* in noble fashion. The *pianissimo* introduces with considerable effect the atmosphere of "the soft moonlight glow of the Judean night" with which the choral part opens. The principal feature of this scene is the supplicatory prayer of the Saviour, "Father! the last dread hour of shame, and death is near," in which Coleridge-Taylor gives the first example of the dramatising of his subject. Throughout the work he violates certain artificial conventions, such as that which forbids any singer to attempt to realise the part of Christ; there being an impression in some minds that the seven words of Christ from the Cross are irreverent if sung by one singer, but are appropriately reverent if sung by a chorus. Coleridge-Taylor ignored this dramatic absurdity, and Christ speaks throughout naturally as one Person; and drama is the pervading character of the whole. His rabble with sticks and staves do not sing melodiously, but shriek "Away with Him!" rancorously, as they may well have done in actual life. Pilate is thoroughly judicial, remonstrative, and scornfully angry; the fury of the crowd is real, and swells as the tragic trial scene proceeds; the mockery is real mockery. Indeed, in the first performance of the work Coleridge-Taylor actually introduced into Pilate's mouth a solo, " Breath of my Life," which is succeeded by a duet between the Roman Governor and his wife of a distinctly "love" character, and therefore utterly unconventional in a religious choral work. These two numbers, however, he withdrew before the work was published. Between the Gethsemane and Pilate scenes is the Prayer of the Holy Women and Apostles, an eight-part chorale with great tonal possibilities, with a properly subordinated accompaniment. A fine semi-barbaric march leads up to the Pilate scene, and the scene itself, in which the Christ is silent throughout, is all drama, and ends in a choral March to Calvary ironical in character. The Calvary section is the longest of the work, detailing the march to Calvary; the sorrow of the faithful; the chorus describing the suffering; the tauntings of the Jews; the prayer of the three Maries, which is given first as soli, then as a trio; the choral description of the darkness; the supplication from the Cross; and, most impressive of all, the combined quartet and chorus, "It is finished."

At the Hereford production of the work the composer was fortunate in his principals, who were Mesdames Albani, Emily Squire, and Kirkby Lunn, and Messrs. Andrew Black and William Green. The chorus had found the work greatly to their liking at the rehearsals: and the resultant performance was a satisfactory one for both performers and listeners. Criticism varied from the statement that the Gethsemane scene strengthened the hope that the composer was "capable of illustrating intensity of feeling with picturesqueness as well as sincerity," to "there are moments when his orchestration is scarcely rich enough to convey the dramatic significance of the words . . . and the constant repetition of certain sentences becomes tiresome, rendering them unconvincing, and marring the impression of the music "; in brief, they were as muddled and contradictory as criticisms of Coleridge-Taylor's works were wont to be.

It was after this performance, in a mood of depression, that he told Miss Leila Petherick he would not undertake another commission for a musical festival. The artistic and physical strain was too great. However, the work was undertaken for performance on the following Ash Wednesday at the Albert Hall by the Royal Choral Society; and, indeed, Coleridge-Taylor told me that thereafter this society had promised to substitute it for their annual Lenten performance of the artistically much inferior *Redemption* by Gounod. From the public point of view, this second performance was an unqualified success, as a letter to Mr. Hilyer indicates:

10 UPPER GROVE,
SOUTH NORWOOD, S.E.
March 6, 1904.

DEAR MR. HILYER,—I received a letter from Mr. Gray yesterday and have written to accept his terms for conducting the S. C.-T. Society.

So I hope to meet you soon. Thank you very much for your letters.

The Atonement has been much abused by a portion of the English Press, but not by the leading papers such as *The Times,* which puts it above Gounod's *Redemption!* The strange thing about it is this, that it was received more enthusiastically at the Royal Albert Hall than ever *Hiawatha* was. I was recalled twice in the middle, and three times at the end, and the audience nearly smashed a magnificent performance by applauding in the course of a trio towards the end —almost an unheard-of thing. The choir, numbering a thousand voices, sang it as they have never done anything before, at least that was the opinion of most people, so *The Atonement* can afford to wait for a little.

Excuse this short, and I am afraid uninteresting, letter.

With kind regards to you all,—Believe me, yours sincerely,

S. COLERIDGE-TAYLOR.

But the "leading papers" were not potent enough to overcome the lesser. Critic after critic murmured that the work was uninspired, was lacking in reverence to the verge of actual irreverence, and much else. Whether from this cause or not I do not know, but the promised future renderings of *The Atonement* have yet to be given. In spite of his reference to them Coleridge-Taylor did not collect these newspaper criticisms. When asked in 1906 for them by an American, his wife wrote: "I am very sorry to say that I am unable to send you what you want in the way of Press notices of *The Atonement.* Unfortunately, we do not value the opinions of our critics as you do in America, for very obvious reasons; but you have the most reliable critiques, if you have *The Yorkshire Post.*" In parenthesis I may say that our composer maintained this high opinion of the musical notices in *The Yorkshire Post.*

CHAPTER IX

VISIT TO AMERICA, 1904

WHATEVER may have been the views of his newspaper critics in England, the chorus of appreciation in America grew considerably in volume within the last few years. In no small measure was this due to the Samuel Coleridge-Taylor Choral Society, of Washington, to the foundation of which in 1901 reference has already been made. This society was without precedent in musical annals in that it consisted entirely of members of the negro race, or of negro derivation, trained by a negro conductor. It is true that the Fisk Jubilee Singers, a choir of liberated slaves, had appeared in Europe a generation earlier on a musical-evangelical mission, singing to great congregations the intensely racial folk-hymns of the slave plantations; hymns which, as we have already seen, had inspired Coleridge-Taylor, and were to inspire him still more; but a chorus of two hundred voices, brought together by negro initiative and sustained by negro resources, and devoted to the study of the choral masterpieces of the world, was a new and significant institution. Thus was its general object stated, but its immediate purpose was the performing of *Hiawatha*. In the first years of its existence the society made great advances, and earned public esteem. The ridiculously erroneous popular conception of the negro as a person of thin, reedy voice, incapable of fine tone-production, was gratifyingly disturbed. Said *The Boston Herald*, after the society's performance of *Hiawatha* on April 23, 1903, before an audience of over two thousand at the Metropolitan African Methodist Church at Washington, "No white society could interpret it as sympathetically as this coloured choral society. The very genius of the composer is their race-spirit, and the music is as their native voice. These, with the peculiar naturalness of their singing, the depth and richness of many of their voices, and their excellent drilling, the result of patience and enthusiasm, give them special advantages."

In some ways this unique chorus was the most interesting thing in Coleridge-Taylor's world. He wrote to Mr. A. F. Hilyer, the treasurer of the society, a week before the concert :

10 UPPER GROVE,
SOUTH NORWOOD, S.E.
April 11, 1903.

DEAR MR. HILYER,—That everything may go splendidly on April 23 is my most sincere wish. No performance has ever interested me half as much as this " coloured " one, and I would give a great deal to be with you all. The notice you so kindly sent has already been printed in several papers here, and if you like, please send anything else connected with the concert.

What an immense undertaking it must be for you all, and I feel sure your enthusiasm and hard work will be repaid by great results.

Please tender a message of thanks and sympathy to all the members of the choir, and at the same time accept my heartiest thanks for all your kindness.

With best wishes.—Believe me, yours sincerely,

S. COLERIDGE-TAYLOR.

Again, after the concert :

10 UPPER GROVE,
SOUTH NORWOOD, S.E.
May 2, 1903.

MY DEAR MR. HILYER,—Ever so many thanks for your deeply interesting letters, and also for all the newspapers dealing with your concert. It must have been a great success indeed, and I am so glad it came off so well both artistically and financially. I know full well how hard you all must have worked to have had such splendid results. I have never heard

Hiawatha without orchestra, and can only imagine it to sound fearfully dull without a band; but then you know I live on the orchestra, and feel lost without it! Evidently your performance was anything but dull, to judge from the flattering newspaper reports. I notice that one paper speaks about the want of a good, reliable orchestra for such occasions. It is the same here in England. Only about half a dozen towns have really good bands, and the others have to hire many of their players from the nearest possible centre. And, as you may imagine, this kind of thing is fearfully expensive.

I have heard a great deal about Mr. Burleigh from people I have met here who have heard him in the States. Everyone agrees that he is a splendid singer, and also—more rare—a splendid musician too. Unfortunately the two things do not always go together.

The quality of tone produced by your chorus must be quite different from what I am accustomed to hear. As you say, I really must try to arrange to pay you a visit in the near future.

I have been asked to write a book on Negro Music by a firm of publishers in the States, and shall probably undertake it.

I hope, more than anything, that the S. C.-T. Society will recommence rehearsals very soon and go from excellent to most excellent and ever onward. You might put Mendelssohn's *Hymn of Praise* or some other classic in practice.

Please give my kind regards and warmest thanks to conductor, secretary and all the others. Mrs. Coleridge-Taylor joins me in wishing you and Mrs. Hilyer everything that is good.—Yours very sincerely,

S. COLERIDGE-TAYLOR.

The desire expressed in this letter, and in the one from the Choral Society itself given in the previous chapter, had been from the first in the minds of the society. It was natural, after the success attending the concert, that an invitation should reach the composer. It came in June, 1903, and it is worth reproducing if only to show the estimate of him held by the members of his race :

2302 Sixth Street, N.W.,
Washington.

June 1, 1903.

My dear Sir,—At a meeting of the Board of Managers of the S. Coleridge-Taylor Choral Society, I was directed to convey its invitation to you to visit Washington and personally conduct one or more presentations of your immortal *Hiawatha*. You have already been informed by our treasurer, Mr. Hilyer, of the high compliments paid by the American Press to the excellence of your work and of the intelligent, sympathetic, and altogether satisfactory interpretation of it given by the chorus. It is therefore unnecessary for me to go into an extended discussion of even so pleasing a subject. Suffice it to say, the state of the public mind is such that your coming to this city, and indeed to America generally, would be greeted by an unprecedented outpouring of the people, and would mark an epoch in the history of music in America.

The S. C.-T. C. S. was born of love of your work, was christened in your honour, and for two years has studied your masterpiece inspired by the hope that you would sooner or later come to America and personally conduct its presentation. Should you visit us, we can assure you of a thoroughly competent chorus of no less than two hundred voices, all in love with *Hiawatha* and its creator. Your coming will be a great boon to music, and will afford you an opportunity to be introduced to the great American public who are rapidly awaking to the fact that a new star has appeared in the firmament of the world's immortals.

We should therefore be glad to receive a definite acceptance of our invitation, stating approximately the date at, and the terms upon, which you could come, and such other information as you deem proper to submit in the premises. While the month of March, or April, would perhaps be the best time from our standpoint, we should of course gladly subordinate our wishes to your own convenience, and shall be glad to arrange for a musical festival, provided we can agree upon terms mutually satisfactory and advantageous.

Photograph by A. N. Scurlock, Washington, U.S.A.

The Coleridge-Taylor Choral Society

Trusting to receive a favourable response, and extending to you and yours the best wishes of the society.—I am, Sir, very truly yours,

ARTHUR S. GRAY
(Secretary).

By order of the Board of Managers.

JOHN F. COOK (<i>President</i>).

No doubt the letter gratified its recipient, and he determined to accept when circumstances permitted, but he recognised unerringly that his work required an orchestra. His reply made this condition, and is a fair example of his business qualities—qualities in which he is supposed, not without reason at times it must be admitted, to have been deficient. As usual, the letter is undated* :

10 UPPER GROVE,
SOUTH NORWOOD, S.E.

MY DEAR SIR,—I received your letter this morning and propose the following plan.

You see, first of all, it is impossible for me to visit you in a professional way unless I am assured of a first-class orchestra.

It is not that I would not come, <i>personally,</i> but I am in touch with so many noted musicians in the States that to conduct a performance of any of my works without such an orchestra would injure my reputation.

Now, could you negotiate with the management of an orchestra in Washington (or, if there is not one there, in the nearest city where there is one)?

Of course the expenses would be great, perhaps, but orchestras are often sent three or four hundred miles here in England—from London to Scotland—and nothing is thought of it.

I notice you say a <i>series</i> of concerts.

Well, if you could arrange for an orchestra to play in, say,

---

* The dates given on most of the letters have been taken from the postmarks. Occasionally Coleridge-Taylor wrote the day of the month; more often he merely wrote the day of the week; but he omitted the year invariably.

K

five or six concerts with your choir, things might be arranged more reasonably.

The best way would be for you to communicate with the principal musical agents in the States, and ask if this can be done.

I should require : 1 piccolo, 2 flutes, 2 oboes, 2 clarinets, 2 bassoons, 4 horns, 2 trumpets, 3 trombones, drums, and 8 first violins, 8 seconds, 4 violas, 6 'cellos, 4 basses.

Of course, some of the strings might be amateur if very good.

If this plan does not commend itself to you, could you find one of the principal agents and ask if he would like to arrange with me to conduct a series of concerts—orchestral, choral, and chamber, in the month of May, the engagement to include Washington with your chorus? If an agent could do this, it would relieve you of all responsibility and make it worth my while to come over to you.

Personally, there is nothing I should like more than to be able to pay you an informal visit and conduct the S. C.-T. Society and then return to England. But, as I told you, a first-class orchestra is absolutely imperative, especially as it would be my first visit to the States.

I hope you will understand my reasons for demanding this, and not think I am a difficult person to deal with! I should on no account be permitted to conduct in England unless a band were in attendance, and the same holds good in the States, or more so.

Will you kindly let me know your views on this as soon as possible.

Strangely enough, I was thinking of writing to some agent regarding a visit to America, but if you would do it for me, it would save much time.

Again thanking you for your letter, and for the honour you do me in sending the invitation,—Believe me, yours very sincerely,   S. COLERIDGE-TAYLOR.

To MR. ARTHUR S. GRAY,
    SECRETARY, S.C.-T. C. S.,
        2302 SIXTH STREET,
            WASHINGTON, D.C., U.S.A.

The letters to Mr. Hilyer that follow indicate that most of the difficulties were adjusted, but that the visit was still to be postponed for a year :

> 10 UPPER GROVE,
> SOUTH NORWOOD, S.E.
> *September* 1, 1903.

MY DEAR MR. HILYER,—I received your kind letter a few days ago. Unfortunately I have mislaid Manager Wolfsohn's address and am therefore asking if you will kindly send on the enclosed to the proper address. I have decided to allow him to manage the visit, and, tho' it is some time ahead, perhaps you will not mind much.

It will enable me to settle my business here much more satisfactorily.

My new work has been produced and the Press had most conflicting criticisms of it. Some of them are good—others nasty !

The fact is that there has never been a religious work written by a coloured man before, and so they had only English and German works to guide them, and my efforts were fearfully misunderstood ! Nevertheless, it held the people very well indeed.

The Times critique was a very fair judgment, I think.

So you'll expect me in the spring of 1905, if all goes well !

Excuse this short letter—you will see how busy I am by the enclosed.

With kind regards to you and yours,—Ever yours sincerely,

> S. COLERIDGE-TAYLOR.

(The new work referred to is, of course, *The Atonement.*)

> 11 DAGMAR ROAD,
> SOUTH NORWOOD, S.E.
> *November* 16, 1903.

MY DEAR MR. HILYER,—A line only to tell you that I do not see my way to come out this season without offending two or three very important musical societies in England. I have written a long letter (for me) to Mr. Lewis explaining the why and wherefore in detail, and he will doubtless tell you about it all.

Thanks very much for the papers; they were indeed interesting, but how is it that the English papers only show one side of the proceedings, and that the Southern side? An amusing incident happened touching *The Daily Telegraph* notices. I had been conducting at Huddersfield, and was returning in a railway carriage with an absolute stranger who did not strike me favourably. Without asking me where I came from (he had made twenty other queries!) he suddenly produced the paper with the extra black heading telling of the President's proceedings. "What do you think of *that?*" he asked.

I said "Bravo President! and shame on you South Americans." Instead of the abuse I had expected and was prepared for, he gave me his hand, and told me how sorry he was he had not a hundred hands each one armed with a revolver for those Southerners! Not a very Christian travelling companion, you'll say! But still a lover of justice evidently, tho' he looked like a bear.

Remember me kindly to Mrs. Hilyer; also, my wife sends her kindest regards, and believe me,—Yours sincerely,

S. COLERIDGE-TAYLOR.

Eventually the autumn of 1904 proved to be more convenient for the visit than the spring of 1905. Meanwhile his occupations seemed to multiply daily. In 1903 he moved his household gods to 10 Upper Grove, South Norwood; less than a half-mile from the various Norwood houses in which he had lived for the preceding ten years, but larger, though still modest, and more in keeping with his needs. It was to his drawing-room here that his friends were frankly and unaffectedly welcome, and in this modestly furnished apartment, decorated with interesting souvenirs of his musical journeyings, he continued his inimitable telling of his experiences. He stood, as always, on the hearthrug, with a cigarette in his mouth, and talked incessantly; and he was always worth listening to; his conversation was as finished and interesting as his music. He was, however, an excellent listener; and even the most absurd remarks would not draw him into a contradictory mood. When statements which he could not believe were made, I have noticed with secret amusement his invariably polite smile and, "Really, do you think so?" And his formula for scandalous stories—which as I have insisted he never told himself—was a laughing, "You really *are* too awful!"

Early in 1904 he told me with sudden enthusiasm that he had just finished "the greatest book he had ever read." This book he lent me, and I received from it the most intimate view of the coloured man's mind I had ever had, except as I saw it in the more or less mysterious workings of Coleridge-Taylor's own unusual mind. It was Dr. Du Bois's "The Souls of Black Folk." Certainly one would not accept Coleridge-Taylor's enthusiastic statement as criticism; he did not mean it to be so accepted; but the book is an eloquent revelation of the "vast sigh of a buried continent," and represents poignantly the sorrows and aspirings of the negro race. Of late years it has found its way into European bookshops and libraries; but it is not read as freely as it might be; and he who would faintly understand the subtle character, the irony and tragedy of the colour question in America, should lay this volume beside the works of Booker T. Washington, and such critics of the negro race as Viscount Bryce in his "Relations of the 'Advanced and the Backward Races of Mankind." It is to "The Souls of Black Folk" that Coleridge-Taylor refers in the following letter:

10 Upper Grove,
South Norwood, S.E.
January 3, 1904.

Dear Mr. Hilyer,—This is only a line to thank you over and over again for so kindly sending me the book by Mr. Du Bois. It is about the finest book I have ever read by a coloured man, and one of the best by any author, white or black.

Expect another line from me shortly. For the moment I have many other letters to write, so I know you will forgive so short an epistle.

With every good wish for the New Year to you and Mrs. Hilyer.—Believe me, yours sincerely,

S. COLERIDGE-TAYLOR.

The year with which this letter opened is in retrospect a maze of engagements—conducting, teaching, adjudicating; the only hours when he seemed to have peace were those of his Sunday evenings, and even then he had a flow of visitors. Consider: he was conductor of the Croydon Conservatoire, the Westmorland Festival, the Rochester Choral Society, the Croydon Orchestral Society, and, in 1903, he had accepted the position of professor of composition at Trinity College of Music. Most of these were regular engagements, but, in addition, he travelled the country from end to end fulfilling engagements to conduct his own work. Some of these engagements were remunerative; a great many were not. He was generous with his energetic help to the point of unwisdom. He would coach singers freely in his vocal works for concerts in which he had no interest; and I have known him conduct the whole of his *Hiawatha* for strangers in a distant town for a fee of two guineas. Not this way are fortunes made, but he never complained. The wonder is that people were willing so to undervalue and underpay him. Moreover, he was willing at all times to help his lesser-known friends. On one occasion, for example, he broke off in the middle of his composing to attend a local concert that he might accompany the singing of his *Easter Morn* by Miss Leila Petherick; on another he acted as accompanist to his friend—and, later, principal violinist—Mr. Stanton Rees, for the more important part of a concert; and all this without fee or the thought of one.

Yet he never paused long from composition. This year, 1904, saw in April the appearance of his *Moorish Dance for Pianoforte,* a delicate, very varied, and finished little work, which is in itself sufficient to prove that the orchestral composer could undoubtedly write effective and original pianoforte work. In June he published his characteristic *Six Sorrow Songs,* which were dedicated to his wife. These, I think, represent the high-water mark of his songs; there were never more poignantly beautiful settings than he has given to Christina Rosetti's lyrics, *O, What Comes Over the Sea, When I am Dead, my Dearest,* and *Unmindful of the Roses,* to name only three of them. On May 18 these songs, sung by Miss Marie Brema, formed the principal novelty in a successful recital of his works given under his own direction at the Public Hall, Croydon. A remarkable recital it was too, consisting almost entirely of new works from his pen. Among them were two new movements of his *Gipsy Suite* for violin and piano; the *Moorish Dance* already mentioned; a *Waltz* for piano, yet in manuscript; a violin *Romance;* violin soli, *Danses Nègres,* consisting of four numbers; a duet, *Keep Those Eyes,* for soprano and tenor; and six new songs, in addition to the *Sorrow Songs.* These six were *The Eastern Morn, Eulalie, Love's Questionings, A Dance of Bygone Days, Ah! Sweet,* and *The Delaware's Farewell.*

Negotiations for his American visit progressed satisfactorily during the summer. It was arranged finally that he should reach America in November. His letters during the intervening months point again to his desire to visit Germany. In August and September he spent some weeks at West Worthing, where he writes, "We are having splendid weather and an altogether delightful time." On September 1 he wrote to Mr. Humphery concerning the conduct of the Conservatoire orchestral class during his prospective absence. He notes as "an excellent man" Mr. William H. Reed, who, in 1911, was to succeed him as conductor of the Croydon String Players' Club; and the remark is typical of his many sayings and writings in appreciation of his fellow musicians. He seemed entirely free from the virulent, and, to outsiders, surprising jealousy which is so common in the profession :

> 6 BURLINGTON TERRACE,
> ROWLANDS ROAD,
> WEST WORTHING.
> *September* 1, 1904.

MY DEAR MR. HUMPHERY,—I certainly think your suggestion an excellent one; and if Mr. Hurlstone can undertake the orchestra it will get rid of many difficulties.

I have been persuaded all round to leave my concerts till my return from the States, so I shall refuse no deputy for that.

I was about to write you, for we are staying here for a few weeks, and I am expecting to go to Cologne before I go to the States; so that I am afraid it will be almost impossible to take the early rehearsals, though my date of actual departure is not yet fixed.

Will you please let me know as soon as everything is settled? If Mr. Hurlstone can't do it, there is a Mr. Reed who visits S. Croydon or Purley every week to conduct some orchestra there. He is an excellent man (R.A.M.), and a member of the Queen's Hall Orchestra—also a promising composer. Dr. Cohen, of Purley, would give you his address should it be necessary to communicate with him.

With our united kind regards.—Yours very sincerely,

> S. COLERIDGE-TAYLOR.

His next letters to Mr. Hilyer deal with the business arrangements for his tour, and show the care with which he considered the details of his programmes. The Marine Band referred to in the first is the orchestra of the Marines at Washington, one of the best-known large bands of the United States, which the Coleridge-Taylor Society had secured for his visit :

6 BURLINGTON TERRACE,
ROWLANDS ROAD,
WORTHING,
SUSSEX, ENGLAND.
August 26, 1904.

MY DEAR MR. HILYER,—Thank you very much for your last letter and enclosed circulars. I wish you would be kind enough to mail me, say, a dozen of the circulars. I shall send them to various interested people and papers.

I suppose my photographs have arrived all right by now. If you should require them I will with pleasure send you two more.

Regarding my coming over, I will certainly be with you as soon as possible. I may come straight to Washington first, but I am not quite sure yet.

I am strongly advised to travel via Boston, as I find that it is cheaper and quieter, and the extra day or two taken will not matter much. Regarding financial matters, I just wrote to Mr. Gray that I would require fifty per cent. in advance, as I have several deputies here to arrange with for the few weeks I am away, and they will require to be paid in advance, otherwise it would not matter. It will be the same to me who arranges the transport. I do not mind in the least.

Will you please tell Mr. Gray to see that Novello's have due notice about the *full scores* and *band parts* of *Hiawatha?*

But don't hire them too long before. The conductor of the Marine Band would probably tell you if any of his men require the parts to look over in advance.

I know Novello's system through and through, and I should advise giving them plenty of notice, but only hiring for as few days as possible, as this will save a lot of money.

Letters will find me at the above address for, say, three weeks, after which I shall be in Germany for a few days; but 10 Upper Grove will always be permanent.

You will be pleased to hear that the " Choral Ballads " are to be done at the Norwich Festival in 1905, with two additional numbers which will be done for the first time.

With kind regards, believe me, very sincerely,

S. COLERIDGE-TAYLOR.

As the time drew near his coloured friends had qualms as to the manner in which Coleridge-Taylor might be received by the white population of America. They feared he might become the target of insults with which the coloured man is too often assailed. Coleridge-Taylor, however, scouted the notion of taking special precautions against any such contingency.

> 6 BURLINGTON TERRACE,
> ROWLANDS ROAD,
> WORTHING,
> SUSSEX, ENGLAND.
> *September* 14, 1904.

MY DEAR MR. HILYER,—Many thanks for your letter. Our arrangements have all been upset, so we have not gone to Germany yet, after all, but I expect to go for a week just before I come to Washington.

I can assure you that no one will be able to stop me from paying you my long deferred visit. As for the prejudice, I am well prepared for it. Surely that which you and many others have lived in for so many years will not quite kill me.

I don't think anything else would have induced me to visit America, excepting the fact of an established society of coloured singers; it is for that, first and foremost, that I am coming, and all other engagements are secondary.

I am a great believer in my race, and I never lose an opportunity of letting my white friends here know it. Please don't make any arrangements to wrap me in cotton-wool. I am not that kind of person at all. I do a great deal of adjudicating in Wales among a very rough class of people; most adjudicators have had bad eggs and boots thrown at them by the people, but fortunately nothing of the kind has ever happened to me yet. I mention this so that you may know my life is not spent entirely in drawing-rooms and concert halls, but among some of the roughest people in the world, who tell you what they think very plainly. Yet I have four more engagements among them for next January.

I suppose one letter of mine must have crossed yours; in it I answered your question about the money.

The address I have written above holds good for three more weeks, till October 1. Communications will reach me quicker than if they first went to Upper Grove, S. Norwood. After three weeks I shall probably be in Germany, but am not sure.

I really must say that your American publishers, Ditsons, are the only publishers who have ever written to express their thanks and appreciation of my work, and yet I thought Americans were much more matter-of-fact than the English.

A white friend of mine at Chicago, who was going to arrange some concerts for me—he is a singer—thought I was not coming after all as he had not heard from me. I, on my part, wondered what had become of him. Yesterday a letter I wrote to him *last June* was returned from the Dead Letter Office, so there will be yet another delay before I can let Mr. Vest know what I am doing.

You will be pleased to hear that the Leeds Choral Society is going to give my " Choral Ballads " in January under my direction. Already quite a number of important societies have put them down for rehearsals—but, of course, the Leeds affair is by far the most important.

I really must stop or I shall lose the mail.

The typewriting was splendid.

With kind regards, believe me, yours sincerely,

S. COLERIDGE-TAYLOR.

6 BURLINGTON TERRACE,
ROWLANDS ROAD,
WEST WORTHING,
SUSSEX, ENGLAND.
September 16, 1904.

DEAR MR. HILYER,—You can't complain of my backwardness in answering your letters this week, at all events!

Regarding the miscellaneous programme, I shall, of course, be most happy to do my *Corn Song*. Who will sing it? Mr. Freeman, I suppose; and if a fine violinist is available, I should like to include my " African Dances " for violin and pianoforte, which will be published on October 1.

Kindly, by return, let me have a pen-and-ink sketch

programme of what is likely to be done at the concert so that I may see if there is time for the violin things.

But while I remember it, I do hope the *Hiawatha* concert will be the second night, and not the first. Also the second number of my " Choral Ballads " should be for solo and quartet, if possible; you have three solo voices— is a good contralto to be had? Please let Mr. Layton know this, as, if a quartet is available, the chorus will not need to learn the second number.

If you want any of my new songs to be done, let me know, please, but I should not advise an over-long programme.

Regarding the money—certainly three hundred dollars in advance will suit my requirements. I want to book my passage early in October, so, as you ask *when,* the sooner I have the cheque the more convenient.

With kind regards to you and Mrs. Hilyer.—Yours,

S. COLERIDGE-TAYLOR.

10 UPPER GROVE,
SOUTH NORWOOD,
LONDON.
October 16, 1904.

DEAR MR. HILYER,—I have to acknowledge your kind letter and enclosed cheque, for which I thank you.

Breitkopf and Haertel have just written to me about the orchestra parts of the three Ballads. They have not time to print, so are lithographing the strings and doing the wind in MS. They have promised them in ample time, and will let you have them at cost price as a special favour.

If you really must have some of my songs, I should suggest " The Shoshone's Adieu " for Mr. Burleigh; " Eulalie " for Mr. Freeman, and " Easter Morn " for Miss Clough, unless she likes to sing two little things of Dunbar's, but this she will let you know. The violin pieces I have already sent to you for the violinist.

Will you kindly see that none of the lighter pieces (i.e. songs and violin pieces) come at the end or beginning of the programme. I am also sending you a copy of the " Choral Ballads " with the exact marks which will be printed in the new edition now being printed; the two new numbers are much finer than the three already out; I think, but any performance is prohibited until after the Norwich Festival.

Regarding my coming—unless you have anything to the contrary, I shall sail by the *Saxonia* (no sea-sickness guaranteed!) on October 25 (Cunard Line). The next boat will be too late. I believe the *Saxonia* arrives on November 2. It is a Boston boat. I am sorry to say that the summer rates are still in force in England—till October 31. I grudge them the extra money very much.

By the enclosed you will see I am conducting "Meg Blane" to-morrow at Staffordshire.

I was amused to hear about my postcard; there was nothing important on it, but they were on sale at Worthing where we were staying, and so I bought one for a joke.

Germany will not see me before I come to you, for I have to attend a general meeting of the Handel Society next week, which is most important. I think I told you they have appointed me conductor.

Of course, I understand about *Hiawatha* coming first; I didn't know Baltimore followed the next day. I hope Mr. Layton will conduct the other choruses on the second evening, as I am anxious to hear the choir from a distance; but this is for you to decide. I am entirely at your disposal, and am never tired of conducting—so don't think of *that,* please.

I shall write again shortly.

With kindest regards.—I am, yours sincerely,

S. COLERIDGE-TAYLOR.

P.S.—Do you want a proper receipt for the money? It is not usual in England among professionals, but may be so in America—please tell me.

SOUTH NORWOOD,
October 22, 1904.

MY DEAR MR. HILYER,—I leave here for Boston on Tuesday next, October 25, and I shall arrive just after your Presidential election! May Mr. Roosevelt be re-elected is my ardent wish!

I have to call at Ditsons, but it will not take long, and I shall then come straight on to you.

While I remember it—will it be possible for me to have quite a separate and private band rehearsal? It will mean a ten times better performance.

I am bringing orchestra scores and parts of "Three Choral Ballads" with me. I like your new arrangements ever so much; there are one or two little errors.

It should have been Leeds Festival Choral Society. *Hiawatha* has been performed more than two hundred times in England, and on December 1 it will be done by the Royal [Choral] Society for the sixth time.—Very sincerely yours,   S. COLERIDGE-TAYLOR.

The voyage was without any incident of moment. His wife saw him off from Liverpool. It was the first time that he had been separated from her for a lengthy period since their marriage, and he wrote that an awful feeling of desolation came over him as he stood at the deck rail and watched the quay recede. He joined in the social life of the passengers quite unaffectedly, and with great enjoyment. In particular he was amused by the antics of a young man, whose intellect could not have been the most perfect, who would enter the saloon and inform the assembled company that he was going to America to buy land, and would demonstrate his ability to do so by bringing out a large bag of gold and running the coins through his hands. "No doubt," remarked Coleridge-Taylor, "he was relieved of the money before it was invested in land." A letter he wrote from 9th Street, Washington, to Miss Goldie Baker, of Rochester, a gifted violinist and a former student at the Royal College, hints at his qualities as a sailor. He writes :

"In the midst of all my engagements I find a moment to write to you.

"First of all I want to thank you *ever so much* for coming on the Sunday before I left. I am perhaps superstitious a little, and things like that go a long way with me.

" We had a most delightful voyage, and I didn't miss a single meal !

" Of course, you know about all the race prejudice here, but I have been well looked after, and spared any trouble up to the present. Quite a lot of *white* people met me at Boston as well as coloured, for which attention I was grateful. You would be surprised to see the actual state of things here. There are 90,000 people of colour—the majority of the official appointments are held by them ; of course, through competition.''

From the day of his landing in Boston until his departure on December 13 from the same port, his life was a whirl of engagements and festivities in his honour of a very gratifying and very exhausting character. "When I stepped off the boat at Boston there were half a dozen newspaper men waiting to devour me," he told an interviewer on his return. " They were very nice too, and what they said in their papers was very nice. My portrait must have been on every citizen's breakfast table the very next morning. After this everyone seemed to know me, and, curiously enough, appeared to take it for granted that I knew them. Still, you soon get used to this kind of freedom in American social life."

A part of a brief stay in Boston he spent at the house of Mr. Lee, a well-known Bostonian, who had entertained many notable people. His daughter, Miss Genevieve Lee, has recalled his visit for me. "A friend came to our home (we were then living in our own home in the city of Boston proper) and asked permission to bring Mr. Coleridge-Taylor to call. It was on the occasion of Mr. Coleridge-Taylor's first visit to the United States, and he was to land in Boston on his way to Washington. I remember so well at the expected time of his call how we waited in the parlour and library. Think of it ! I was to meet one of the greatest musicians living—greater than any in the United States ! And then, when Mr. Coleridge-Taylor entered the room, and we were introduced, one forgot that he was a great musical genius, and realised that here was a man unassuming and of great personal magnetism. His call was short, but he arranged with my parents to take breakfast with us when he returned to Boston."

The tour included visits to Washington, New York, Chicago, Baltimore, and Philadelphia. About a week was spent in Washington, and this, as may be inferred from his letters, was his central engagement.

His first ordeal was that of the handshaking. On Sunday, November 13, he attended the service at a negro church; and the Metropolitan A.M.E. "Church Notes" on this event, given in the Washington paper, *The Record*, are sufficiently naive to bear transcription:

" Though Sunday was such a very inclement day, quite a number of people were present; according to promise S. Coleridge-Taylor joined in the service. Dr. Scott preached a very eloquent, impressive sermon from John xii. 32—' And I, if I be lifted up from the earth, will draw all men unto Me.' After the recessional, ' Holy, Holy, Lord God Almighty,' Mr. Taylor received all who wished to shake his hand in the pastor's study. Hundreds seized this opportunity to greet the man whose name is a household word wherever true worth is appreciated. Children pressed forward for a peep at his kindly face. The old, middle-aged, and youth felt honoured to know they had received an introduction to Mr. Taylor. He is in every way a credit to the race, and the ovation he received was justly his."

No doubt Coleridge-Taylor carried through the ceremony with a good grace and with smiling face; but I know that he regarded these handshakings as "dreadful." Another incident connected with another church may be recorded. Walking in the street one Saturday, he was accosted by a man whom he did not recognise.

"Ah, Mr. Taylor," said he, "we are all coming round to-morrow evening."

Coleridge-Taylor expressed his surprise, and inquired

to what place the man was coming, and why; and learned to his consternation that the enterprising pastor of a well-known church had announced not only that Coleridge-Taylor would be present at the evening service, but also that he would address the congregation. This was too much for our composer, who retired to his room for the whole of Sunday evening, locking himself in for greater security from his kindly and well-meaning, but rather too pertinacious friends.

The Coleridge-Taylor Festival, as it was called, occupied two evenings at Washington and a third at Baltimore. The Washington concerts were held in the Convention Hall, a building with a capacity for concert purposes of nearly three thousand. This not meagre accommodation was taxed to the uttermost. "I daresay you will be interested to hear about the sale of tickets," he wrote to Miss Goldie Baker; "it is unprecedented in Washington." The orchestra is described as "an enlarged U.S. Marine Band Orchestra of fifty-two pieces," and it had been well rehearsed by its conductor, Lieutenant William H. Santelmann. Coleridge-Taylor, however, left nothing to chance, and secured his own "separate and private rehearsal," which he had suggested to Mr. Hilyer. The first concert, on November 16, was devoted to *Hiawatha*. His principals, as his chorus, were all coloured, the soprano being Madame Estella Clough, of Worcester, Massachusetts, a well-known operatic singer, the tenor Mr. J. Arthur Freeman, of St. Louis, perhaps the foremost of living negro tenors, and the baritone Mr. Harry T. Burleigh. Mr. Burleigh, of whom Coleridge-Taylor had already heard much, and with whom hereafter he was to remain on intimate terms, was a pupil and friend of Antonin Dvořák during the latter's sojourn in America, and it was he who had supplied to Dvořák the melodies of negro origin introduced into the *New World Symphony*. This intimacy with Dvořák would in itself have attracted Coleridge-Taylor as much as the poet Browning was attracted by

L

the radiantly fortunate being who once "saw Shelley plain"; but, beyond this, Burleigh is the possessor of an enviable voice and a dramatic instinct.   In Coleridge-Taylor's own opinion, Burleigh's interpretation of his work was only approached by one other singer, his later colleague and friend, Julien Henry.

The crowded audience was in the proportion of two-thirds coloured and one-third white, in itself an evidence that the intense interest in Coleridge-Taylor was by no means confined to his own race.   This fact must always be estimated in the light of the subtle race antagonism which apparently exists in Washington, and which, so far as the detached Englishman can judge, creates marked lines of cleavage in their social and artistic life between White and Black.   President Roosevelt had hoped to be present, but public engagements—the Presidential election had taken place only a few days before—detained him in New York.   His secretary was present, however, as were other members of his Government.

The papers of the white folk commented upon the whiteness of the cultivated negro, and the remarkably little difference to the outward eye that the groupings of the races presented.   Never did a composer receive a greater welcome from his own people.   The audience and the newspapers stopped little short of delirium in their enthusiasm.   To them he was the living realisation of their highest ideal, the indisputable and accepted proof that the more exalted ways of creative art were open to and attainable by the negro.   One newspaper extract sums up the festival, and will suffice.   Says the Washington correspondent of *The Georgia Baptist*:

" When Samuel Coleridge-Taylor, of London, walked upon the platform of Convention Hall last Wednesday night, and made his bow to four thousand people, the event marked an epoch in the history of the negro race of the world.   It was the first time that a man with African blood in his veins ever held a baton over the heads of the members of the great Marine Band, and it appeared to me that the orchestra did its best to respond to every movement of its dark-skinned conductor.   There, too, was a chorus of more than two hundred voices, the best aggregation of singers, white or coloured, Washington has ever had, according to the testimony of all our leading people in the world of music.

" And what a wonderful performance did band, chorus, soloists and leader give ! The whole affair was simply indescribable, and we may never see or hear its like again. For there can only be one first time. . . . The audience which had gathered to witness this performance was brilliant and distinguished, composed of leading men and women of both races, many from far-away cities, South, East and West. The whole occasion was an inspiration. No one was disappointed in what he heard and saw that night."

The second concert was of a more miscellaneous character, but included an important new work, his *Choral Ballads*, written for and dedicated to the Samuel Coleridge-Taylor Choral Society.   The work consists of settings of some of Longfellow's poems on slavery for solo voices and chorus.   Those presented were *Beside the Ungathered Rice He Lay, She Dwells by the Great Kenhawa's Side,* and *Loud He Sang the Psalm of David..*   Two other numbers, notably *The Quadroon Girl,* perhaps the most haunting of them all, were added later ; but there was something peculiarly appropriate in the first production of this choral suite by a negro chorus, and its reception was all that its composer could have desired.

The third concert was given at the Lyric Hall, Baltimore, and was in programme a repetition of the first, and was an equal success.   After each of these concerts a reception was held in the concert halls, and Coleridge-Taylor again shook hands with enthusiastic hundreds.

Next day the proceedings were varied by a concert given in his honour by the Treble Clef, a society of musical coloured ladies, and the Æolian Mandolin, Guitar and Banjo Club, the Amphion Glee Club, and other musical fraternities which had combined for this purpose. One is inclined to wonder what may have been the effect upon so essentially an orchestral composer as Coleridge-Taylor, of a potpourri of *Tannhäuser* by the Æolian Mandolin, Guitar and Banjo Club, which opened the programme. A pleasant evening it was, however, in which, besides the members of the bodies mentioned, his friends Miss Lola Johnson, Mr. J. Gerald Tyler, Mr. Clarence C. White, Professor John T. Layton, Mr. Fred Freeman, and Mrs. Kathryne Skeene-Mitchell all co-operated for his entertainment. Curiously, but to his satisfaction, his own works did not figure in the programme.

The visit ended with an elaborate public reception on November 21, at the Coloured Oddfellows' Hall, given by the Choral Society in Coleridge-Taylor's honour. The hall was brilliant with bunting, the flags of Great Britain and America and palms, and an orchestra hidden in a border of palms discoursed music, while in the centre stood Coleridge-Taylor with the officers of the society and others, to receive their callers, who, we are told, "entered at the east door, passed through an aisle of palms on each side of which the members of the chorus were banked, and passed out at the west door." This gratifying but formidable public reception over, the reception of the chorus followed. The central incident of this was the presentation to Coleridge-Taylor of a handsome silver loving-cup, bearing on its panels the following inscription :

A Token of Love and Esteem
To Samuel Coleridge-Taylor, of London, England,
in appreciation of his achievements
in the realm of music.
Presented by the S. Coleridge-Taylor Choral Society
of Washington, D.C., to their distinguished
guest on the occasion of his first visit
to America to conduct " Hiawatha "
and " Songs of Slavery," No-
vember 16, 17, and 18,
1904.
It is well for us, O brother,
That you come so far to see us.

The reception closed with musical honours for him in the shape of an ode, written by the secretary of the Choral Society, Mr. Arthur S. Gray :

Tune.—" God Save Our Gracious King."

O thou illustrious one,
Whose genius as the sun
Illumes our race ;
'Twas love that brought thee here
To fill our heart with cheer,
And may our love sincere
Repay thy grace !

Thy music, wondrous sweet,
With beauties rare replete
Charms every heart ;
Though praises we have won,
Our work has but begun ;
We'll study on and on,
Each one his part.

As meeting brought its cheer,
So parting brings its tear,
Its grief and pain ;.
And when the ocean wide
Shall bear thee on its tide,
May winds propitious guide
Thee home again !

Though earthly joys must end,
And friend must part with friend,
Yet love abides.
Our hearts where mem'ries dwell
Would fain their story tell,
But speechless, beat farewell,
A fond farewell !

The stay at Washington was marked by visits to many of the homes of his coloured friends; and, in particular, he was persuaded to pay visits to Howard University and to various schools, among them the Washington Normal School and the Armstrong Training School, both of which institutions have done much to elevate the coloured American and to equip him for the highest citizenship. At each of these he found much to interest him, but it need hardly be said that he was an object of intense interest, almost of adoration, on the part of the students as an example of recognised achievement. From each, too, he received characteristic and interesting presents. Present-giving and receiving, indeed, were prominent features of this visit. Another school at which he received cordial welcome from the pupils was the M. Street High School for Girls, where he listened with appreciation to the singing of the girls, and complimented them upon it, saying that such singing could not be heard in English schools. A souvenir of this particular visit was a baton made of cedar from Cedar Hill, the estate of Frederick Douglass, the negro leader, bearing upon it in gold the symbol of the school, the fleur-de-lis. At one such school visit a charming young girl was deputed to present him with a bouquet on behalf of the scholars. Next day he chanced to pass a house, and beheld the damsel coming out of the gate, carrying her bag of books on her way to school. She stopped Coleridge-Taylor, and remarked naively, "My name is ——, and this is where I live. You may write to me from England, if you like." I believe he did write to her later, but at any rate the little incident amused him greatly.

As a climax he was received at White House a day or two after the concerts by President Roosevelt, who had been re-elected to the Presidency of the United States. They had a long talk, in which they seemed mutually appreciative, and a memento of the interview was an autographed portrait of the President. The liberal attitude of the latter towards the coloured peoples Coleridge-Taylor regarded as of happy and hopeful augury.

As he had told Miss Baker, he himself had been too well looked after by his friends to suffer any annoyance because of his complexion. His managers had feared that he might not be well received; but for some curious reason the prejudice was not active against a negro British born, and both managers and Coleridge-Taylor were gratified at his comparative freedom from trouble. I say comparative advisedly, for on one railway journey he was drawn into conversation with a Yorkshireman who happened to be a fellow passenger, only to find himself a few minutes later the centre of a heated quarrel, the origin of which he could not fathom. Next day the papers were full of the incident, and they one and all championed him. From later hints he gathered that the quarrel was a preconcerted arrangement of one of his enterprising managers, who had in view a sensational advertisement of the composer.

To an interviewer on his return he had other remarks on this all-absorbing colour question. "As soon," he said, "as people found out I was English they were quite different. Of course, at first they could not reconcile the absence of the Yankee twang in a man of colour like myself. At the same time, I was sorry for coloured people generally. I heard some pitiful stories about their treatment. I met a young coloured lady of great educational attainments and of refined tastes. She was travelling south of Washington, and was turned out of the car. Coloured people and white are separated when travelling on the other side of a line drawn south of Washington. In the car for coloured passengers a hulking lounger wiped his feet on the hair of her head. Other indignities, too, were perpetrated, for which there was absolutely no redress. Think of it, if the aggrieved parties were whites! When I go to Tuskeegee, it will be in Mr. Booker Washington's own private car, and consequently I shall avoid being insulted. What is so deplorable to me is that there is as yet very little discrimination between the educated and decent-minded black and the idle and semi-civilised man of colour. This, understand me, is from an English point of view. The fact is, no Englishman can get quite inside the question, it is really so subtle."

He left Washington tired, but gratified and entirely happy. His own people had acclaimed him, and the white people, too, had acknowledged that he was, a living prophecy of the possibilities of his race.

From Washington Coleridge-Taylor proceeded to Chicago. He was much concerned by the recklessness of American railway travelling. "Human life," he remarked afterwards, "seems very cheap indeed when in transit. I happened to pass the scenes of three recent smashes. As I have lived in England all my life, and have never seen one here, naturally I did not trust myself with blithesome confidence to the tender mercies of the railway staff and the rolling-stock." But he greatly appreciated the comfort and elegance of the cars.

His concert at Chicago had been fixed up at ten days' notice by his agent; yet, in spite of this and of the awkward fact that nine other concerts were announced for the same evening in Chicago, the Music Hall was full. This concert on the whole pleased him more than any of the others. "My best time," he said, "was in Chicago. The audience was made up almost entirely of those whom you would call really musical people, and there was no mistaking the immense German element among the listeners. Coloured people always put in a large attendance, and they were most enthusiastic." His assistants were Miss Mary Peck Thomson, Henry T. Burleigh, and Theodore Spiering, in a programme consisting entirely of his shorter compositions. It was at this concert that Coleridge-Taylor cemented a life-long friendship with the fine violinist, Spiering, whose playing of his *Gipsy Movements* and *African Dances* he frequently spoke of in terms of high appreciation. Interesting, too, is the fact that Coleridge-Taylor not only accompanied, but actually appeared as pianoforte soloist in his *Three Negro Melodies Symphonically Arranged from Set of Twenty-four*, a new work upon which he had recently been engaged, and in his oriental valse, *Zulieka*.

By way of New York and Philadelphia he returned to Boston. At New York he was well received, but the nights he spent there were sleepless: the never-ceasing noises of the great city almost shattered his nerves, and it was with intense relief that he rested later in quieter surroundings. At Philadelphia he gave a recital at Witherspoon Hall on the evening of December 8, in aid of the building fund of the Douglass Memorial Hospital. In this he had the assistance of three Philadelphia musicians of repute, Miss Marie Louise Githens (soprano), Mr. Edwin Evans (baritone), and Mr. Frederick E. Hahn (violinist), and the programme, which was received with the usual favour, consisted entirely of his own works. Here again he figured as solo pianist with satisfaction to his audience.

At Boston he found royal welcome amongst a thoroughly congenial set of musical people. A dinner was given in his honour by Dr. and Mrs. Samuel Courtney, at which several guests of musical inclination were present. Of the singing societies he seems to have attended various rehearsals; in particular, one of the Cecilia Musical Society, which had been the first society in the United States to perform *Hiawatha's Wedding Feast*. He also fulfilled the promise made when he landed to take breakfast with Mr. Lee. Miss Genevieve Lee writes:

" Mr. Booker T. Washington was the other guest. It was rather chilly that day, and we had a grate fire in the library, and I remember so well how much like home Mr. Coleridge-Taylor said it made him feel, as it was the first one he had seen since he had been in the United States. I remember I sang some little song about which he complimented me."

Coleridge-Taylor greatly enjoyed the intercourse with Booker Washington, and although he could not accept Washington's ideal of limiting negro activities to the utilitarian and abandoning the creative and artistic—being, indeed, rather of Dr. Du Bois's view that all spheres of human endeavour should be free to his race—he yet recognised and appreciated the enormous importance of the work of the principal of Tuskeegee in making possible any progress at all. Dr. Washington pressed him to visit Tuskeegee, and although it was impossible owing to his English engagements for him to accept then and there, he accepted for his next visit, which he had already arranged for 1906. Unfortunately circumstances then unforeseen prevented the fulfilment of his promise; he never reached Tuskeegee.

On December 13 Coleridge-Taylor sailed for home. Of the voyage he told me many stories, amusing and characteristic, which, however, depended for the greater part of their interest upon the way in which he told them. Many of them, too, have been forgotten; but one may be transcribed.

During the voyage a French lady insinuated herself into his notice, and called his attention to another lady. "You see ze lady wiz ze red 'air. She 'ave lef' 'er 'usban'. Before ze ship go, she telegraph to him, ' Good-bye; I 'ave gone for evair.' When ze ship was two mile from land she receive ze answer by ze wireless, ' Zank ze Lord ! ' "

The ship was somewhat delayed by fogs, but Coleridge-Taylor reached home safely on Christmas Eve, to find his doorway decorated with holly and the inscription "Welcome Home." It was a glad returning for his wife and children and for himself. He was laden with souvenirs and with presents for them; but more satisfactory to him than the presents was the feeling that he had been completely successful in his journey from the points of view of his race, his art, and his reputation. It may appear that I have lingered too long over this American visit; but I cannot believe this to be so, when I recall its immense influence upon his outlook and his future work. A new world, indeed, had been opened to him.

In America he told me he had found a more widely-spread and more frank recognition of pure music than in England; he had found surprisingly splendid orchestras, instrumentalists, and vocalists, and a public taste which enabled these to exist for their art. For some time, indeed, he contemplated the desirability of emigrating to this land of the future.

CHAPTER X

THE reader has seen that for some time before his visit to America Coleridge-Taylor had engaged concurrently in many activities. The most important of these was undoubtedly the professorship at Trinity College of Music, which he accepted in 1903, and which he was to retain, although not so actively in later years, until his death. After a short period he was elected a member of the College Corporation, and was "recognised," as the term is, by the University of London as a professor who might prepare for the musical degrees of the University, a distinction which, I am told, is much coveted by teachers.

During the early years of his professorship I was in daily contact with one of his intimate pupils, who rejoiced greatly in his lessons, and so was able to learn something of his work in this direction. As may be expected, Coleridge-Taylor dealt with composition. His methods seem to have been informal in the extreme, and to have been calculated—if such a word may be used in this connection —to disarm completely any nervousness on the part of his students. The attitude he commonly adopted in talking to them was one of sitting on the table, while discussing the work in hand with great earnestness. He seldom, if ever, used harsh methods, and destructive criticism was perhaps too alien from his lessons. I remember noting particularly that individuality in the student was what appealed to him, and was the characteristic that he endeavoured to enlarge and to develop. Usually he allowed students to choose their own themes and their treatment, and he restricted his criticism to the whole effect and to the methods by which the students could better interpret their own ideas. I can remember the emphasis he placed upon important, but admittedly not original notions, such as "the greatest thing in music is silence" in inculcating the value of rests, and the desirability of a sound-climax at the conclusion of a composition. He also occasionally, with special pupils, talked about their future dealings with publishers; and in these talks, as I understand, he showed a clear conception of the just rights of both composer and publisher. In precept, at least, he showed none of the uncarefulness in business with which he is sometimes credited. "His mark as a successful teacher is found in some of our old students," writes Mr. Shelley Fisher, the secretary of Trinity College, "who remember him both with affection and gratitude for his earnestness and painstaking endeavours on their behalf." Even to indicate those amongst his pupils who owe much to him is impossible. His attitude was generous always; in his own orchestral concerts at Croydon, and at the Croydon Conservatoire concerts he occasionally introduced the compositions of capable students, as a quotation from a letter to Mr. Humphery shows: "A very advanced pupil of mine at Trinity College, who has written some excellent full orchestral work, told me she had written a short piece for strings. If it is all right, I'll get her to have the parts copied for trial. I understand that it only takes five minutes."

I find amongst his papers several programmes carefully preserved of recitals of Miss Bluebell Kean, a young composer of much promise, who was one of his pupils, and whose career in music he followed with the deepest interest. Similarly, my friend Mr. E. Beck-Slinn received the most enthusiastic encouragement from him, and so generous was the composer, that he would allow him to call at his house at any time of day to ask his advice upon points in composition. In fact, one pupil at least told me that he moved from the north of London to South Norwood in order to be near his master. In the college itself this atmosphere prevailed. Several of his compositions were performed by the college orchestra, and on one or two occasions he conducted them himself at the students' concerts which were given at Queen's Hall.

In February, 1905, he accepted a further teaching appointment, when he became professor of theory and harmony at the Crystal Palace School of Art and Music. This position, in spite of several half-formed resolutions to relinquish it, he retained until his death. His pupils were, in general, young ladies, whom he used to take in small classes on Saturday mornings; and, as a rule, only exceptional students, who had mastered their art to a large extent, were placed under his care. He preferred such students, indeed, as he had done earlier in connection with his violin teaching at the Conservatoire. "But," said the Principal, Miss E. M. Prosser, in a recent conversation with me, "I never knew him to refuse to do anything that I asked him to do." The disposition indicated here had effects on his pupils such as I have already shown to have been usual with him. He was idolised by them, and at the same time they knew little of that fear which is common in the learner when in contact with a famous master. He was an engrossing teacher, and to quote Miss Prosser again, "I never knew a man who was so careless of the value of time or of money; not, indeed, that he wasted either, but that in giving his lessons, for example, he would often linger over them far longer than he ought to have done." It was no uncommon thing for him to enter the school with the remark that it was imperative that he should catch a certain train. He would proceed to his classroom, and when the time was so advanced that by running he could just catch his train, the Matron would go up to the classroom to find him absorbed in the lesson, and quite oblivious of the movements of the clock. He was the same with his fees. He never demanded the strict payment of his hours, and though, fortunately, he did not

suffer in this instance, in some circumstances his carelessness might have been troublesome to himself. It was not
exactly laxity; it was rather a devotion to his work which
caused him to neglect its just monetary recompense. "He
was," says Miss Prosser, "careless of pounds, shillings,
and pence." I believe he enjoyed these lessons as much
as any he ever gave.

I have already said that he had no burning affection
for teaching, and believed that it used up too much of the
vitality of the teacher; and no doubt in his own case he
was right, but he allowed himself to be persuaded to continue these lessons after he had ceased to give any others,
except such as were connected with his work at the Guildhall School of Music. His pupils, too, were always ready
to meet him by changing the hours of their lessons to fit
in with his often sporadic engagements.

There was besides an attraction after Coleridge-Taylor's
own heart in the situation of the classrooms. The view
from the Crystal Palace Towers is famous, but one does
not realise that the classrooms of the School of Art and
Music, loftily perched as they are in the loftiest building
on the loftiest hill in the South of London, command a
range of country unsurpassed in England. Coleridge-
Taylor would never enter the room without going to the
window and exclaiming in unaffected delight at the beauty
the scene. · Beauty indeed it is, in which the eye leaps un-
concernedly over the not inconsiderable, but withal leafy,
ranges of streets in Anerley and Norwood to a vast reach
of varying loveliness of umber heaths, shining green fields,
hills over which woodlands run in every shade of green
from silver birch to sombre fir, dales that hold glistering
pools like discs of silver, and beyond rising and fading in
blue mystical distance the South Downs. Such scenes
wrought themselves into the very heart-fibres of the man.
In words, they found the simplest expression from him.
"What a lovely view!" with large emphasis on the first
word. But the deepest experiences that reveal themselves

in his music were found in a few such places as these;
in such moments of simple deep delight in the beauty of
the world he found his best inspirations.   Beyond these
hills it is easy to dream are the illimitable forests through
which his Hiawatha wandered; and it was from contact
with natural beauty and not from any hours of indoor
learning that he gained the powers through which "ages
unborn shall hear his forests moan."   The sea only, as it
finds its expression in *Meg Blane,* a work which yet awaits
the simple justice of recognition, affected and inspired
him as strongly.   I believe that this view was a large
element in reconciling him to continuing his teaching
at the Palace long after he supposed, and justly supposed, that there were more universal claims upon his
days.

At the Palace his memory is fragrant.   "He was the
most unaffectedly innocent man I have ever known," the
Principal tells me.   His coming was one of the most welcome episodes of the week.   Standing at the window of her
reception room, and gazing over the hills of Kent and
Surrey, he would talk to Miss Prosser of his projects for
composition, a confidence which he kept for those whom
he esteemed most intimately.   And the impression he made
was deeper than that a person merely charming makes.
"Many," says she, "might consider him greatly talented
only, but one felt instinctively in talking with him that
there was always something behind him that must have
been genius."   I have only met one person whom he did
not impress in this way, in spite of his transparent child-
likeness—perhaps because of it—and that man was of the
breed that supposes that genius can only evolve by way of
the public schools.

In November, 1905, he distributed the prizes to the
students at the Streatham School of Music, and on this
occasion he delivered one of the very few speeches he ever
made.   It was an extempore address from notes, but a
fairly full newspaper report was made.

"ON MUSIC

" I do not think that the study of what I may term the unpractised side of music—by which I mean harmony, counterpoint, sight-reading, and extemporisation—can be too strongly insisted on for all who are studying music, whatever branch it may be. It is remarkable that in these days of speciality, musicians, at any rate, are travelling in the other direction, and are becoming broader instead of narrower. While saying this, of course, I do not forget that the old style of music master, who teaches piano, violin, organ, 'cello, guitar, mandoline, banjo, singing, and a few other subjects, is becoming a thing of the past—luckily for all of us. I mean broader in another sense. The expert in one practised subject is more often than not highly accomplished in the side-lights of his art. I think it would be difficult to name a single great, or even good, violinist or pianist of the present day who is not also fully equipped with a technique for composition, though he may not be able to compose. They are all masters of harmony, counterpoint, extemporisation and the orchestra, and the art is all the better for it, though they may not be able to use these practically. Organists I need not mention, because with them the study of theory is a practical thing. An organist without a knowledge of harmony is not an organist. He cannot get on without it, whereas any other kind of instrumentalist may do so. But there is one class of musicians to whom these subjects are of especial use. I refer, of course, to singers. It is astonishing that good musicianship so rarely goes hand in hand with a good voice. For some reason or other, singers seem to think that all their shortcomings in this respect will be forgiven so long as they have good voices. To many, the poor person whom they call their ' coach ' is someone, good-tempered, who will literally draw the notes of all their parts into their heads. This is all very well, providing things go straightforwardly and without accident when the singer is before the public. But when something happens—and in our complex music something usually does happen—where is the vocalist who is not better for a thorough grasp of the whole

M

work, instead of his or her little part? I can illustrate the point from my own experience at a musical gathering in the North of England, when a soprano, who was not strong on the theoretical side, got slightly ahead of the orchestra in a composition in which, at a certain point, occurred a six bars' rest. For a time all went well, but when the lady attempted to proceed there were some rather unpleasant sounds. Singers, therefore, should acquire a good knowledge of theory to save themselves from any *contretemps* of this kind. Sight-reading, again, ought to be much more practised, though in this respect things are at a very high level in the North. I was adjudicating at the great Blackpool Festival, and for the sight-reading competition two choirs of about a hundred voices each entered. Copies of things they had never seen before were put into their hands—not easy things, by any means—and no one was allowed to look inside until the bell rang, on which they had to start away. First they sang without words, then with words and expression, etc. The winning choir sang the piece almost perfectly the second time. I think there are few choirs around London that could do anything of the sort—and all of these were amateurs. This brings me to another thought—there are people naturally gifted, many of them, who oppose a set study of harmony because it naturally results in dullness and commonplace respectability. Some little time ago I was reading a book of travel on the districts which border Europe and Asia. The writer—I have forgotten his name—mentioned that large bands of gipsies were to be found in the neighbourhood, and that in each band one could always discover at least three or four excellent violinists and guitar players, not to mention singers. The writer went on to say that these fiddlers and singers were wonderful in transposing melodies into words, and that this discovery gave him a shock, as it seemed to point to the fact that music was a very low and brainless accomplishment; otherwise, how could these people excel as they did? I posted the passage to a friend, and casually remarked that they would not be worse musicians if they had a knowledge of the scientific side of the art. To which my friend replied that were they to study such things as harmony; etc., they would be better off. But I warn you not to allow harmony and theory to cramp your artistic development, because it should be remembered that these must always be subservient to the beauty of sound. Therefore, those who are studying harmony should take care that these excellent things become not the end, instead of means to an end, and that they are not mere mechanical paper work, without any regard to sound. I have had a number of pupils who were able to work a difficult paper with ease, but who could not distinguish the most simple chords played in succession on the piano. Too often a wonderful knowledge of text-book harmony deprives the person who possesses it of the enjoyment of mere beauty, and this is a great pity. Imagination should also be far more thought of than it is in the playing of music. Technique is not everything, and everyone has some small amount of imagination. But imagination wants bringing to the front. We want to get away from the dull, conventional, respectable and matter-of-fact performances, and to go in for something better. We require less of the lady and gentleman, and more of the man and woman. We must look upon music from a more impersonal standpoint—there is too much of the everlasting heralding going on. It is becoming too much admiration for the man, and too little love for his music. I appeal for more enthusiasm.''

Contemporaneously with all these energies his local work in Croydon went on. For nearly six years he had conducted the Croydon Orchestral Society, with results which gave him not unqualified satisfaction. The society was large, and it was very miscellaneous in quality, and presented all the difficulties that a society composed entirely of amateurs is wont to do. The amateur wind which the committee insisted on retaining was the cause of many sad hours. Once, irritated by the tuneless noises emanating from an enthusiastic horn player, he asked, "What instrument are you playing?" and received the answer, "The He-'orn, sir." Again, his tympani player was a well-meaning, but myopic individual, who had some difficulty in seeing the conductor's beat, and had also an unfortunate tendency to drop a cymbal on the floor in the middle of soft passages.   Coleridge-Taylor managed to endure these irritations good-humouredly for some years, and rarely came into conflict with either the players or the soloists engaged by the society.   At one rehearsal, however, a singer with a great sense of her importance mounted the platform and presumed to dictate the time of her song —one of the best-known works in vocal music—to the conductor.   "Madam," remarked Coleridge-Taylor, "on this occasion I am the conductor, and *I* will set the time."   The lady refusing thereupon to sing, Coleridge-Taylor told her courteously that he would be compelled to engage another singer; at which the lady left the concert room in high dudgeon.   Such incidents were so rare that they should be recorded.

The cumulative disadvantages of the Croydon Orchestral Society grew too heavy to be borne, and with Coleridge-Taylor's resignation its existence came to an end.   However, he could not bear the notion of the complete ceasing of good concerts in Croydon, and he set to work immediately to arrange symphony concerts on a new basis.   He invited the best of the string players to join him in giving what were known as the Coleridge-Taylor Symphony Concerts, and arranged that wind and tympani should be engaged from London.   Much enthusiasm on his own part and on that of the players went to these concerts.   His wife acted as secretary; the wind players and soloists were always chosen with great deliberation and with excellent results artistically; and the Public Hall at Croydon was crowded on concert nights.   So far as stage management and business details were concerned, a hitch never occurred.   In spite of these things, at the end of two or three seasons Coleridge-Taylor had gained a large local appreciation and had lost about eighty pounds.   The hall, then the only one available, was too small for receipts to cover expenses; and at the end of 1905 Coleridge-

Taylor was forced to review his position. The foundation of the String Players' Club in 1906 was the outcome.

Other conducting appointments which he held concurrently with this were that of the Rochester Choral Society and that of the Handel Society. He became conductor of the former in 1902, and held the position until 1907; and during these years he accomplished much for music in the Kentish city. "Mr. Taylor," writes a correspondent, "threw himself into each work with tremendous enthusiasm. The race to which, on his father's side, he belonged was an intensely musical one, and with such blood in his veins he was able to throw himself into the music with entire abandonment. We remember how he conducted *The Golden Legend* and *The Spectre's Bride* and *The Banner of St. George* at the Choral Society, and how vividly he emphasised their points. . . . His *African Dances for Violin and Piano* were heard at Rochester with much delight at Miss Goldie Baker's concert, when, for the first time, these were played in England. Miss Baker was the violinist, and Mr. Coleridge-Taylor himself was at the piano, and these characteristic dances, full of colour and wild melody, were most rapturously received."

Two years later, in 1904, the well-known Handel Society invited him to become its conductor. The society, which has a membership of fashionable West London music-lovers, was at that time in a poor way artistically. It existed ostensibly for the performance of the works of the composer after whom it was named; but while it sustained this character to a limited extent, it may be said to have devoted its energies to more modern music. Coleridge-Taylor did not express his opinions on Handel directly to me; but Mr. Beck-Slinn tells me that he regarded the great seventeenth-century composer as crude and bare, a result, of course, of his advent before modern orchestration. This was his principal fault, but Coleridge-Taylor was further irritated by his unblushing plagiarism, his use for sacred purposes of secular themes, and the invariable ending phrase—a phrase, by the way, which Handel borrowed from Purcell. However all this may be, Coleridge-Taylor gave to the Handel Society the care and enthusiasm which he usually bestowed upon his work, and in a few seasons he had redeemed the society from the worst of its weaknesses. The social prejudices of some of the members amused him greatly, and he had stories to tell us of the unfortunate member who was unlucky enough to remark to a number of members who spent their holidays at Mentone that he spent his own at Westcliff-on-Sea, and of the cold manner in which the remark was received. "I always avoided mention of my holidays," Coleridge-Taylor told me, laughingly.

It is difficult to estimate the place of Coleridge-Taylor as a conductor. Such evaluation can only be of the comparative, and therefore of the offensive, order. I am told by Colonel Walters that one of the best-known English orchestral players averred in 1911 that of the three greatest living British conductors, Coleridge-Taylor was one. This may be so, but his exact place scarcely matters. What we do know is, that he possessed an unusual magnetic power in conducting; that he threw his whole soul into the work, and loved it. So great were his efforts that he found it necessary to change his collars, which were wet with perspiration, sometimes twice during a single concert. Players, too, found his direction stimulating and inspiring. Especially was this true in connection with his own works. There is a tradition, whether well or ill founded I am not prepared to say, that composers are rarely good conductors of their own works; but of Coleridge-Taylor "it is safe," remarks Mr. Julien Henry, "to say that he could get a better performance of his own work than any other conductor." So far as he could, when he was to conduct one of his works, he insisted upon conducting a final rehearsal himself; and the influence of this one rehearsal was said often to be greater than weeks of previous study.

His principal work of 1905 was not the result of a festival commission, but of an introduction to Mr. Ernest Hartley Coleridge, the grand-nephew of Samuel Taylor Coleridge, the poet. Coleridge-Taylor took tea with Mr. Coleridge, and after tea the latter read the exquisite lyrical fragment *Kubla Khan*, and it was suggested that the composer should make it the theme of a choral work. The result was his *Kubla Khan: a Rhapsody for solo, chorus, and orchestra*, which appeared towards the end of the year. It is one of his shorter cantatas, consisting of a fairly long orchestral prelude, in which the later themes of the work are announced and developed, and a choral setting of the words with two contralto interludes. Music has rarely been married to immortal verse more fittingly. The shadowy mysticism of the great poet's dream appealed most strongly to the composer, and the result may be classed with his finest efforts. It received a satisfactory performance at the concert of the Handel Society in 1906, and another shortly afterwards at the Scarborough Festival. For an interval of years, however, until 1914, the work was scarcely heard. This was mainly owing to the collapse of its publishers. In the last year or two it has been acquired by Messrs. Novello and Co., and already it is receiving that attention from choral societies which its characteristic beauty merits.

Letters written in 1905 to Mr. Hilyer may fitly be inserted here :

10 Upper Grove,
South Norwood, S.E.
April 25.

My dear Mr. Hilyer,—Many thanks for Easter remembrance and also newspapers. I am glad the tickets have gone so well.

You will see by the enclosed that my new work will have its initial performance at Queen's Hall on May 23. Several other performances are already booked.

At the Philharmonic Society, London (the Premier

Orchestra), my new *Variations on a Negro Theme* will be done for the first time on June 14.

Did you know that *Hiawatha* was performed in Constantinople a few days ago? And that the principal orchestra in Rome will do some of my stuff in May?

Please forgive this short letter—the mail goes out in ten minutes' times. I'll write you a longer letter next week.

With kindest regards from us both to you all.—Believe me, yours very sincerely,   S. COLERIDGE-TAYLOR.

> 10 UPPER GROVE,
> SOUTH NORWOOD, S.E.
> *May 2.*

MY DEAR MR. HILYER,—I am so glad to know things went well with the chorus. Thank you for sending the cuttings. A newspaper wrapper arrived here two or three days ago, but, alas! its contents were lost, stolen, or strayed.

I omitted to enclose the notice of the Handel Society's concert in my last letter, but am doing so now.

We had a magnificent rehearsal of *The Spectre's Bride* at Rochester last Monday, and we ought to have a fine performance on Monday next. I am also conducting the same work at Queen's Hall, as you will see by the enclosed.

It is a frantically difficult work, especially as regards the orchestration.

With our united kind regards to you all.—Believe me, yours very sincerely,   S. COLERIDGE-TAYLOR.

> 10 UPPER GROVE,
> SOUTH NORWOOD, S.E.
> *September 30.*

MY DEAR MR. HILYER,—There were two queries of yours which I left unanswered in my last letter—one about the *Clarinet Quintet* and the other about the Marine Band.

Regarding the first, the work would only interest people who play chamber music, such as Mr. Lent, to whom I have already written. Therefore I should not like to accept any subscription from anyone else, on my publisher's account.

Moreover, the matter is now well in hand, I am glad to say, and quite satisfactory.

Now as to the other matter. If any kind of festival really can be arranged for next fall, I would suggest the following plan. It would be a thousand pities to let the chorus drop in any way, as I felt it was really an immense thing for everyone, especially the coloured people.

But I must say that the band last year was not a tenth good enough for the chorus, especially in its string department. The wind was not so bad.

So I suggest that a sort of compromise be arranged. That is to say, the strings should be engaged from some other place, and possibly the wind also, but failing the latter, the Marines might supply it. Or another proposition is that a certain number of really fine string players be engaged, and the wind be entirely dispensed with. Of course, this would not be so good in some ways, but much better than a non-capable orchestra, and the wind parts could be filled in on the pianoforte and organ, by that extraordinarily clever Miss Europe and someone else.

If you think anything of my scheme, would it not be better to have the concerts in a church, instead of that hall, and let them run over three, or even four, evenings, as is done in England, to make the financial part come right?

As for programmes, possibly something like the following would do :

> *Alexander's Feast* (Handel), a short and very attractive work, which we did last year in London.
>
> Mendelssohn's *Hymn of Praise,* which, of course, you know, and which the chorus certainly ought to study.
>
> Part of *Hiawatha,* perhaps, if wished for, or part of *The Atonement.*
>
> Miscellaneous Works for Male Voices alone, and Female Voices alone. I can let you have the names of some splendid little things, which I have adjudicated at the Welsh eisteddfods.

And, of course, some songs, violin pieces, and pianoforte solos.

I am sure this would prove very attractive, and would offer

more variety than last year's programme, excellent though it was.

If all this strikes you, Mr. Gray, and your committee in a favourable light, I should advise that Mr. Lent and Mr. Clarence White be asked kindly to select the strings. They are both excellent gentlemen, and would probably get hold of some fine people. Mr. Burleigh would, I am sure, do likewise as regards the selection of the soloists.

I think if all this can be carried out, the affair would be a really noteworthy musical celebration, and one which would do us all credit.

Please remember me most kindly to Mr. Gray, Mr. White, and Mr. Layton, whose splendid work was a triumph last year.

Also, of course, give my kindest regards to Mrs. Hilyer and the family.—Yours very sincerely,

S. COLERIDGE-TAYLOR.

P.S.—I expect Miss Harriet Gibbs will call here very shortly, and I will tell her more explicitly than I can write anything else that occurs to me.

Strange to say, my new setting of " She Dwells by Great Kenhawa's Side " for female voices is the favourite of the " Five Choral Ballads," which are being done under my directorship at the Norwich Festival, October 25. They sing them all magnificently.

10 UPPER GROVE,
SOUTH NORWOOD, S.E.
December 7.

MY DEAR MR. HILYER,—Thank you for your kind letter, to which I can only reply very briefly.

I can definitely promise to come over at just the same time as I did last year. I have already heard from one or two other people, and as we do nothing much here before Christmas, I can make it convenient to come then. If you think this will do—and the necessary arrangements can be made—kindly let me know, and I will send you the detailed programme I propose. I shall have no objection to conducting the reduced orchestra, as I suggested, provided the members are all good.

(I am writing this for my husband, as he is very busy with

his music for Mr. Tree.* Please don't be too critical. We both send warmest greetings to you and Mrs. Hilyer, not forgetting the boys and Kathleen. Perhaps I may have the pleasure of making their acquaintance next year!)

Wishing you all a very happy Christmas, and with love from the chicks to you and yours.—Believe me, yours very sincerely,

S. COLERIDGE-TAYLOR.

Of the year 1906 few records or personal reminiscences survive; yet it was a year of great movement in many ways. It was a year of concert engagements; it saw the first three performances of *Kubla Khan*; in it was written the *Nero* music, which has been the most successful by far of the orchestral suites into which he transformed the incidental music he wrote for His Majesty's Theatre; it saw his second visit to America; and, greatest event of all in his eyes and in the eyes of many, it saw the death of Hurlstone.

In February we find him again acting as adjudicator at a musical eisteddfod. Some of his notes survive, and, if space permitted, a large selection of these might be given to illustrate his method. As the competitors performed, he wrote comments on sheets of foolscap or in a large exercise book, adding underneath, with many alterations as his judgment altered with listening, the marks awarded. Three brief judgments on the singing of "Novices" will suffice :

(1) "Excellent voice—her *sostenuto* was one of the best points—especially considering her youth, or apparent youth—her position might have been a little better—and she might have looked away from her copy now and again. There was not much variety of expression, however, and the impression was a little wanting in conviction."—42.

(2) "Voice not altogether satisfactory—it was all too suppressed and throaty—on the other hand he sang with much more freedom of expression than the preceding com-

* This letter, though signed by Coleridge-Taylor, was written by his wife.

petitor—and he sang with a certain amount of conviction, and his phrasing was excellent—had his voice been better he would have obtained rather high marks."—43.

(3) "A naturally beautiful, though not—at present—a very big voice—it is equal throughout its compass—she has the posture of the singer too, and there was a good deal of quiet strength in her rendering—she sang much better this afternoon than this evening, and acquitted herself excellently in every way."—45.

The epithets he uses in some of his judgments are picturesque. One voice he finds " too stringy," a female choir is "a little sticky at the beginning," and another is "inclined to be too chippy in utterance." On occasions when "Onaway, Awake" was the competitive theme he was wont to complain that the singers were almost invariably too slow, and often "not quite lover-like enough."

In addition to his symphony concerts he gave each year in Croydon a recital of his own compositions, engaging famous performers to help him. These were usually devoted for the greater part to his new smaller compositions, songs, violin pieces, and similar works. It is significant that of all the concerts that he gave in Croydon one of these was the only one from which he received a financial return. This was a recital at which Madame Ella Russell was the vocalist and John Saunders the violinist; and the net profits were £33, a sum the mention of which disposes of an opinion at one time current in Croydon that Coleridge-Taylor must have been making a considerable income from his music. His recital at the Public Hall on March 31, 1906, is typical. His assistants were Miss Clara Dow, Albert Garcia, John Saunders, and Charles Draper, and the programme included, in addition to his earlier *Clarinet Quintet,* a new arrangement for violin, 'cello, and pianoforte of five of his *Characteristic Negro Melodies,* and no less than eight new songs : *If I Could Love Thee, Genevieve, Dreaming for Ever, The Young Indian Maid, Beauty and Song, Once Only, African Love Song,* and

She Rested by the Broken Brook. Two of the lyrics are
by Robert Louis Stevenson, a fact which recalls his saying
that he had made several attempts to set that writer's address to his wife, the well-known verses which open thus :

> *Trusty, dusky, vivid true,*
> *With eyes of gold, and bramble-dew,*
> *Steel-true and blade-straight,*
> *The great artificer*
> *Made my mate.*

and was unable to satisfy himself. This confession he
made at a Croydon eisteddfod, at which as judge he set
the lyric in the composition competition.

In June his college friend, W. Y. Hurlstone, died of
consumption. Lately the two composers had not been in
daily intercourse, but their friendship had been real and
sincere, and based upon complete mutual appreciation.
Coleridge-Taylor wrote for *The Norwood News* the short
tribute, from which I have quoted already, but which it
seems worth while to reproduce here in full :

" Like many another highly gifted musician, the late Mr.
Hurlstone, whose death we all so deeply regret, was remarkably prolific in composition. This seems to be one of the
surest proofs of an imagination above the ordinary. Truly,
quantity is not quality, but with the single exception of
Chopin, all the famous composers have left a vast amount
of work behind them. We have only to think of Schubert
and Mendelssohn, both of whom were in the thirties when
they died, to realise the truth of this assertion. I think
there were very few branches of composition in which Mr.
Hurlstone was not successful. So far as I know, he never
published any choral work, and I well remember how, in
our college days, we both used to despise this form of music,
and how, only six months ago, we laughed over our youthful
prejudices. It was in chamber music (which, after all, is
the highest form of composition, in spite of the present-day
fashion) that Mr. Hurlstone shone so conspicuously, and in
his college days he had an extraordinary passion for writing

for out-of-the-way combinations of instruments. To me his works were quite matured so long as ten years ago, when I first knew him at college, and all of his early works show exceedingly fine workmanship. I don't suppose he wrote half a dozen bars of slip-shod stuff in his life. I recall that in our student days we each had a musical god. His was Brahms; mine was the lesser-known Dvořák. We agreed that, when either of these composers was really inspired, there was not much to choose between them; but he (Mr. Hurlstone) insisted that when Brahms lost inspiration he became merely dull, whereas Dvořák became commonplace. How we used to argue over that vexed question, as to which was the greater crime, to be dull or commonplace! Mr. Hurlstone was exceedingly critical, in the best sense, and had a way of seeing through superficiality which must have been rather alarming to anyone who tried to deceive him as to his or her attainments musically! On many occasions have we sat next each other at concerts, and during the progress of a work we would both look up at each other at the same moment. I doubt if there is anything that can draw musicians, or, for that matter, any artists, to each other more than the knowledge that they each appreciate the same points in other people's work.

"In these days, when it is customary to applaud all that is ugly and meaningless, and to decry the beautiful and natural, it is a relief to find music that always has melody, and more important still (though, alas! we are in danger of forgetting it in painting as well as music) *form*. Such is the music of W. Y. Hurlstone. A kind friend, a shrewd observer, a brilliant pianist, and a scorner of humbug—such was Mr. Hurlstone personally, and his early death is no less a real loss to English music than it is a great grief to his many friends."

The event in drama of the early part of 1906 was the production by Mr. Tree of Stephen Phillips's *Nero* at His Majesty's Theatre. Coleridge-Taylor received the commission for the incidental music, and found in the theme even greater opportunities than he had found in *Herod* or

Ulysses, and the results have certainly proved to be more widely appreciated. He attended almost daily at the theatre, watching the rehearsals, and getting the atmosphere of the play, but he was so occupied with other engagements, teaching and conducting, that he could rarely stay a rehearsal through. There were delightful half-hours, however, when he and Mr. Adolf Schmid could steal away to a neighbouring restaurant to discuss the theatre and music, to the accompaniment of the inevitable coffee and cigarettes; and to these he owed much, since there were times when he found the greatest difficulty in fulfilling the exacting requirements of the theatre, and the suggestions and encouragement of the popular conductor helped him materially. Not that he ever complained of Mr. Tree's requirements. On the contrary, he recognised the superb organising genius of the actor-manager, and realised that when once it was satisfied he could feel assured that he had done a really good work. In an interview with Mr. Raymond Blathwayt he is explicit, " My work for Mr. Tree has been invaluable to me as a composer. It has helped to broaden, to deepen, to elevate my whole musical outlook. Mr. Tree is a wonderful man. He gave me every possible assistance, and it is to him that I owe any knowledge I may possess of dramatic writing. How does one begin? Well, first one goes to hear the play read through, to get hold of what the painters call the ' right atmosphere.' Then the ideas begin to come! And, curiously enough, though Mr. Tree may not be a musician —that is, from the technical point of view—yet he always makes one understand exactly what it is he wants. I attended many of the rehearsals." And, in answer to a question as to whether he enjoyed writing for the stage, he added : " I like it now and then, for it comes as a welcome change and relief, and, as I say, it helps to broaden one's whole outlook. And then, again, the music is played every night, and it is played well, too, by such a band as His Majesty's. Now, you don't get your ordinary symphony or overture played nearly so frequently. I consider there is a great future for the composers of theatre music, and such a man as Mr. Tree benefits not only the drama, but also all the other arts which go to make up a great play, by insisting that everything shall be of the best."

The *Nero* music has true dramatic character, and the sensuous oriental elements in Nero's character are presented remarkably. In connection with this he remarked to Mr. Blathwayt, "Of course one does not copy music of that day too closely, for people wouldn't listen to it. All that you can do is to try and get hold of and to convey a certain oriental impression now and then. That was my aim, rather than to provide people with what actually occurred." Its main features are an effective prelude, which opens with a trumpet theme, a complex Nero theme, a suggestive bacchanalia interlude, and a processional march of real magnificence. The critics wisely remarked, too, on the appropriate character of the little themes used for entrances. The orchestral suite from this music, which was published in the same year, has been performed more frequently than any of Coleridge-Taylor's incidental music. In this later form the work has been greatly altered, the prelude is replaced by an entr'acte representing "a woman without pity, beautiful," Poppæa, and the remainder is made up of three movements, the second being an *Intermezzo* (andante moderato), the third *An Eastern Dance,* and the fourth an *Entr'acte* (andante). Parts of the incidental music, including the stately processional march, made their appearance as a separate work.

A concert which gave him great pleasure during this year was a Special S. Coleridge-Taylor Concert at the Tower, New Brighton. The programme included *Kubla Khan,* the *Symphonic Variations on an African Theme,* the *Nero Suite,* and the *Processional March,* interspersed with songs from other composers by Madame Ella Russell. *Kubla Khan,* as we have already noted, had its first pro-

Mrs. Coleridge-Taylor with her children, Hiawatha and Gwendolen

(*The loving cup, presented to the composer by the Samuel Coleridge-Taylor Choral Society in* 1904, *is shown on the table.*)

duction in May, when it was produced under Coleridge-Taylor's own baton by the Handel Society. It was a success; but a performance which gave him even greater joy, since it revived in a manner after his own heart his personal connection with his alma mater, was one in the same month which he conducted at the Royal College of Music.

The String Players' Club was a co-operative effort, in which Coleridge-Taylor was the energising force. As we have seen, the Croydon Orchestral Society and his own symphony concerts died of the usual financial deficit and of the varying quality of the players. Coleridge-Taylor called together the better players, and the club was formed on sound business lines. In the first place, the players agreed to submit their playing to examination, and no one was to become a performing member who could not survive the ordeal. It was resolved at the outset that the activities of the club were to be confined, as its name implied, to works for strings only, except for an occasional orchestral concert to be held at the close of the season, at which professional wind and tympani players would be engaged; and, in order to secure success rather than profits, the prices of seats were to be one shilling and a limited number at sixpence. Every member undertook as a condition of his or her membership to dispose of tickets to the value of five shillings. These principles were adhered to as long as Coleridge-Taylor remained the conductor, and the result was immediate and lasting success, and so firmly was the Club established that with very minor modifications, it remains the principal feature of musical activity in Croydon to this day. The examiner was the late Mr. Otto Manns, and the test was sufficiently severe to exclude the worst offenders in Coleridge-Taylor's former concerts. One or two of the rejected were piqued considerably, but in general the findings of the examiner were accepted with candour, and the disappointed players became supporters of the movement. Some notion of the influence of our

N

musician may be gained from the fact that he had no difficulty in persuading a Fellow of the Royal College of Organists and of Trinity College to officiate in the not very glorious rôle of triangle-player. He was especially fortunate, too, in securing a most gifted leader in Mr. Stanton Rees, a violinist well known in the south of London for the beauty of his tone and his admirable technique. His personal friends acted as his stewards and ticket-collectors, and, indeed, the concerts were events anticipated and attended by many of us with intense pleasure. His theory, which has already been touched upon, that a beautiful player is usually a beautiful person, seemed to receive some sanction in the club; and, although I feel that it is a delicate matter to recall, he told us that he chose the fairest of his players to occupy the front of the platform. The result was certainly successful.

His programmes were worked out with almost mathematical exactness to his absolute limit of two hours, beyond which time he held that it was not fair to expect an audience to listen; and the interval of ten minutes was rigidly limited to ten minutes. These intervals were the social side of the concerts, when, in the artistes' rooms, coffee and cakes were dispensed, and friends could find their way in to talk with the members and with the conductor himself, who moved about amongst them chatting and laughing in the most accessible, boyish manner. His thoughtfulness and readiness were apparent at these times; he would go out of his way to introduce to one another people whom he thought had interests in common, and smoothed the way to conversation between such strangers with a skill which was enviable in its natural simplicity. As for the concerts themselves, they were varied in character as far as the not unlimited field of music for strings only allowed, and there was usually one singer and one solo instrumentalist at each. A high level was aimed at both in the concerted and in the solo work, and I remember his annoyance when a singer introduced into his interpretation of a song a rather cheap suggestiveness of gesture. "That is not the sort of thing we wish to introduce," he remarked to me.

Such details as the work of the stewards received his attention almost equally with the higher work; and he was gratified when on one occasion they ejected two members of the audience who, having dined too well, persisted in making audible comments during the pieces. "It is good to have one's friends as helpers," was his remark; "for their own interest in the music makes them wish to prevent the least annoyance to others, and they are not afraid to do this in a way that paid stewards would be afraid to take." He particularly detested the humbug with which some artistes embellish their performances. For instance, a singer desired to impress the audience by a prearranged presentation of a bouquet to herself. She therefore ordered a bouquet from a florist, which she required to be addressed to herself at the Public Hall, in the expectation that it would be handed to her publicly after her singing as a tribute from an enraptured audience. To her chagrin her turns passed without the appearance of the floral tribute. Coleridge-Taylor had seen the arrival of the box containing the bouquet, and recognising its intention, had it secreted in a corner of the artistes' room, whence, at the close of the evening, he brought it forth, and handed it to the lady with a smiling, "I believe this is for you, isn't it?"

As at his earlier Croydon concerts, he gave a hearing to the works of several young British composers; but he was, as usual, reticent in the performance of his own. Occasionally, however, some brief work from his pen appeared; his *Novelletten,* some *Variations for 'Cello,* which have since vanished mysteriously, and a number of songs can be recalled as having figured in the programmes. Sometimes he adopted pseudonymity at a first performance of a work, as was the case with four songs, *Life and Death, Prithee tell me, Dimple-Chin, An Explanation,*

and *The Vengeance,* which were announced as by
" F. R. C."   The mention of these songs raises a point
of some interest in connection with the expression and
sentiment of the words of songs, and Coleridge-Taylor's
insistence upon a definite interpretation of the words.
The Vengeance has not been published; the publishers to
whom it was offered found the music interesting and appropriate, but "the words were too strong."   The rejected
words are as follows :

> *I met him, Lady of my Dream,*
> *Where rainbow torrents flashing stream ;*
> *I saw his eye with laughter gleam,*
>   *His proud lip curl with scorn ;*
> *With laughter at thy maiden fame,*
> *And words that mocked thy fairest name ;*
> *Then leapt my heart with hate to flame*
>   *As breaks a stormy morn.*
>
> *He mocked at thee ; I saw him jeer ;*
> *He cursed at thee ; I raised my spear,*
> *And like a tempest I drew near,*
>   *And like a tree he fell ;*
> *Three times I thrust the traitor through,*
> *A thrust for every curse of you ;*
> *His corpse lies rotting 'neath the blue,*
>   *His soul abides in Hell !*

The lyric was one of a set of would-be Arabian lyrics,
of which the posthumously published *Low-Breathing
Winds* forms one, and the writer fondly hoped that
Coleridge-Taylor would slur over quickly the somewhat
violent

> *His corpse lies rotting 'neath the blue,*
> *His soul abides in Hell !*

but with unerring dramatic instinct the composer introduced a pause after the unpleasant word, "rotting," and
repeated it with great emphasis.   A moment's study of
the lyric will show how true this is as an interpreting of

its spirit; and, when the verdict of the publishers was known, all the efforts made at his request by the writer of the lyric to produce a less "strong" climax were rejected by Coleridge-Taylor, because the first "gave, after all, the right effect to the song." His insistence upon perfect accenting was invariable, and he would stop in his composing when he encountered a word the exact pronunciation of which evaded him until he had assured himself that his conception of it was correct. I remember his amusement at a song of the sea in which the composer had set the word "sailors" with the accent upon the second syllable, and I am told that he thought Mendelssohn's beautiful *O Rest in the Lord* suffered gravely from the way in which the elocution of the words was ignored in the music.

On October 15, 1906, we find Coleridge-Taylor at Walsall Town Hall, in the capacity of accompanist at a violin recital given by his college mate, Mr. Willie J. Read. The two men had drifted from one another in late years, and this recital is interesting as marking the renewal of a connection which was to be strengthened by nearness of neighbourhood when Mr. Read became leader of the Duke of Devonshire's Orchestra at Eastbourne, and which was to last until death dissolved it.

The letter to Mr. Hilyer of December 7, 1905, foreshadowed Coleridge-Taylor's second visit to America, which was the important event with which 1906 closed. He did not leave any impression of his voyage as vivid as were those of his first voyage; it seems to have been without incident. His purpose was to conduct the S. Coleridge-Taylor Society again, this time in *The Atonement, The Quadroon Girl,* and *Hiawatha;* but he also arranged a brief tour in company with Henry T. Burleigh. This commenced at the Mendelssohn Hall, New York, with a recital of his smaller compositions, the programme of which may be given, as he repeated it, with little variation, throughout the tour :

Violin Soli   .   .   .   .   Mr. Felix Fowler Weir
    (a) Intermezzo
    (b) Entr'acte No. 1
       (From the Music to *Nero*.)

Songs for Soprano   ·   .   .   .   Miss Lola Johnson
    (a) "The Young Indian Maid"
    (b) "Beauty and Song"

Songs for Baritone   .   .   .   .   Mr. Henry T. Burleigh
    (a) "Love's Passing"
    (b) "A Corn Song"

Piano Soli   .   .   .   .   .   S. Coleridge-Taylor
    Two Oriental Waltzes:
      (a) Andante con Sentimento
      (b) Allegro Moderato

Violin   .   .   .   .   .   .   Mr. Felix Fowler Weir
    Romance in E flat

Songs for Soprano   .   .   .   .   Miss Lola Johnson
    (a) "Spring had Come"
    (b) "Minguillo"

Songs for Baritone   .   .   .   .   Mr. Henry T. Burleigh
    (a) "She Rested by the Broken Brook"
    (b) "Beat, Beat, Drums!"

Violin Soli   .   .   .   .   .   Mr. Felix Fowler Weir
    African Dances:
      1. Allegro Moderato
      2. Andantino (based on a real negro melody)
      3. Allegro vivace
      4. Allegro energico

It is interesting to learn from *The New York Herald,*
in connection with this Mendelssohn Hall concert, that
"many coloured persons were in the audience, but probably through fear of making themselves conspicuous they
failed to give the composer an enthusiastic demonstration.
There was, however, no lack of applause, because the
whites in the assembly did not hesitate to express their
approval heartily."

In spite of its strenuous character, Coleridge-Taylor
always regarded his American visit of 1904 as in the
nature of a pleasure tour. This visit of 1906 was of a

different character; it was crammed with engagements. The programme outlined above was presented to audiences at Washington, Pittsburg, St. Louis, Chicago, Milwaukee, Detroit, Toronto, and finally at Boston. He received, too, an invitation from the Litchfield County Choral Union at Norfolk, Connecticut, to give a complimentary recital at the Village Hall, Norfolk, in recognition of his election as honorary member of the Union.

"He accepted at once," writes Mr. Carl Stoeckel, "and my first personal meeting with him was when he alighted from the train at our station, accompanied by the men who were to assist him in the concert, which was given on December 17." His assistants were Reed Miller, Henry T. Burleigh, and Felix Fowler Weir, and the programme, which was of his own works, was a variation on that given above, with the addition of five of the *Negro Melodies*. "The audience," continues Mr. Stoeckel, "consisted of two sections of our organisation, the Norfolk Glee Club and the Winsted Choral Union, with other invited guests. Mr. Coleridge-Taylor was received by a rising salute from the audience, and was introduced by President Clark. I told him that this was to occur before he went on to the stage. He was pleased, and remarked, 'I will do anything but make a speech,' and I told him that this would not be expected, but whatever he wished to say could be done through his music. The audience was most enthusiastic, and after the concert Mr. Coleridge-Taylor and several officials of the organisation came to my house to supper. Everybody who met him was charmed with his personality, with his intelligence, graceful conversation, modesty, and sincerity. In the report made in the following year this appears : ' We recall with pleasure the opportunity given to so many of us to see and hear one of our distinguished honorary members, Samuel Coleridge-Taylor, in a recital of his own compositions. Delegations from the various chapters came to the Village Hall, and were delightfully entertained. A few were privileged to meet Coleridge-

Taylor socially, and he proved himself a cultured gentleman, modest, charming, and interesting, and an inspiration to his own race, and, sincerely it may be said, to the white man also.' "

At Washington the S. Coleridge-Taylor Society's Festival occupied three days, November 21 being devoted to *The Atonement* and *The Quadroon Girl*, November 22 to *Hiawatha*, and November 23 to the miscellaneous recital. The *Hiawatha* performance was the thirteenth that had taken place in Washington. The festival was held in the Metropolitan A.M.E. Church, and the audiences were as great and as appreciative as they had been on his first visit. The composer was in excellent health and vigour throughout the tour, and enjoyed to the full the experiences it afforded. He returned, as from his first visit, laden with souvenirs and good-wishes, reaching Upper Grove in the last days of the year. His musician friends gathered at his house to give him a welcome in the form of a brief concert in his honour.

His second visit confirmed his opinion that musical taste in America was very good. "Especially in the great cities," he told Mr. Blathwayt, "though it is not generally so good in the country. Nor are there nearly so many small choral societies as we have here, and it is our choral societies which have done the real spade-work during the last fifty years in England. Most of the good music in America is due to the enormous German element in the larger cities. They never have the commonplace English ballad, for instance, and much of their taste in music is built upon the German *Lieder*—and the very best basis too ! "

The first day of 1907 found him in Wales in his favourite capacity of adjudicator, at the Dolgelly Eisteddfod. It was a genuine mystery to his friends that he should accept so many of these engagements, and especially that he should post off to one so soon after his strenuous American tour, but, apart from the economic question involved, he seems to have found suggestions of value in the musical experiences they afforded; and, as I have shown, he had a delight in these years in their social side. He usually met other adjudicators there of sound knowledge and experience, with whom he spent a few days agreeably; and he received undoubted pleasure from the singing of the Welsh choirs. It is characteristic of him that he seldom, if ever, was without enthusiasm for the work in hand, and, to meet him on his return from one of these eisteddfods, as I frequently did, was to hear a great deal about the correctness and the fine tonality of the Welsh singing. The choirs from the mining districts were his special admiration, and not a few of his part-songs owe their existence to them.

It would be a wearisome task, and unprofitable except that it shows his unwearying industry, to detail his many engagements in 1907. He travelled to many parts of the country during the year, conducting, adjudicating, rehearsing. On February 27 he conducted his *Variations on an African Theme* at Liverpool, and in reference to this concert he made some interesting remarks to Mr. Blathwayt : "The other day I conducted one concert in Liverpool, the programme of which was what used to be called ' classical,' and yet there were present at that one concert no less than four thousand five hundred people, of whom certainly not more than a hundred quitted the hall before the long and fairly-difficult-to-listen-to programme came to an end. And I have no hesitation in saying that the most genuine and enthusiastic appreciation came from the cheap, one and two-shilling, seats. That is why Henry Wood's Promenade Concerts are so popular. In my opinion the half-guinea stalls will soon cease to exist, where music pure and simple is concerned." He added, "It is to the great masses that I feel that we owe it here in England to-day that music stands on the high level it undoubtedly does."

This theory of the musical appreciation of the masses,

which he thought to be the logical outcome of the thirty years of popular high-class concerts, he tested in practice through his Croydon String Players' Club. On May 23, the fifth concert of this body was given at the Large Public Hall, Croydon, and with it the first season concluded. It will be remembered that the prices of seats had been one shilling, and sixpence, respectively; and, in spite of the commonly-received notion that the public appreciates only music for the hearing of which it pays expensively, the experiment had justified itself from every point of view. Expenses had been paid; that is to say, all first costs had been recovered—although, be it noted, Coleridge-Taylor's own work was purely gratuitous; there had been crowded and highly appreciative audiences throughout; and in the actual playing his method of choosing his players and music had been vindicated thoroughly. It is well to give this concluding programme, as it is typical:

ASGER HAMERICK, Op. 38:
Symphonie Spirituelle (No. 6 in G major)
(a) Allegro moderato   (c) Andante sostenuto
(b) Allegro molto vivace   (d) Allegro con spirito

Songs . (a) " To Althea "   .   .   .   . C. H. H. PARRY
          (b) " Oh, Lowly Earth " .   .   . MONK GOULD
          (c) " Ebb and Flow "   .   .   . MONK GOULD
                    MR. DAN PRICE

Solo Violin . " Ballade et Polonaise " . HENRI VIEUXTEMPS
                    MR. STANTON REES

JULIUS A. HARRISON:
" Ballad " (MS.) for String Orchestra (first performance in Croydon)

EDGAR BECK-SLINN:
" Waltz " (MS.) for String Orchestra (first performance)

Interval of Ten Minutes Only

ALEXANDRE GLAZOUNOW, Op. 35:
Suite in G major for Strings (without double basses)
(a) Introduction et Fugue   (c) Orientale — Andante
(b) Scherzo — Allegro   (d) Tema, con variazione
          (e) Valse — Moderato assai

Songs . (a) " Eleanore " . S. COLERIDGE-TAYLOR, Op. 34, No. 5
(b) " Beat, Beat, Drums ! "
S. COLERIDGE-TAYLOR, Op. 41, No. 6
EDVARD GRIEG, Op. 40 :
Suite for String Orchestra, " Aus Holberg's Zeit "
1. Prelude — Allegro vivace
2. Sarabande — Andante
3. Gavotte — Allegretto
4. Rigaudon — Allegro con brio

It will be seen that throughout a welcoming hand was offered to younger composers; and the Waltz by E. Beck-Slinn, which figures here, was only one of the several promising new compositions which had their first hearing at these concerts.

Press interviews are not entirely satisfactory sources of information. With such a man as Coleridge-Taylor, easily impressionable, fluent in speech, and willing to please, it is not difficult for the interviewer to direct the thoughts of the interviewed into channels not of his own choosing; there is also no consecutive thought expressed as a rule. These probabilities granted, the interview with Mr. Blathwayt, from which quotation has been made, may be said to give certain interesting dicta which I know Coleridge-Taylor approved, because, when Mr. Blathwayt submitted proofs for his inspection, the composer handed them to me for examination, smiling a little at the genial pertinacity of interviewers in general, but admitting the statements the proof contained. It is therefore desirable to quote a few of them. In it he returned to the theory that Beethoven had coloured blood in his veins. The supposition, he thought, was supported by the great composer's type of features and many little points in his character, as well as by his friendship for Bridgewater, the mulatto violinist. And he could not avoid a sarcasm : " I think that if the greatest of all musicians were alive to-day, he would find it somewhat difficult, if not absolutely impossible, to obtain hotel accommodation in certain American cities."

When asked his opinion of modern musical comedy and of the future of English music, he remarked, "The good and the bad always march side by side for a time, but in the end the good comes in a long way ahead. And very likely musical comedy itself displays a great advance on what used to be popular in the 'sixties and 'seventies. I certainly think and hope that music will not become very much more complex than it is in the latest examples of our great living composers' genius. Yet, after all, you must take into consideration the fact that music and the appreciation of music, as old Sir August Manns told me, stand on a far higher level in England than fifty years ago. That is, in most respects, though not, perhaps, altogether. In giving lessons to the few pupils I have time to teach, I am constantly being surprised by the uniformly high level that is maintained. It is a level distinguished by culture, originality, and imagination, a level impossible of general attainment fifty years ago, let us say."

"Church music," he thought, "is one of the branches of the art that has not made any progress. Most of the latter-day Church music is certainly no better than it was thirty years ago, and much of it is not nearly so good. I think one reason for this is, that whereas the technique of nearly every other branch of music has advanced so tremendously, in church choirs it has stood comparatively still. The amateur church choir singer has not made the same strides as the amateur violinist, for example. And our best composers are not, therefore, very much attracted at present, though, of course, there are brilliant exceptions."

He was of opinion that greatest progress in the last half-century had been made in our orchestras. "Curiously enough, I attribute this to Russian influence. It was the Russians who first sounded the death-knell of the old-fashioned English writing of orchestral music fifty years ago. The influence of Tschaikowsky and other Russians is leavening the whole mass, pretty much, indeed, as Ibsen influenced the writing of English drama. The Russian influence has converted orchestration from being a stereotyped element in musical composition into a very serious element indeed."

An examination of the correspondence that he received during the year shows a tendency in music-lovers, which he appreciated, to offer suggestions of subjects for musical setting. Although it may be affirmed that the highest creative genius is known by its enormous fertility in ideas, yet the greatest have often been grateful for suggestions. Some of those he received were, of course, impracticable, indeed, almost amusing, as for instance a polite request from America that he should provide the entire music of a play by a writer entirely unknown to him, the proceeds of the performances of which were to go to a charity. I have been unable to learn what he replied, but he had a just indignation at the too prevalent notion that in the sacred cause of charity musicians may be expected to give their services as a matter of course. At the same time, he appeared at large numbers of concerts for one cause and another. In an earlier letter to Miss Petherick he remarks about a concert he was persuaded to arrange for some "cause" in Croydon : "No one is receiving a fee, but I pressed the people who are arranging the fête very much, and told them it was unfair to expect professionals to play for nothing. Of course you know it is for a ' charity ' (everything is, it seems, in Croydon !), but they will pay each of your expenses at half-a-guinea. I tried for more, but had to give in ! "

This ground has been gone over again and again by professional musicians, but unfortunately professional musicians are the helpless cause of their own sufferings. By giving the lessons by which they earn their livelihood to amateurs to whom performing music is a means of amusement, they create a race of competitors who would occupy the platforms that they refused. Moreover, the struggling professional musician needs publicity above all things, and to obtain it is willing to appear without fees; and while such a system prevails it will be difficult to convince the public of the necessity of giving his daily bread to the musician.

Other suggestions showed more discernment, as, for instance, one from Liverpool "that an effective subject for musical treatment would be the life of Toussaint l'Ouverture, the Haytian patriot"—a suggestion after the event as we have seen. Another letter, from an American correspondent, presses upon him, as being "just your sort of stuff," *The Story of the Slaves in the Desert,* by Whittier, and brought him a transcript of it. Amongst these letters I find one from New York: "Will you accept thanks for your public condemnation published in this morning's paper of the abominable rubbish called ' coon songs ' and ' rag-time.' There has been no greater detriment to the race in this country, nor can there be a greater impediment to its future progress."

Late in the year Mrs. Mary Church Terrell, of the Board of Education at Washington, a gifted American writer, adds a postscript to a letter which suggests the kind of attention that Coleridge-Taylor occasionally received: "How dreadful you must feel to be deprived of the pleasure of lending impoverished Americans some of your English pounds! I am afraid you are being snubbed by your American friends, if nobody asked you to lend him anything during a whole summer. You had better see what is the reason you are being deserted in so wholesale a fashion."

On July 7 he conducted another special S. Coleridge-Taylor concert at The Tower, New Brighton, which was chiefly notable for the first appearance of a new work from his pen, a *Fantasiestück in A major for Violoncello and Orchestra,* which was played by Miss Mary McCullagh.

The work is in the form of variations upon a theme, but has greater homogeneity in treatment than is usual in such works, and is marked by the restraint with which the orchestral accompaniment is scored and the consequent effective prominence given to the solo instrument. The work opens with twelve bars of arpeggii and sustained chords, and the theme is announced by the violoncello at the thirteenth bar. The key is A major, and the theme "comprises a first phrase, a responsive phrase, and a return of first phrase."* The tempo increases at the first variation with an eventual change to F major; the second variation, which is approached by accelerated passages and a transition to F sharp minor, begins with a chromatic phrase, which introduces a singing violoncello melody contrasted by another melody held by the violins and flutes. A brief slow movement of peculiar beauty follows in A flat major, and this is succeeded by a vigorous allegro on the principal themes of the work, in which the solo part becomes elaborate. A quiet passage then forms an interlude, before a largamente passage of much power leads up to the brilliant and rapid coda with which the work ends. Few even of Coleridge-Taylor's instrumental works are marked by a finer sense of proportion.

It was during this year that he became president of another musical society, and how eventually he became its conductor is told in some notes with which I have been furnished by Miss Florence Montgomery, its organiser and secretary :

"In 1907 I endeavoured, with the help of my friends in South London, to form an orchestral society, afterwards known as the Blackheath, Brockley, and Lewisham Orchestral Society. Mr. Coleridge-Taylor was the president, and when we had been in existence for a couple of seasons, he kindly consented to conduct his *Nero Suite* at one of our concerts. Never shall I forget the effect of his personality on the orchestra, which, with the exception of a few first-rate instrumentalists, was of the usual suburban mediocrity. The *Nero Suite* is written in his most

* Herbert McCullagh.

characteristic vein, and the last number especially roused the enthusiasm of orchestra and audience alike, who rose *en masse* and cheered him to the echo. He had many recalls, which he took in the most reluctant manner, appearing at last with one boot on and an evident desire to escape. I remember the principal viola player coming to me, with streaming face and kindling eye, and declaring that he had never played so well in his life, and had certainly never felt so hot and exhausted.

"Some time after the concert the society became in need of a conductor, and the daring idea occurred to me of asking Coleridge-Taylor himself to fill that position. I have often wondered at my temerity in doing this, and still more at his ready compliance. We had then only about fifty members, no financial guarantee of any kind, and all the organisation rested on the shoulders of an enthusiastic girl. I am positive that it was just his ready sympathy with this enthusiasm and his own warm, chivalrous nature that made him undertake a work which can have meant little beyond loss of precious time and energy; and it is just this kindly and generous action that should be placed on record. I, of course, hoped that the number of active and honorary members would increase by leaps and bounds, and it was one of my greatest disappointments to find that such was not the case. We gave several altogether delightful concerts with an orchestra improved beyond recognition, yet our finances were so low that we were never able adequately to repay our conductor.

"After a while the rehearsals and concerts were held at Blackheath, and Mr. Coleridge-Taylor used to go to the Brighton New Cross Station to catch the Waddon train. He told me several times that the ticket-collector at New Cross used to take a fiendish delight in assuring him that the train had gone, when with a little hurry he could easily have caught it. But when I suggested telling the collector that he was treating a celebrity in this disrespectful manner he always said : ' No, not on any account; it would spoil his fun.' He generally had a cup of coffee and a cigarette after rehearsal, sitting on the edge of my secretarial desk (which he called the coffee-stall), and there he would talk of any subject under the sun, always in the raciest and most vividly interesting manner. On one occasion we placed a new baton on his desk, with silver mounts, and his name inscribed upon it, and much to the chagrin of the orchestra he used it without making any comment whatever, afterwards explaining that it had never occurred to him that it was meant as a present. He was always loth to have his name on the programme, and when on several occasions he accompanied his own songs, he invariably objected to the words ' accompanied by the composer.' I remember when Miss Evangeline Florence sang his *Fairy Ballads,* he absolutely refused to share the applause with her, and only an energetic push from the wings, and a ' Oh! really you are too modest for anything ! ' brought him forward.

"He had an extraordinary memory for names and faces, and a charming facility for not only putting others at their ease, but deferring to them in such a way that he invariably brought out all that was best in them. He was absolutely sincere, with something of the child's frank fearlessness. Indeed, I think he retained much of the child's beautiful nature, although he was in many respects a keen man of the world."

The mention of his appearance with one boot on reminds me of certain effects of the preoccupation to which I suppose every creative genius is more or less subject. His regard for and attention to personal appearance were great ; but things might intervene between his dressing-room and the concert platform. I remember that on one rainy night he had turned up his trousers several inches to avoid mudstains, and he came before the footlights blissfully unconscious of the fact that one trouser-leg remained turned up and allowed a generous display of sock, while, to com-

o

plete the picture, a white pocket handkerchief dangled from the tail-pocket of his evening dress coat.

At the Crystal Palace, he not only gave lessons; he also received them, in the German language. He had long possessed an admiration for things German, which had its foundation in the music of Germany, and in the organised national regard for the art, which seemed to him to give opportunities for the development of the native musician, of which the British composer could only dream rather pathetically. He took up the study of the language with his usual intensity and enthusiasm, and within a year we find him writing letters in German to his friends. Amongst them was the well-known Berlin violinist, Theodore Spiering, who visited England during 1907, and who occasionally played Coleridge-Taylor's works at his recitals. His letters to Spiering are brief enough, but show his appreciation :

SOUTH NORWOOD,
July 4, 1907.

MY DEAR MR. SPIERING,—You played splendidly last evening, and I haven't enjoyed a concert so much for years. My leader, Stanton Rees, was simply *delighted*.

I couldn't come in last night, as I had to see two ladies home, and then to get to Victoria by 11.40, and I knew you had a crowd in the artistes' room.

Are you going back immediately? If not, please let me know, and tell me if the Berlin address I have will always find you.

Kindest regards from both of us; and renewed congratulations.—Yours always,   S. COLERIDGE-TAYLOR.

10 UPPER GROVE,
September 12, 1907.

I shall write to Mr. Godfrey to-morrow, and shall write to you again when he answers. I have a new piece (a ballad) for violin and piano, and I hope that you will soon play it if you like it enough.

10 Upper Grove,
October 12.

My dear Mr. Spiering,—I really must write and congratulate you on your splendid playing last evening.

It is not often that a London audience is roused to such enthusiasm.

Sitting next to me was a former leader of the Royal College Orchestra, a most brilliant player himself, and he was simply delighted.

Might I trouble you to send me a postcard with the number of the Arundel Street address by return?

I am so sorry to trouble you. I shall come straight from the Crystal Palace, and will be with you just before one.

Kindest regards and renewed congratulations.—Believe me, yours very sincerely,

S. Coleridge-Taylor.

The work referred to in the second note was his *Ballade for Violin and Piano,* which received its first performance at the hands of Zacharewitsch at his recital at Leeds on October 29, when the piano part was played by the composer. The work is highly characteristic and of singular beauty and variety, and is in five movements, *Molto moderato, Allegro, Piu andante e tranquillo, Allegro vivace,* and *L'istesso tempo,* which have a sequence in ideas, and have moments of grave depth, although the whole leaves the impression of being a sort of rhapsody.

During the late season he conducted various concerts at Devonshire Park, Eastbourne, and assisted Mr. William J. Read at recitals in the town. His letters and notes to Mr. Read are models of conciseness, and a few may be included here, with the excuse that they illustrate his practice of omitting unessential things from his correspondence :

August 4.

My dear Read,—*Evening dress Sunday?*—Yours always,

S. Coleridge-Taylor.

August 19, 1907.

I'm coming down to Eastbourne, Sept. 5, to conduct. I shall be only too delighted to play for you on that day—what do you propose doing? "Gipsy Pieces"? Let me know, please.—Yours always, S. COLERIDGE-TAYLOR.

10 UPPER GROVE,
SOUTH NORWOOD,
September 1.

MY DEAR READ,—I am coming down to Eastbourne on Tuesday afternoon to rehearse at 3.30.

Will you please let me know at what time you'll be free to run through the fiddle things?

My train leaves London at 12 noon, arriving about 2.30, or so.

But, if you prefer to wait till after the orchestra, I can easily wait, as I have a very good train as late as 8.30.

Great haste and kind regards.—Yours very sincerely,

S. COLERIDGE-TAYLOR.

SOUTH NORWOOD,
September 4.

Hope you've received fiddle pieces.

On November 12 he distributed the prizes to the students at the Beckenham and Bromley School of Music, and following a musical programme by the students, he delivered another brief address:

" There are many things connected with music that I might talk about, but as I recently examined the harmony papers of this school I shall confine my remarks to that most important subject, and the one or two things that arise directly from it. That every student—whatever his or her subject—should study harmony and counterpoint thoroughly goes without saying. There are some people, perhaps, specially gifted, who really appreciate the ins and outs of original and beautiful harmonies without knowing anything of technique, but they are very much in the minority. It should be remembered that the great difference between music and the other arts (with the exception of dramatic poetry) is that the former always requires a third person—that is to say, a medium—between the composer and the listener. To argue that that third need know nothing of the composition from a harmonic or structural point of view is obviously ridiculous, but whether audiences are better left in the dark or not is a question I should not care to answer. But I will mention a matter which often comes under my notice. I very frequently adjudicate in Wales and the North at eisteddfod meetings. Six choirs, say, will sing one composition; now an audience applauds for two things—a liking for the music itself, and an appreciation of the rendering of the music. I will take the position of the first and last choirs. The people, when they hear the first choir, have not begun to like the composition very much—on the other hand, they have not had a chance to compare renderings, so a certain amount of applause is granted. Things go on until the last choir sings. By this time the audience know and like the music, and are inclined to applaud much more on that score, but at the same time are ten thousand times more critical as to the renderings, because they have had a good chance of comparing one rendering with another; consequently, about the same amount of applause is given, but, as you will see, for a very different reason. That is why most adjudicators insist that the audience's reception of the various choirs is the very worst basis on which to give marks. A certain knowledge of harmony would cure to a great extent such mistakes on the part of the listeners.

" Many students do harmony perfectly well on paper, but if they are asked to name those very same progressions when played on the piano, they are completely lost. That, it seems to me, is the main reason why harmony is considered a dull thing by so many students, a thing to be got over quickly, and with as little trouble as possible—it means nothing to them as regards sound. In many cases it is all but impossible for the professor to do anything in that way at lessons, because harmony is generally taught in a class, and there is consequently no time to spare. I strongly advise harmony students to go through their work carefully on the piano after they have done it as well as possible on paper, and to alter anything that sounds unmusical even though it be correct, taking care, of course, that no new mistakes are made by so doing. On the other hand, a student should not rely on the piano, and ought to be able to do a correct and fairly musical paper away from any instrument. A fairly advanced student ought also to try to analyse the piece he or she is studying. Harmony would not then seem to be (as it so often does) a thing apart from the voice or instrument, but something very much connected with it indeed.

" Harmony, too, is of great use to those who would read at sight. It is doubtful if anything is so really useful to the musician as that. To the orchestral player it is, of course, imperative, and it is astonishing to find what a splendid lot of good amateur violinists there are who can read at sight. But with pianists and vocalists it is another matter. How humiliating it must be to the pianist who, after playing a Liszt rhapsody, on being asked to accompany a simple song, has to ' own up.' Seriously, many singers tell me how impossible it is to sing some of the more modern songs of such writers as Strauss, Debussy, and Hugo Wolf at concerts, because of the accompanists. In these overcrowded times it would be surely a good thing in every way if some of the young pianists made a special study of this. The tendency with modern composers is to make their piano parts quite as important as the solo. Accompaniments are no longer a placid background for the display of the soloist, and yet, notwithstanding this, it is very rarely that one meets the soloist who cares to go through the music more than once with the accompanist; therefore, the accompanist who would succeed to-day must, in addition to being a good pianist technically, have a complete grasp of the whole thing. Singers are by far the worst people in that respect. The inability of even good professionals to keep a part in a quartet, for instance, is one of the most disconcerting things a conductor has to get used to. Nearly all conductors are afraid of the singer coming in too early, or too late, or not at all; or, if at a proper moment, then on a wrong note."

In October Coleridge-Taylor tired of Upper Grove, and moved away some two or three miles to "Hill Crest," Norbury. The house lies on the London Road, from which it is separated by about fifty feet of front garden. The district is leafy, and is pleasant, as suburban districts may be reckoned; but the change soon began to reveal its drawbacks. Trams, motor-omnibuses, traction-engines, and all the manifold traffic of this main road from London to Brighton rattled and rumbled by with brief intermission all through the twenty-four hours. He hoped, however, by keeping the front windows and doors closed, and by working at the back of the house, to escape the worst consequences of these distracting noises. The experiment was not very successful, and his friends noticed, with some apprehension, that the noises were beginning to affect his nerves considerably. The effects were nightmare-like. The London Road has an incline towards Croydon from Norbury, and "Hill Crest," as its name implies, stands at the top of it. His dreams became obsessed by the figure of a horse, drawing a loaded vehicle, who grinned horribly as it came up over the slope; nor would any remedies of rest or otherwise that he could devise rid his nights of this incubus. When telling me of it, he laughed at what he said was the ridiculous humour of the thing; but it was not difficult to see that his body, which through long days he over-worked systematically, demanded quiet nights imperatively.

Another matter which I heard from him in those days is interesting as showing a certain fear of himself. "I am naturally a lazy man," he remarked. "It's a good thing that I have to work, for if I hadn't I should probably sit and read and smoke all day." He had, also, a curious horror of sleeping sickness, and really believed that abundant industry was absolutely necessary to the health of his mind and body. The fear is pathetic in the face of his tremendous activity and fertility.

CHAPTER XI

NOTWITHSTANDING the disadvantages that have
been enumerated, Coleridge-Taylor was wont to call
"Hill Crest" his "lucky little house." The luck was not
obvious during its occupation; indeed, a specially malig-
nant fortune seemed to pursue him there, but it had its beginning earlier in the year when he told us with some
glee that at last he had acquired an opera libretto that was
worth setting and that appealed to him. This was a
poetical rendering of a modern legend, which was first
entitled *The Amulet,* but afterwards changed to *Thelma.*
The story had no reference to Marie Corelli's novel of the
same name, but revolved, he told me, about a Norwegian
saga-legend. I have not seen the libretto as a whole, and
am not able to form an opinion of its constructional merits.
Such verse as I have seen, however, seemed to me to be
hopelessly mediocre, but this was after the event, when
such an opinion was futile. He had reason to hope that a
suitable opera from his pen would receive the attention of
the Carl Rosa Opera Company; and he commenced work
upon it with all his characteristic energy and enthusiasm.
For nearly two years he made it the centre of his interest;
working at it constantly, and revising to a bewildering extent; whole scenes were written and re-written in entirely
new forms again and again, and the finished manuscript is
beautiful in its minute neatness and legibility.

It is for this reason that his published works are fewer
by far during 1907 and 1908 than usual. His multi-
farious conducting, teaching, and similar activities absorbed no small amount of his time, and although the
intervals were spent in intense composing, the public re-

sults seemed to be small. At the String Players' Concert on November 30, 1907, Mr. C. A. Crabbe played from the manuscript and for the first time some *Variations on an Original Theme for the Violoncello,* a work which proved that this instrument received very special attention from him during the year. I have been unable to see the copy of this work, as it has disappeared mysteriously; but at that single hearing we formed the opinion that it was a fine, sustained, characteristic work, and the audience, which recalled player and composer some half-dozen times, more than shared the opinion.* These, and the compositions referred to in the previous chapter, and a few songs, "written when he had need of money," alas! form the principal works of these years other than the opera music.

It was towards the middle of 1908 that he received a further commission from Sir Herbert Tree; this time to provide music for a prospective production of the version of *Faust* by Stephen Phillips and Comyns Carr. This incidental music gave him unusual trouble. Comparisons, he knew, would be instituted between his work and the *Faust* music of Gounod and Berlioz; but the possibility did not daunt him: He haunted the theatre during rehearsals, staying half an hour at a time, getting the atmosphere of the play in a way that was impossible at the "reading," which took place at the theatre before it was put in rehearsal. He succeeded not only in avoiding the disparagement which might have arisen from the inevitable comparisons, but also in adding something vital to British music.

Though strenuous, no singular event marked 1908. In January he adjudicated at a musical festival at Queen's Hall; in February at Horbury, in June at Rhymney. On March 27 he was present at a Rimmer Quartet Chamber Concert of his own works at Liscard; nine days later he was conducting his *Ballade in A minor* and *Hiawatha's Vision*

---

* Since the above was written I learn from Mrs. Coleridge-Taylor that the work has now been recovered after eight years, and it is hoped that it may be published.

at Bournemouth. April 6 found him sharing a recital at Wolverhampton with Mr. W. J. Read and Frank Mullings. The list seems interminable, and is probably such as falls to the lot of any successful composer. One recognises in this travelling from one end of the country to the other the possibilities of fatigue from which it would have been well if he could have been shielded. He rarely showed any symptoms of fatigue, and I remember meeting him, full of laughing vitality, at East Croydon Station at close upon one o'clock one winter morning. He had missed his last train from Brighton, had resolved to travel by a slow one to Norwood Junction, and faced with a light heart the more than two miles' walk in the small hours from there to Norbury. I accompanied him part of the way, and I do not remember him to have been more cheerful at any time, although he had moved about all day and had conducted a heavy rehearsal in the evening.

He preserved a letter from Mr. Hilyer, the honorary treasurer of the Samuel Coleridge-Taylor Society, which he received on April 26 :

> 2352 6TH STREET, N.W.,
> WASHINGTON, D.C.

DEAR MR. COLERIDGE-TAYLOR,—I am enclosing some newspaper clippings to let you know that we have had another presentation of your *Hiawatha*. It has a wonderful hold upon all of us. The interest in the society on the part of the singers themselves had been distressingly small, the attendance averaging from forty to fifty at rehearsals. We were plodding along with *The Messiah,* and when the time came to make arrangements for our spring concert, it was evident that the society did not know *The Messiah* well enough to attempt it—especially since the white Choral Society here had rendered it every year for twenty-five years. Besides, something was needed to rally the chorus. We decided that *Hiawatha* would do it, went out, blew the bugle call, "Hiawatha! Hiawatha!" and they came. We soon had a splendid chorus of about 125, which did most effective work. Not all seats were sold, but expenses were smaller than usual, Miss Mitchell having contributed her services free; so our deficit will be materially reduced. We are also planning to render *The Atonement* at a Sunday night song service (by subscription), and also in Baltimore, for the benefit of the coloured branch of the Young Men's Christian Association, on the evening of May 21.

In composing *Hiawatha* you have done the coloured people of the U.S. a service which, I am sure, you never dreamed of when composing it. It acts as a source of inspiration for us, not only musically but in other lines of endeavour. When we are going to have a *Hiawatha* concert here, for at least one month we seem, as it were, to be lifted above the clouds of American colour prejudice, and to live there wholly oblivious of its disadvantages, and indeed of most of our other troubles.

I suppose, of course, that you have heard of the many Samuel Coleridge-Taylor societies being organised all over the country. Your compositions are often rendered by prominent white orchestras and musicians. Last week the *African Dances* were rendered at a fine concert by some white artiste—a lady, by the way. Mr. C. C. White is planning a big concert with the daughter of B. T. Washington, Mrs. Pittman, as the star. . . .

Mrs. Hilyer, Franklin, Gale, and Kathleen all send kindest greetings to you and family.—Very sincerely yours,

ANDREW F. HILYER.

In the latter part of the summer he told me that he had met a young baritone who sang his works "better than anyone else." The subject of this enthusiastic comment was Mr. Julien Henry, who had called upon him, and had received a hearing from the composer. Coleridge-Taylor conceived the greatest possible admiration for the singing, which was supplemented by personal attachment to the singer, which followed immediately, and grew through the four remaining years of his life. In the course of his career he had formed many friendships, but this became the most intimate of them all. Several of his succeeding works were composed with Julien Henry's voice in view, such as the solos in the *Bon Bon Suite* and Yoichi Tenko in *A Tale of Old Japan;* and there is no doubt that the singer repaid this interest in the sympathetic study and beautiful interpretation which he gave to these and other of Coleridge-Taylor's works.

Faust was presented at His Majesty's Theatre on September 7, and the new version of the play achieved great success. The whole of the music produced was not from Coleridge-Taylor's pen, the second entr'acte being Berlioz's *Minuet des Folles* and *Ballet de Sylphes,* and although he provided organ music in the cathedral scene, the unaccompanied vocal music he drew from Roman Catholic sources. For the rest, with the exception of the Prelude to the Prologue, and entr'actes between the first and second and the third and fourth acts, the music was entirely incidental; and throughout he exercised such restraint as is shown in his avoidance of any display that would have challenged the supremacy of Gounod in the Garden scene. The Prelude to the Prologue is a long, subdued, but dignified work, which has the Angels' Chorus for its second subject. The first entr'acte has for its theme the drinking song with which the second act opens; and the entr'acte before the fourth act is a wild rhapsody anticipating the Brocken scene. The other points in the music are the sinister male voice chorus heard in the Kitchen scene, the really grotesque *Dance of the Apes,* and the beautiful new setting of *A King there Lived in Thule.* Throughout musical suggestion is employed with much power, as in the various love motives heard at the end of the first act and in the Garden scene, the different shades of character shown in the choruses when the four visions of the queens of beauty rise before Faust, the low theme representing Mephistopheles, and the chromatics representing the witches.

From the *Faust* music Coleridge-Taylor arranged an orchestral suite of three good numbers, *The Dance of the Witches, The Four Visions,* and *Dance and Chant from the Devil's Kitchen Scene.*

Extracts from a letter to Mr. Hilyer written at this time may be given :

" I have been very busy indeed lately, and I am afraid my correspondence has become neglected. My typewriter has been out of order for the last fortnight, and the man hasn't yet been to see to it—hence my pen and ink letter, which I hope you will be able to understand.*

" Perhaps you know that Mr. Tree engaged me yet again to do the music for *Faust,* which has just been produced in London. It is certainly Tree's greatest success, and it will be difficult to get a ticket for weeks.

" It came at a very bad time for me. I am in the middle of my first opera, so I had to leave it for the time, but I am getting it well in hand now, and it probably will be produced here next June. It is, of course, grand opera, and on a Norwegian subject.

" I have been conducting a good deal in different towns. I thought the newspaper enclosed would interest you; we had close on five thousand people present, and quite six hundred were turned away (a purely orchestral programme too).

" I pay my first visit to Guernsey (one of the Channel Islands), soon after Christmas, to conduct a concert. I'm looking forward to it very much.

" And how is Washington and all the people there? It seems so long since I was there. Mr. White and I see quite a deal of each other; he is studying with Zacharewitsch, a very fine player and one of my best friends.

" It would be so nice if you could both come over for a few days—after all, England is a much greater country than America can ever be !

" How is the Choral Society coming on? I do hope it is flourishing still, and that the members are all enthusiastic.

" I think you know we're in a new house now—exactly a year since we came in. We like it much better than our old one.

" It seems that quite a lot of Washingtonians and others

---

* It should be said that his American friends had presented him with a typewriter some time before.

have been over to England this season. I suppose the Exhibition has had a great deal to do with it. Some I've seen and some I haven't. I've something else to do than going to and giving entertainments, and the natural excitement is repressing to one's imagination—though I simply love the excitement of the stage rehearsals at the theatre. There, you see, everyone is doing his or her best for one great end, and it inspires one immensely.

"Just fancy, the principal woman part (Margaret) is taken by a Miss Marie Lohr, only seventeen and a half years old, in London's greatest and most artistic theatre!

"I should like to go on writing for hours now I have begun, but other things are waiting."

It was after this that he journeyed to Nottingham to lay his opera before the director of the Carl Rosa Opera Company. The director and he worked over the score together, and the former recognised with real enthusiasm the fine character of the music. When, however, the libretto was studied from the standpoint of the stage there was a graver note in his voice; and in the end he pronounced it to be utterly unsuitable for representation. Coleridge-Taylor returned bitterly disappointed; the blow was a heavy one. The greater part of two years had been wasted. Other competent opinions were sought, and they coincided with that of Mr. Van Noorden. There was not only the artistic disappointment; there was the more pressing material one, and Coleridge-Taylor was for a little time, as he told me afterwards, in low financial waters. Many men would have been embittered considerably by such a result, perhaps crushed, but his resilience was proverbial. He had failed through want of expert guidance in a singularly difficult form of art in the initial stages of the work; he now put the opera aside and turned industriously to other tasks. Since his death attempts have again been made to place the·opera; it has been suggested on good authority that the work deserves a new libretto, and it has been further suggested that it should be transformed into a cantata, but until now these suggestions have not borne fruit. Its only appeal to the public was the performance of the *Prelude to Thelma* by the New London Symphony Orchestra in March, 1910.

The *Bon Bon Suite,* which was the principal published work of 1909, was the outcome of his necessity. When he learned that his opera could not be produced, he turned to the writing of a work which was likely to have a popular appeal, and chose for his purpose a series of six brief lyrics from Thomas Moore. They were *The Magic Mirror, The Fairy Boat, To Rosa, Love and Hymen, The Watchman,* and *Say, What Shall We Dance?* Their chief merit lies in their variety; and a study of the lyrics, apart from their setting, shows how little the composer owed to their intrinsic inspiration; nowhere do they rise beyond the level of the drawing-room ballad. Yet out of this unpromising material he produced a work for baritone solo, chorus, and orchestra, in which melodic variety, poetic expression, and vivid orchestration are combined with an etheral lightness of touch, and a spontaneity which he rarely surpassed. It was concerning this work that he and I had one of his infrequent talks over the business side of his music. His publishers seemed to have doubts about its prospective popularity, which were perhaps founded on the unmerited neglect into which *Meg Blane, Kubla Khan,* and others of his really fine choral works had fallen. He was a little indignant in a half-humorous way. "They knew I was hard up," he said, "and they offered me ten guineas for the copyright. I told them, however, that I wanted fifty pounds on account of royalties." I give these, his actual words, not to add to the criticism which has been bestowed upon his publishers, but to show Coleridge-Taylor's own personal difficulties.

The name of the work was unusual. Suite is a term confined, generally speaking, to instrumental music; but, although the chorus predominates here, the suite-form is preserved, and the dance, as is usual in the suite, is the most prominent measure.   The name, indeed, militated against its popularity in the early days of the work, from the misconception as to its character to which it gave rise; and to counteract this Coleridge-Taylor issued a small prospectus saying, "It has been deemed advisable to point out that this suite is *not* orchestral, but choral. . . and is in every way like a cantata, excepting that it is divided into six short numbers."

The first performance was given at one of the Brighton Musical Festival Concerts at the Dome, on January 15, under his own baton.   Julien Henry sang the solos, as few men besides himself sing Coleridge-Taylor's work, and the choir sang with the verve which he seemed able always to instil into the south coast singers, and the many colours of the work were brought out in a manner that roused the audience to equal enthusiasm.   The second performance was also conducted by himself, and was given by the Central Croydon Choral Society the next evening.   I remember the difficulty one had in getting entrance to the Public Hall, so great was the demand for admission, and large numbers of people were turned away in disappointment.   This performance, too, was all that could be desired.

It is whimsical to note that the most striking feature of this second performance was an unrehearsed effect having little dependence upon musical considerations.   In the watchman number the guardian of nocturnal peace breaks in between the stanzas with his cry of the hour.   The character was taken by a member of the chorus, and when his entry was due the audience was aware of a pause which was not in the score, and at which the conductor smiled. Then a wavering voice, redolent of sack, and seeming an intensely realistic conception of the character of this Dogberry, gave forth

"Past twelve o'clock, past twelve."

The audience was delighted with the singer's perception of the vocal possibilities of a watchman who might have visited several taverns in the course of his duty. The artistry, however, was unsought by the artist. As the passage is unaccompanied, and follows a difficult interval, the singer felt so uncertain of getting his note that it was arranged that the 'cellist sitting immediately below him should give it softly. In leaning forward to catch the sound, the unfortunate vocalist dropped his artificial teeth. The pause was occasioned by their re-adjustment, and the dislocation and his nervousness had produced the admired realism.

The *Bon Bon Suite* is dedicated "To Little Sunshine," and the dedication recalls his love of children and its reciprocal influence. He was at Worthing for a brief holiday during the preceding summer. Staying at the same boarding-house was a pretty, bright-eyed, brown-ringleted little girl of nine, who conceived a great liking for Coleridge-Taylor at sight, and found a simple means of introducing herself to his notice. One morning she crept near to watch him where he sat in a beach-shelter, and overheard him say after searching his pockets vainly for his matches in order to light his cigarette, "Bother it! I haven't a match!" "I'll get one for the gentleman," exclaimed the eager little maiden, and she ran down to a boatman, begged the necessary means of ignition, and returned with it to the composer. They became great chums immediately, spending much time together; and "Little Sunshine," as he called her, was restless and unsatisfied when his work detained him in his rooms; she would invent simple excuses for returning to find him. On one such occasion she had to return "to fetch a rug," and entered the room where Coleridge-Taylor was writing, stole upon him from behind, and clapped her hands over his eyes with "Guess who it is?" It is characteristic that the game was as joyous to him as to Little Sunshine; and it was appropriate when the *Bon Bon Suite* was finished— which was planned first as a work for children, but developed into something else—that he should dedicate it to her.

P

The year 1909 was almost as uneventful from the point of view of the biographer as 1908. A copy of his engagement book would show that his activities were almost without number, but I have already dwelt several times upon this side of his life, and further reference to it would weary the reader.

One example of the peculiar "luck" connected with "Hill Crest" occurred in this summer. During a holiday which he was spending with his family at Leigh-on-Sea, he had occasion to make a flying visit to London; and, calling at "Hill Crest," he found that burglars had entered the house in his absence, had stolen some articles of jewellery that Mrs. Coleridge-Taylor had left behind, and had wantonly smashed several batons which he had received from the various musical societies he had conducted. The event annoyed and depressed him greatly. The batons, indeed, were riveted and restored to usefulness, but the house never had been a home to him, and this new circumstance determined him to leave it as soon as his lease permitted.

In October Mr. Carl Stoeckel was in England, and met Coleridge-Taylor. His description of the meeting is interesting :

"When we decided to give a gala performance of his *Hiawatha* music in June, 1910, I called on Mr. Coleridge-Taylor when in London in October, 1909, but did not find him at home. I left my address, and the next afternoon he came to call on me at Claridge's Hotel. When his name was announced, I opened the parlour door and saw him walking rapidly towards it. His pleasant smile of welcome and his distinguished bearing as he advanced over the red-carpeted hall made a picture which will not soon fade from my memory. He had tea with us, and then I made a business proposition to him that he should come to America in the following June and direct the final rehearsals and concert performance at Norfolk. He accepted at once, and while I was conversing with him, the thought came to me that it would be an interesting time to ask him to compose an orchestral selection, as it would be profitable to compare such a composition with his earlier style. He agreed to this also at once, and said that he would not think of taking anything more than the original honorarium offered him in the beginning of the interview, and would include the new composition in the total amount, which was certainly most generous of him; in fact, in our business transactions he was always ready to do more than his half.

"On our return to London, during the same year, Mr. Coleridge-Taylor and his wife came to call at Claridge's Hotel, and invited us to have tea with them at their house the next afternoon. We motored out there, and found them pleasantly situated, the house giving evidences of refined taste. The children, Hiawatha and Gwendolen, were brought in, and with their parents made as pleasant and unaffected a family group as one might well wish to see. My wife had brought with her from America a little Indian suit with moccasins and tomahawk for Hiawatha, and a little jewelled pin for Gwendolen. Both the children were tremendously excited at seeing a real Indian suit; Hiawatha at once retired to don it, assisted by Gwendolen. A little while afterwards there was a knock at the door, and Hiawatha literally shot into the room, appearing as an Indian with a tomahawk in his hand and an Indian whoop in his voice. Gwendolen was behind him, as much excited and pleased as Hiawatha. We stayed about an hour, had some delicious tea, bread and butter and cakes, all prepared and gracefully served by Mrs. Coleridge-Taylor, and as we left both my wife and I could say in all sincerity that our visit was as pleasant as any we had ever made in our lives."

Amongst the few things I am able to recall of this year is a story he told me when in a reminiscent mood. After a great choral concert, a number of guests, including the principal soloists, were taking supper at the house of the conductor, who was one of the best-known of living chorus-masters. The conductor was standing at the head of the table, engaged in the carving of a cold fowl, when a spirited discussion arose on the relative virtues of choirs. Someone disputed the merits of his favourite choir, and he became demonstrative, and oblivious of the fact that his left hand grasped the handle of a fork that was deeply embedded in the fowl he was carving. "I tell you," he exclaimed, "that the Sheffield choir is the best in England!" and he lifted his hand, excitedly waving the fowl on the fork to give force to his assertion. The latter instrument lost its hold, and the fowl described a parabola across the table and landed in the lap of the principal soprano. The lady, Coleridge-Taylor added, was possessed of enough humour to appreciate the situation, even at the expense of her concert dress.

In September he undertook to conduct the rehearsals and concert of the Central Croydon Choral Society. This involved every Monday evening from October until the middle of January, and one is tempted to wonder again how he found time to accomplish this new task; but it is certain that the society never had a better season, or a more successful conclusion to it, than this. Some part of its attraction to Coleridge-Taylor was undoubtedly due to the fact that amongst the works chosen was Dvořák's *Stabat Mater*.

My work has been done ill if the reader has not gathered that Coleridge-Taylor was of a perennially happy and cheerful disposition. Nothing, and not even the great blows of his life, such as the unmerited neglect of his great choral works, or the shock of learning that his opera was unplayable, could depress him for long. Such sorrows as he suffered he sedulously and successfully hid even from his intimate friends. If, however, a period of his life could be regarded as happier than any since that which saw his initial success and his marriage, it was that which began in 1910; and it is from this circumstance perhaps that he called "Hill Crest" his lucky house. For in these years he recovered rapidly and in a high degree his hold on the public; they were filled with inspiration, ideas and plans, which grew more and more until the last month that ends my story. The year opened busily, as we see from a letter written to Mr. A. T. Johnson, which refers to the unsatisfactory relative arrangement of orchestra and chorus made necessary at the forthcoming Central Croydon Choral Society's concert by the form and capacity of the platform, and acknowledges a suggestion from his correspondent that the stage might be arranged as that at the Streatham Hall had been for a recent concert.

> HILL CREST,
> NORBURY, S.W.,
> *January* 5.

DEAR MR. JOHNSON,—Thank you for your last letter with sketch of the platform at the Streatham Hall.

We shall do all we can to arrange our people on the 15th, but, you see, the arrangement of the Central Croydon Choral Society is in one block, so it may be impossible to alter positions.

The enclosed may interest you—especially where I " dust my own music " ("direct" was meant).

The band played magnificently, and they had the biggest audience of the season.

I am doing my " Ballade " at the Jaeger Memorial Concert, London Symphony Orchestra, Queen's Hall, January 24. " Endymion's Dream " is at Brighton on February 3. I adjudicate and conduct at Warrington on February 4 and 5. Coliseum, Sunday, January 30. Birmingham Symphony Concert I am conducting throughout on February 26. So, you see, I couldn't have done the String Players very well with my Handel rehearsals twice a week as well.

Landon Ronald will do my overture to " Thelma " (the opera) at Queen's Hall early in March (New London Symphony).

With all good wishes for 1910.—Believe me, yours very sincerely,   S. COLERIDGE-TAYLOR.

It is scarcely necessary to explain that the "dusting" of his music was a printer's error, made in a cordial notice in a Bournemouth paper of his conducting of the *Variations of an African Theme* and the *Faust Ballet Music* at the Winter Gardens on December 30.

After the Central Croydon Choral Society's concert he writes again to Mr. Johnson:

> HILL CREST,
> NORBURY, S.W.,
> *January* 17.

DEAR MR. JOHNSON,—I hope you approved of my orchestral arrangement on Saturday. I certainly think the change of position of the brass made all the difference (and the change of players, too, of course).

I wonder what you think of the Dvořák—personally, it impresses me more than any other religious work I know, and I think the last number stands by itself as a really noble inspiration—but I'm always a champion for Dvořák!

There was only one weak man in the orchestra, and he has some connection with the society, and I couldn't get him out, though I tried hard!

It was impossible for me to arrange the platform as you suggested, but I think if Mr. Richards will in future put his brass in a less prominent position as I did, there will be less to complain of!—Kindest regards, yours very sincerely,

> S. COLERIDGE-TAYLOR.

During January Mr. J. H. Smither Jackson brought to his notice the works of 'Alfred Noyes, and Coleridge-Taylor was arrested at once by the poems of one who, perhaps more than any living poet, has that quality of singableness in his works which is essential to successful musical treatment. Mr. Smither Jackson, who had for some time past constituted himself a champion of the composer, challenging his various critics, controverting their views, and occasionally extending their knowledge materially, was also one of those helpers appreciated by Coleridge-Taylor who endeavoured to find him verse suitable for musical setting. He informed Mr. Noyes of the interest his works had aroused, and the poet responded readily : "I should certainly be most pleased to hear of the composer you mention, for I have been contemplating something of the sort for some time," adding : "My cordial thanks once more for what you say about my books, and for the information, which naturally gives me great pleasure, and will, I hope, lead to something being accomplished as you . suggest." The something which came of this beginning was the exquisite setting of *A Tale of Old Japan* and other works which I shall have occasion to mention.

A signal event in the early part of 1910 was the first performance of his new work, *Endymion's Dream*, at the Brighton Musical Festival on February 5. It is, of course, a version of the Hellenic myth of the priest whose prayer for immortality was granted, but with the addition of eternal sleep, and who is loved by the moon, Selene. The situation of the work is the drawing near of Selene to the cave on Mount Latmos to awaken Endymion, his awakening, their mutual surrender, and the cataclysm that results from Selene's deviation from her appointed course :

> *See, see the universe totters to its fall,*
> *Lo, chaos reigns—chaos dire, exulting over all.*

From this expression of universal chaos the quality of the libretto may be gauged, and one cannot but feel that Coleridge-Taylor was for the last time devoting his great powers to work unworthy of them ; the words are entirely undistinguished. A typical stanza is that in the solo, "Who art thou ! " and this is neither higher nor lower than the general level :

> *Last evening, when the setting sun*
> *With mingled gold and crimson dyed the West,*
> *With one I lingered, whom I then*
> *Deemed fairest of the fair—of men*
> *I thought, nay, would have sworn myself most blest.*

Ah well, that could not have been love,
Or, if it were love, that love now is dead,
Slain by the message from thine eyes,
And from its ashes doth arise
Love! love for thee, that in my heart thou'st bred.

Mr. Fagge tells me that in company with the *Bon Bon Suite* the work was refused performance by the London Choral Society because of the marked inferiority of the words to the music.

The work is a mild imitation of a Greek tragedy with the orthodox single scene, a commenting and narrative chorus, and the two protagonists, Selene and Endymion, who are represented by soprano and tenor respectively. Into the libretto Coleridge-Taylor read much of the beauty of the original myth, and *Endymion's Dream* must rank with his finer works. The tenor recitative and solo, "Who calls!" of which two versions have been published differing considerably from one another, he thought an even finer work than "Onaway, Awake," and, without admitting this estimate, it is a superb tenor song. From its quiet, suggestive prelude of twenty-two bars to its close *Endymion's Dream* is full of melody, light, colour, and dramatic beauty.

In connection with the work Coleridge-Taylor had a conversation with Mr. Johnson, in which he explained his intention. The scene was conceived for dramatic representation, and could be performed without difficulty. Only the two characters would appear, and the chorus would be concealed, and he thought that the final catastrophe would not present any special problem to the ordinary stage-manager. He was under the impression that if the work succeeded at Brighton, Sir Herbert Tree would produce it at His Majesty's Theatre. He himself was astonished and delighted at the unanimity of the approval with which it was received at Brighton and by the critics. One critic, hitherto rarely favourable, was very cordial, and gave as his reason the qualities of restraint and proportion which were shown. "Perhaps," remarked Coleridge-Taylor, "he didn't know that it has been written twice over, which accounts for that." The second writing was the result of a change of plan. Originally he wrote the choruses for female voices, but, deeming it advisable to give them to the four voices, he seized the opportunity to rewrite the whole.

A lady ventured to ask him for tickets for the performance. He replied, kindly enough :

" Regarding Brighton; I'm afraid they are adopting the Coliseum rule, ' If artists cannot attract their own friends, how can they attract the general public? ' Have you seen it posted up anywhere? So bad is it that I had to pay for *eight* friends about a month ago at the Coliseum, as they flatly refused to give me a single one. But Sainton may be able to do it for me, and directly I see him I'll ask him, as I should like you to hear my latest muddle ! "

The String Players' Club concert in February was not remarkable, except in that it drew a remark from the conductor to Mr. Johnson : "I hope you were pleased with the concert. Don't you think it is a great compliment to us that so many *men* turn out to hear these affairs—and sit them out too ? " Another remark showed his pleasure in the good opinion of Zacharewitsch : "M. Zacharewitsch came all the way from North London to hear us, and stayed to the very end. He says the playing was magnificent, and as for amateurs—well, he said that if many first-class professional orchestras in England could play so well it would be nice. He was particularly pleased with the rhythm and attack, of which he himself is such a master."

On February 26 he was at Birmingham Town Hall, conducting what was virtually a Coleridge-Taylor festival, when the Birmingham Symphony Orchestra produced his *Overture to Hiawatha, Incidental Music to Faust,* and the *Nero Suite.* He had often appeared in Birmingham, but this was the first time he had conducted an avowedly popular concert there. His success may be gauged from a sentence or two from the account given by Mr. Robert J. Buckley in the *Birmingham Gazette*:

" After the *Nero Suite*, Mr. Coleridge-Taylor was recalled, and, though it must be admitted that the musical prigs are against him, he may take comfort from the assurance that the people are on his side, as they always were, and are, with Grieg, another composer reviled by the ' superior.' "

He continues :

" The Birmingham Symphony Orchestra fully merited the high opinion of their talent expressed to us by Mr. Coleridge-Taylor, who is familiar with all the best orchestras, and whose emphasis as to the capability of the forces he had just conducted was unmistakable. All the improvement he could suggest related to numbers, not to quality. Naturally he would like a larger orchestra. So would anybody. Such, from the beginning of bands, has been the aspiration of every composer and conductor. Berlioz suggested an orchestra of two thousand, with twelve large organs, and two hundred drums, and that, one fears, would not have contented him for long."

In March he contemplates a recital of his own compositions, and calls upon his old college friend for assistance.

HILL CREST,
NORBURY, S.W.,
March 9.

MY DEAR READ,—I am thinking of giving a Benefit Concert at the Public Hall, Croydon, on Wednesday, April 6, *if* I can get the artists together. I should like you to play my fiddle things very much ; but the worst of it is I can only afford an expenses fee, and I don't know if you can manage to come for that.

If you *can*, will you please let me know. I would with pleasure come to Eastbourne for an hour or two to rehearse if you could only manage the evening of the day here.

I go to America early in May, but shall be back again about June 12.

Please let me know about this matter as soon as ever you can.

With kindest regards to you, Mr. and Mrs. Cooper.—
Believe me, yours always,
                                                    S. COLERIDGE-TAYLOR.

P.S.—Don't hesitate to refuse if you feel you cannot come. I shall *quite* understand.

As the next letter shows, Mr. Read consented.

March 13.

MY DEAR READ,—It is awfully nice of you to promise to play for me on April 6, and I appreciate it immensely. I should like you to do the *Ballade*, if possible (you need not memorise this, as it is mostly a duet), *Gipsy Pieces,* or *African Dances,* and a set of four very short and not difficult dance movements, which I will send you in a few days, and which you need not necessarily memorise.

I think I can arrange Thursday, 24th, and should like to hear you do my *Quintet* very much. I might be able to stay Good Friday until about 3 P.M.—or would you rather I come on Wednesday and go back Thursday? (I can only manage two days from home, as I am dreadfully busy with a new orchestral work for the Connecticut Musical Festival. . . .)

Please let me know about days—*when* do you do 5tet, afternoon or evening?—Kindest regards to you all,

                                        S. COLERIDGE-TAYLOR.

The next two letters refer to the concert.

                            HILL CREST,
                                NORBURY, S.W.,
                                        April 1.

MY DEAR READ,—I've written a new middle part for the slow number of the three MS. movements which I am sending on.

You will see exactly where it fits. The other one seemed a little slow and not enough contrasted.

Also, in the third number—43 bars from beginning—I wish you would please add two bars thus :

instead of :

This comes over twice—just before 39th bar from the end.

We are looking forward so much to having you here. Please let me know what time you intend coming.—Kindest regards to all, yours always sincerely,

S. Coleridge-Taylor.

Hill Crest,
Norbury, S.W.,
April 8.

My dear Read,—This is only a line to thank you once again for so kindly coming and playing so beautifully.

A certain Mrs. Watson—a fine musician—simply raved over your playing of the *Ballade* when I happened to meet her yesterday.

I don't suppose I shall come to Eastbourne till July, so I'll score it while I'm in America and have it ready in ample time.

As you are so nasty about it, I shall not press the cheque upon you, but I shall take care you get it back. . . .

Try and call here on your way to Walsall, if only for an hour or two, but let me know, please.

Kindest regards and renewed thanks.—Yours always,

S. Coleridge-Taylor.

The concert took place at the Public Hall, Croydon, and Coleridge-Taylor, who presided at the piano as accompanist, was supported by Miss Effie Martyn, Julien Henry, and Miss Myrtle Meggy, the Australian pianist, in addition to Mr. Read. It consisted mainly of his smaller recent compositions, which show how active his brain and pen must have been during the past year. The new songs were *A Lament, A Birthday, A Lovely Little Dream, Sons of the Sea, The Fairy Ballads,* and *Five-and-Twenty Sailormen;* and the instrumental pieces included the piano soli *Valse Orientale,* and *Zuleika,* and *Three Dances* for the violin, and a variety of other works in small compass rarely met with in music. The concert proved amply that his work in miniature was at least worthy of his powers. In this connection a word should be said concerning his pianoforte works, which have not yet come into their own. The works just named, and his *Scènes de Ballet,* his *Three Fours,* and his *Forest Scenes* are a few typical compositions. They make none of the enormous demands upon the technical skill of the performer that are made by the works of such masters of the instrument as Liszt, Chopin, and their compeers; they nearly always suggest, too, that the composer is "thinking orchestra" rather than pianoforte; but they grow upon one in an unusual manner, and it is not too much to say that they are as individual as are the works of Grieg.

He paid his third visit to America in May and June in order to conduct the first two parts of *Hiawatha* and the *Bamboula,* an orchestral rhapsody written for the occasion, at the Litchfield County Choral Union Festival at Norfolk, Connecticut, where, as we saw in the last chapter, he had already conducted in 1906. The Litchfield Choral Union, it should be said, consists of a number of choral societies in the villages about Norfolk, which owe their existence mainly to the initiative and financial encouragement of Mr. Carl Stoeckel, an American gentleman whose wealth is largely devoted to his love of music. To celebrate the twentieth year of the existence of the Union, the works for performance were chosen by a ballot of the members, Mr. Stoeckel promising to invite the composer of the work chosen to conduct it. The two works receiving most votes were Verdi's *Requiem* and Coleridge-Taylor's *Hiawatha*. "Well," said the President, "circumstances effectually prevent the appearance of Verdi, but we can get Coleridge-Taylor." This was the genesis of the visit; and the festival was arranged on royal lines. Kreisler was to appear as violinist, and some of the best soloists and orchestral players in America were engaged. Moreover, to his delight he was to have a whole week of rehearsals, including two of the choir, one of the orchestra, and two full ones with orchestra, choir and principals.

He looked forward to the voyage with glee, laughing gaily at the prospect open to him as a good sailor of discussing the excellent menus of the Leyland liner *Cestrian*, on which he was to travel, on the Sunday morning alone while the rest of the passengers remained in the sad seclusion of their berths. Before his departure he conducted a performance of the *Te Deum* of his favourite master, Dvořák, at the Handel Society; and undertook to provide a musical accompaniment for Keats's *Eve of St. Agnes* to be produced at the Keats-Shelley Festival which was to be held in London on June 10. He sailed from Liverpool on May 7, reached Boston after a pleasant voyage, and went to Detroit, where he conducted a successful concert before proceeding to Norfolk.

Mr. Carl Stoeckel, to whom I owe so much already, provides me with a chronicle of his doings at Norfolk.

"He reached this country in June, by way of Boston, came to New York, and I met him at the first rehearsal at Carnegie Hall, just at the close of the first rehearsal of the *Bamboula* Rhapsodic Dance, the new composition which he had made and brought with him, and of which he had corrected the parts on board ship. He leaned over from the conductor's stand as I came up the aisle and shook hands, mopped his brow, and remarked: 'This is a wonderful orchestra. I never directed anything like it. They can read anything beautifully at first sight.' And after the rehearsal the men in the orchestra were quite as

complimentary to him. They called him the African
'Mahler,' as it is generally conceded by orchestral
musicians that the greatest conductor who ever visited
this country was the late Gustav Mahler of Vienna, who
was for some time conductor of the Philharmonic Society
of New York. Before engaging the orchestra, I took the
precaution to sound the Musical Union as to whether there
would be any objection to playing under an Anglo-African
conductor. I was told that there would be no objection,
that he would come under the rule of ' visiting conductor.'
He had three rehearsals in New York, and then came with
me to Norfolk. We had lunch on the train, taken from
a hamper which we had taken precaution to take with us.
We had plenty of wine in the basket, but Mr. Coleridge-
Taylor would not take any of this, and, in fact, did not
take a drop of wine or liquor of any sort during the week
that I was with him. He drank ginger-ale, and smoked
a moderate number of cigarettes. Some months before his
visit we had informed the members of our society that he
was coming, and that he was an Anglo-African, and if
anybody had any objection to singing under him would
they please state it at once. Of nearly eight hundred
members only one withdrew. One of the soloists, being
of Southern birth, also withdrew, but there were many
volunteers more than willing to take his place and to have
the prestige of performing the part under so great a composer as Mr. Coleridge-Taylor. I suppose that it is difficult for you in England and Europe generally to
understand the unfortunate and unreasonable prejudice
which still exists against Africans in the United States;
but the fact is here, we must face it and do our best to
overcome it, and I know of no incident, in my life at
least, that has done so much to dissipate this feeling as
the visit of Mr. Coleridge-Taylor to this country in 1910.

"We had at Norfolk two rehearsals of the *Hiawatha*
music. Four hundred and fifty singers were on the stage
and four hundred and twenty-five in the audience. Mr.

Paine, our conductor, made a speech of introduction, and then Coleridge-Taylor advanced to the conductor's platform.   All of the chorus on and off the stage rose, with vigorous clapping and shaking of handkerchiefs, and welcomed him.   He was greatly pleased with his reception, but quickly settled down to business, and started off the rehearsal.   He only made one slight change of tempo, and had very few suggestions to make at either of the rehearsals.   As he said, ' It was a letter-proof chorus.'   He had three rehearsals with the New York orchestra, of seventy-five pieces, and also the soloists.   He had tried the soloists at our house in the afternoon, and was greatly pleased with the way in which Madame Alma Gluck sang her part.   When he came from the library, where he had been rehearsing with her, he remarked to me in a low tone, ' That girl is the best Minnehaha I have ever heard sing the part.'

"At the first concert we gave Verdi's *Requiem Mass.* Mr. Coleridge-Taylor was present, and was so good as to say to Mr. Paine that his rendition of the work had given him many new spiritual ideas that he had not observed before in the work.   He was the only Anglo-African in the audience, and naturally attracted a great deal of attention, bearing himself with great dignity, modesty, and affability.   The next night we gave the Indian music, and as the composer entered he was given the rising salute by two thousand people, who made great applause, which he acknowledged gracefully, and then we had a truly magnificent performance of his work.   Everybody was in an enthusiastic and receptive state of mind, nobody more so than the composer himself, and when he came off the stage he said, ' I do not believe that my work has ever been better done, and I know that I have never directed it so well before, because I felt that everybody, the chorus, orchestra, and audience, were with me.   This is one of the happiest days of my life.'   There was a great demonstration again after the close of his work.

"My wife had invited a number of people to be our guests during the concert season and to meet Coleridge-Taylor, who also was our guest during his stay in Norfolk. We had a delightful supper party after the concert, at which the house party and other guests, to the number of twenty-five, sat down at the supper in honour of the composer. Some of the most prominent musicians of America, accompanied by their wives, were present at this supper, and several highly complimentary speeches were made to Coleridge-Taylor, eulogising him as a man and a musician. Knowing of his disinclination to make a speech, I did not ask him to say anything, but as we were about to leave the table he arose somewhat timidly and said, ' I never make speeches, but I do not feel as if I could leave this table without expressing the gratitude I feel for all which has been done for me by my hosts, the Litchfield County Choral Union and its conductor, Mr. Paine, and the others who have been so good as to be interested in my work. I never in my life have known anything like it. It has been simply royal, and I thank you.' We then adjourned to the library, where we had a jolly time and some impromptu music. The various composers, George W. Chadwick, Horatio Parker, and Coleridge-Taylor, playing a lot of lively stuff, and Madame Gluck singing a number of African songs, in which our visitor was greatly interested.

"The next day we took an automobile ride, and got off of some of the main roads and drove through some of the fields of laurel (Kalmia), then in full blossom. Coleridge-Taylor was greatly delighted with the wild, picturesque scenery of north-western Connecticut. When he came home that evening he retired at once to his room. When I went to call him for supper, I knocked on his door. He answered, ' Come in.' As I entered I saw him shoving some little sheets of musical notes into the desk. He said nothing about it at the time, but some months afterwards wrote me that these were his first sketches of *A Tale of Old*

Q

Japan, and that he had been inspired to make them by the floral display that he had seen that afternoon."

His intercourse with Mr. Stoeckel was of the most pleasant character, and the latter has preserved several notes of his conversation and letters.

"In reference to the first performance of *Hiawatha,* under the conductorship of Sir Charles Villiers Stanford, Coleridge-Taylor told me that he listened to it from the outside, occasionally peeping into the room, but he felt too timid and fearful about its success to go into the hall. He also remarked several times : ' If I had retained my rights in the *Hiawatha* music I should have been a rich man. I only received a small sum for it.'

"While at our house he had breakfast in his room every morning, then came downstairs, and played on tne piano for an hour, and then walked by himself or with me for an hour or two, strolling about or making calls. He was very particular about his personal appearance, being carefully groomed, and invariably putting on his gloves as soon as we issued from the house. He carried a small cane, and was apt to be smoking a cigarette. He became very fond of the tea which we have at our house, and also of the pens which my wife had placed on his desk, which he said were better than any he had used in England. At table he was rather a small eater, and quite careful of his choice of dishes. He always showed a lively interest in everything and everybody about him while at Norfolk. He did not ask many questions, as his pleasing personality and modest demeanour almost always resulted in drawing out those who conversed with him.

"In a conversation concerning contemporary music, Coleridge-Taylor spoke highly of Dvořák and Grieg. He did not seem to care much for most of the modern Russian music, saying that he had spent several pounds on scores, and wished he had the money back again. He did not include Tschaikowsky in this category, and spoke especially of Rimsky-Korsakoff, whose works he considered largely made up of brilliant and clever orchestration. He was much interested in some new works by American composers, notably those of Chadwick and Parker, which had been written for our festivals, and which were just fresh from the printers when he was here. He spoke of giving *King Gorm the Grim,* by Parker, and Chadwick's cantata, *Noel,* with some of his societies in England. I mention this as it shows his liberal and progressive disposition.

"One of his personal attributes was his graceful attitude when on the conductor's stand. This has been commented on by great numbers of people who saw him conduct here. To see him on the conductor's stand, where he presented all the appearances of a well-restrained war-horse panting for the fray, was a contrast from the appearance he made when he stood up to be introduced at his first recital, and seemed almost to shrink within himself—his diffidence made a marked impression on the audience, who considered it pathetic; but as soon as he was where anything had to do with music he was all himself.

"He brought with him to this country what he termed a conductor's jacket, and was particular about changing from street attire into this jacket, although many of the orchestra and most of our conductors, at that season of the year at least, worked at rehearsals without coats. I told him that it would be entirely good form if he chose to work without his coat at rehearsals, but he always went at once to his dressing-room and donned his conductor's coat."

It should be added that Mr. Stoeckel treated Coleridge-Taylor not only with great hospitality, but with the greatest generosity as well. The conductor received substantial fees for conducting, as also for the works he wrote specially for the Litchfield Choral Union. Moreover, the scores of such works were returned to him scrupulously after their first performance, to be published or disposed of as he would. "He insisted on my keeping, however," says Mr. Stoeckel, "as my own property and not for publication, the rendition of *Keep Me From Sinking Down,** as he said it was our music, and he did not feel like exercising any publishing right in it."

On his return to England he took a brief holiday at Eastbourne, if that could be called a holiday in which he worked incessantly, and from here he writes to Mr. Johnson on June 21 :

> "AVONDALE,"
> ROYAL PARADE,
> EASTBOURNE,
> *June* 21.

MY DEAR MR. JOHNSON,—Thanks for your letter. I expect we shall be back home on Saturday, and, of course, pleased to see you.

My American affair has been the greatest delight of my life—the orchestra was simply superb—18 first fiddles, 16 seconds, 12 violas, 12 'cellos, and 8 basses—the pick of America.

As one of the artists said to me : "It is a more unique festival than Bayreuth itself," and I've much to tell you of the wonderful arrangements when I see you.

I enclose a cutting which Mr. Carl Stoeckel has just sent. —With kindest regards, yours very sincerely,

> S. COLERIDGE-TAYLOR.

He seems at this time again to have been contemplating a visit to Germany; but again the intention was frustrated, for he complains in a letter that "Tree prevented my going to Der Vaterland this time," and on July 3 he writes Mr. W. J. Read, "I am so sorry to tell you that although I've got the *Ballade* half done, I can't possibly complete it in time to get the parts copied out, as I am already thick with the theatre." The explanation was that he had been commissioned by Sir Herbert Tree to provide the musical setting for *The Forest of Wild Thyme*, the charming poetical fairy drama by Alfred Noyes, and had to attend the readings of the play and await the various instructions

* *See* Chapter XIII., page 272.

that arose from rehearsals. The music was completed as far as it was possible to do it, but ultimately the play was abandoned, owing, I understand, to its too great similarity in theme to Maeterlinck's *Blue Bird*. This was not the only work of the poet on which he was engaged. All this summer he made progress with his setting of *A Tale of Old Japan,* working at it with delight in the words and great conscientiousness. He would, for instance, come down to his wife from his room to verify the pronunciation of certain words; the word "peonies" in the chorus commencing :

" Peonies, peonies, crowned the May "

was one which made him pause. Besides this, he made a fine scena out of the dramatic lyric, *Red of the Dawn.* So far, however, this has not seen the light.

In this incessant activity the summer, and indeed the year, passed. In August we find him interested in the proposed abandonment by the Duke of Devonshire, who had hitherto sustained it, of the orchestra at Devonshire Park, Eastbourne. An attempt was made to secure sufficient municipal support to continue the orchestra, but with disheartening results. The orchestra appealed to him to add his testimony to its worth. He replied :

Regarding the orchestra, though such a course as you suggest may do no good, on the other hand, it can do no harm, and I am sure everyone who has been down to conduct would write all sorts of nice things. Personally, although I am not an ' eminent musician,' alas ! you know I am always at your service, and that of the other gentlemen of the orchestra. It will certainly look pretty bad if light music-hall turns are allowed to supplant a fine orchestra, and will give the lie to the oft-repeated assertion that the English are really musical, only they don't get the chance to hear good stuff.

On September 8 he wrote to Mr. Read, "Of course your people may call on me for anything at Eastbourne (excepting money !) and I shall be pleased to do my best."

The following letters to Mr. Read deal with a benefit concert at Eastbourne at which he conducted, and an amusing trifle of diplomacy appears in the first:

"ALDWICK,"
ST. LEONARD'S ROAD,
CROYDON,
September 27.

MY DEAR READ,—Is your Benefit Concert coming off all right on October 15?

I want to know for certain because I'm doing the Queen's Hall Sunday concert, October 16, and want to arrange rehearsals.

I proposed doing the postponed *Bamboula* and also the new Dances which will by then be ready.

I wish you would casually invite me to spend a day or two with you at Eastbourne in case some undesirable people come here to see us. Of *course,* I should pay, but it must seem like an invitation. Any time up to October 6 would do. This is, of course, strictly private. . . .—Kindest regards, yours always,   S. COLERIDGE-TAYLOR.

P.S.—I might not be able to come for a few days—it depends on the theatre.

"ALDWICK,"
ST. LEONARD'S ROAD,
CROYDON,
October 9.

MY DEAR READ,—Didn't you ever get my letter in which I said I would be pleased to do the "Nero" stuff and the "Gipsy" pieces?

Of course, I am willing to do anything (Qy.) you wish—and, in any case, it seems as if the Rhapsody is not for Eastbourne; for it hasn't come from America *again,* where it has just been done at Worcester Musical Festival (Mass.) by Boston Symphony Orchestra.

If you mean the *Nero Suite,* I should propose doing only three movements, the Prelude, Eastern Dance, and the Entr'acte you often do.

Your secretary asked me for a photo-block. I can't find mine anywhere—Novellos flatly refuse to lend theirs, so I am wondering if your people can do anything with *The Musical Times* photograph I am sending. If they can't, tear it up.—Kindest regards, yours always,   S. COLERIDGE-TAYLOR.

It will be noticed that these letters have a new address. After much searching and consideration he had chosen as his new home a pleasant little house, in a quiet cul-de-sac, close by Duppas Hill, and bounded by the leafy gardens of larger houses. "I think we've got the quietest house in the town," he wrote to Mr. Hilyer at the end of the year, and certainly quiet is the note of the place. On the west side of it is a green bank, which holds flowers; and on the slopes of this is a wooden, corrugated-iron-roofed outhouse, which Coleridge-Taylor transformed into a music room, furnished with an upright piano, decorated the walls with the photographs of his friends, and in this "music-shed," as he called it, in summer he used to write, where, through the wide-open window, he could look at the roses which crept towards it, and across pleasant greenery. Of the several houses in which he had lived this was undoubtedly the most agreeable,* although in the winter evenings he found it rather too far from the railway stations of Croydon, and more than once I have heard him express the wish to live in London, so as to be near to his work, and, I believe, to his friend Julien Henry, who then had a house in Maida Vale. He was, however, quite happy at "Aldwick," and he showed me the house, with its prettily-situated dining room, its little study where he kept his books, its drawing room where stood his grand piano near the window-doors which opened on to the garden, with obvious pleasure in them. Although the "music-shed" was his official place of study, and was used as such, no small part of his work, and especially his later work, was done in the drawing room. Ideas would come to him at night in the train, or as he walked home from

---

* The house has now been presented to Mrs. Coleridge-Taylor mainly by the coloured people of America, and it is hoped that a memorial tablet may be placed upon the front of it.

the railway station, after his engagements in London. He used the top of the grand piano as a desk, and would write in a standing position, balancing himself on one foot, with the other crossed over it. Only occasionally would he try a brief passage or resolution on the instrument.

A work which belongs to this year deserves special mention. This is the highly dramatic and concentrated *Sea-Drift,* an eight-part rhapsody for unaccompanied voices. Within its limits it challenges comparison with the very finest of his choral work, and maintains a character of expectant tragedy such as few men are given to utter. It is perfectly singable, in spite of the demands it makes upon the efficiency of the voices, and the only criticism that has been levelled at it is the doubtful one that its gloom demands some relief. As a writer of part-songs Coleridge-Taylor has not yet received rightful recognition. His mastery of colour in vocal music, and his rarely mistaken appreciation of the dramatic value of words, are qualities which place him high in that branch of the art in which English music is supreme. It is rarely remembered that Englishmen have written the greatest madrigals, glees and part-songs which the world possesses, but the works of Thomas Morley, Willebye, Boyd, Webbe, and a dozen others can be cited to prove this fact; and amongst latter-day musicians few deserve to occupy a higher place than Coleridge-Taylor in *Sea-Drift,* in the brief, but picturesque *The Lee-Shore,* where the surging of the gale is graphically indicated in the bass, and the tragedy of the words merges into hope in the beautiful final resolution of the music, and the poignant earlier song, *Dead in the Sierras.* His religious and church music, although limited, breaks away from the sentimentality and suburbanism of such work in a real attempt to give expressional value to the words. It is not likely that his morning and evening services will become universally popular, seeing that generations of sentimentality in such music have made music with real meaning seem secular and foreign to church worship; but they are worth a score of the sweet, tuneful examples of rubbish which are so used.

In addition to *A Tale of Old Japan,* which was his principal occupation during the last half of 1910 and the early part of 1911, he was "thick with the theatre" not only in *The Forest of Wild Thyme,* but later with incidental music for Sir Herbert Tree's projected presentation of *Othello.* When I met him in these days he was full of his old enthusiasm for the magnificence of spoken Shakespearean language, and spared himself not at all in his work upon the play. The *Children's Intermezzo,* which is introduced in Act III., was a real trial to him, but luckily he was willing to try unto seventy times seven if necessary to accomplish his purpose. What was wanted was a subdued chorus to be sung behind to convey a definite atmosphere to the scene. He made many attempts; would bring a setting of it into the rehearsal, which Tree would pronounce to be good, but not quite what he wanted; and next day he would re-appear with an entirely new version, to meet with a like verdict. This process was repeated until he almost despaired of producing the effect desired. One day, however, when in the train on his way to Bath to conduct a concert, the unexpected light came, and at the first stop he left the train and telegraphed to Mr. Adolf Schmid, "I've got it!" Next day the delicately beautiful chorus, which was so charming a feature of the play, was received at His Majesty's Theatre.

In November he writes a letter which is a mixture of fun and a real desire to be of service to his correspondent:

"ALDWICK,"
ST. LEONARD'S ROAD,
CROYDON,
November 4.

MY DEAR READ,—I meant to have written long ago to thank you for sending my old coat which I stupidly left at your house!

Regarding the " testimonial," how in the world can I write anything for you? It seems such colossal cheek for me to attempt any such thing, and besides, everyone in Eastbourne knows you so well by now.

If you insist on my doing it, of course I will, but it would be better to get Mr. Cooper to write something nice—he has the happy knack—and I'll sign it !

Most certainly, if you give a Recital, I am at your service with *no* fee, but please don't arrange it on any Tuesday or Thursday—Friday or Saturday are particularly good days.

You must feel it strange not to have to go to rehearsal; and do you miss seeing all the happy (?) faces in the audience?

I'll try to come down for a half-day if I see a 2s. 6d. train running before Christmas.

Please give our united kind regards to Mr. and Mrs. Cooper, and with all good wishes.—Believe me, yours always,

S. COLERIDGE-TAYLOR.

One of the last letters of 1910 indicates that he had entered into another engagement of some importance at the end of the year :

"ALDWICK,"

ST. LEONARD'S ROAD,

CROYDON,

December 26.

MY DEAR MR. HILYER,—I am afraid all your Christmas and New Year's festivities will be over before you have received this, but I thought I must write you a word to wish you and yours everything nice for 1911.

You will note we have changed our address and are now living in Croydon instead of just outside. I think we've got the quietest house in the town.

Possibly the next time I come across I shall get down to Washington. For Mr. and Mrs. Stoeckel, for whom I came to Norfolk last June, have commissioned me to write a work for Madame Maud Powell to play there for the first time—the date rests with me, as I would not be hurried.

You will also be pleased to know that I have just been appointed principal professor of composition and sub-conductor

Photograph by Mr. Ernest Dennis

Coleridge-Taylor's Home at Croydon, with the "shed" in which he wrote most
of his later works

of the orchestra at the Guildhall School of Music, London. Mr. Landon Ronald is the new Principal of the school (which is one of the best in England), and I am his first appointment. He has always been a tremendous friend to me. He, of course, takes the orchestra, being Principal of the whole concern, but he'll be often away, and I feel greatly honoured by being deputy, as he is, perhaps, our finest English conductor.

Sousa and his band will be here for a week, starting next Monday.

Are any of you coming over for the World's Convention next June? I hear Professor Du Bois is to represent the American coloured people. We both hope you are all well. I can always picture your house—up that hill which was always so muddy after it had been raining.

Please give my best wishes to Mrs. Hilyer and all your family, and remember me to anyone you may meet that I know, especially Miss Europe, Mr. White, the Terrells and the Grays and the Wormleys. Kindest thoughts.—Very sincerely,

S. COLERIDGE-TAYLOR.

An after result of the third visit to America was an article upon a subject very near to his heart, which he contributed to the American musical magazine, *The Etude*,* in January, 1911 :

IS TECHNIQUE STRANGLING BEAUTY?
(From an English Point of View)

" ' You English musicians always seem to be *thinking*. Why do you not sometimes feel also? '

" So remarked a Spaniard after having heard a particularly advanced specimen of the modern school of composition, and both statement and question seem to the writer to be very pertinent.

" There appears to be a most desperate craving for technical dexterity in music, and all other sides of the art are being woefully left to take care of themselves. Simplicity, the

* I am indebted to the Editor for permission to give this article a permanent form.

greatest proof of real strength, is for the time being, at all events, in hiding, ashamed and afraid.

" Undoubtedly the most striking thing about the work of the men of the younger school (and I refer throughout to this new and younger school) is the wonderful ability, one may say genius, in orchestration.

" For the young composer to have a complete mastery of the most complicated machine in the world—the modern orchestra—is the rule and not the exception, and the once weakest spot in the equipment of the English composer is now the strongest.

" It is now the fashion in the London musical smart set to decry Tschaikowsky, but this extraordinary improvement in English orchestral writing is distinctly traceable to the influence of that great man—at any rate, it commenced immediately after the advent of the *Symphonie Pathétique,* which work was, until quite recently, far more often heard than any of the composer's other compositions.

" Most English composers of fifteen or twenty years ago were content to use the organ-pedal-like bass in the orchestra, and the majority of the scores were drab and colourless things.

" This cannot be wondered at, perhaps, considering that so many writers held church appointments, for church music has had a tremendous influence on all music in England ; and unlike other countries, there has never been any real operatic hold, until recently, to counteract it.

" But even then, it is strange that nothing much happened to orchestral technique till the time I have mentioned, for there were hundreds of beautiful French scores in existence, not to speak of those of Wagner himself. The explanation may lie in the fact that Wagner's scores were all music-drama and the French mostly operas and suites, so the type may have been considered foreign and operatic, and therefore not exactly suitable material from which the English composer could get hints for this particular kind of work. There may have been some truth in the supposition, but be that as it may, miserably rigid harmonies—even more rigid and mono-tonous bass parts, and orchestration without life or meaning were often the hall-marks of the English school of some years back.

"All this has been blown away as if by magic, and we have come to what? One of the most extraordinary positions imaginable !

" With the wonderful advance in general technique and orchestral writing, there seems to have come a deliberate stamping out of everything melodically beautiful, and too often there is an utter absence of *charm*.

" Not only is much of the music of the younger English school devoid of what is commonly called ' tune,' but in nine cases out of ten there seems to be no melodic outline. Chaotic design, harsh, meaningless harmonies, an almost overwhelming complexity, together with a brilliant score, seem to form the watchword of much of the present-day work. And it is this brilliant orchestration, combined with an apparent want of melodic invention, warmth and real charm, that is so astounding a feature. Complexity is not necessarily a sign of great strength ; on the contrary, it often denotes weakness.

" It is very easy to call the slow movement of the *New World Symphony* of Dvořák (a composer, by the way, shamefully neglected in London) ' a commonplace hymn tune ' ; but how many composers who are adepts at combining twelve or more ' melodies ' could write anything half so poetic, half so beautiful and moving? How many of their melodies would stand the test of being heard alone, out in the sunlight, as it were, with only a few simple harmonies to support them? For few recent compositions really move one—though many of them astonish. It seems as if the composers would wish to be classed with the flying man in his endeavours to ' go one better ' than the last, somehow or other, and in many ways much of the music of the period reminds one of the automobile and the airship. It is daring, clever, complex, and utterly mechanical.

" The question is—Should an imaginative Art follow such lines? Should it not rather come from the heart as well as the brain?

" Of course, a fine technical equipment is a very desirable thing, and nothing of worth can be accomplished without it ;

but should ' What do you think of my cleverness? ' be stamped
so aggressively over nearly every score that we hear?

"The lack of human passion in English music may be (personally I think *is*) merely transitory. It is being pushed
aside only while the big technical Dreadnought is in its most
engrossing stage of development. Soon the builders will have
the time to love again—when the turmoil is hushed somewhat—to give the world a few tender and personal touches
amidst the strife, which will ' make us feel again also.'

" And my Spanish friend will be happy once more ! "

CHAPTER XII

THE record of Coleridge-Taylor is inevitably sprinkled with references to his connection with his own race, and these, in consequence, have been very frequent throughout the foregoing pages; but, even after these references, a biography of the man would be farcical which did not record deliberately and in sequence his relation to the negro and his accomplishment for him. Pride in and his championship of his race developed with his manhood. The little dark-skinned lad who played the fiddle to his white schoolmates was perhaps scarcely conscious of the gulf between himself and them; but the student at the Royal College had all the passionate irritability of the genius, combined with an inordinate sensitiveness, and a power of realising the tragedy of his colour, which was an added tragedy. He hated the early criticisms which dealt equally with his skin and his music; insomuch that he told Colonel Walters that he was a British musician with an English education, and that he desired to be estimated in his relation to music and not to the music of the negro only. The matter is easy to understand. By the nature of his race he was timid, and the isolation in which he stood made what seemed the line of least resistance, the avoidance of any discussion of race questions, the best course for his youth. The atmosphere of the Royal College, his growing success, and the interest gained by actual contact with his own people, combined in early manhood to show him the nobler course of accepting the will of Providence and of adapting himself to the furthering of the darker races in so far as his art allowed. Once taken, the resolution became one of the passions of his life.

Its expression was both subjective and objective, conscious and unconscious. It was not merely fancy which discovered to the critics a strain of barbaric splendour in these early works which in their intention had no relation to the barbaric; the barbaric note was undoubtedly there, just as much as barbaric splendour is generally present in the imagination of the elder Dumas. It came out not only in the rich, unusual character of his orchestration, his short, often staccato, musical phrasing and new rhythms; it was even more apparent in an atmosphere which is peculiarly his own, and is undoubtedly racial. A facet of this race characteristic is his love of queer-sounding names, such as he found early in *Zara's Ear-rings* and in Longfellow's *Hiawatha,* and ultimately in Alfred Noyes's *A Tale of Old Japan,* where, as was the case with *Hiawatha,* the strange names Yoichi-Tenko, Sawara, O Kimi San, were the first factor of attraction in the poem. A cursory study of the negro shows how true this is to his temperament, and a glance at a list of the names chosen for themselves by negroes will increase the assurance. These works are not our concern at the moment, so much as those which are consciously upon negro subjects.

"The production of such men as Mr. Washington, Mr. Dunbar, and Mr. Taylor by the negroid race gives a new complexion to the problem of black and white." This declaration of a well-known London journal illustrates the point of view which was gradually developing in Coleridge-Taylor; and his earliest conscious connection with his race as a musician was, as we have seen, his collaboration with Paul Laurence Dunbar as early as 1897 in the series of songs, *The Corn Song, 'At Candle Lighting Time,* and the *African Romances,* which first secured him an audience as a song-writer whose work could not be neglected; as, also, in *The Dream Lovers,* the slender but interesting operetta which was their joint work in 1898. The whole significance of Dunbar lies in his expression of the "souls of black folk," and Coleridge-Taylor recognises and utters his affinity with him in his music.

His earliest orchestral piece on a more ambitious scale which was consciously directed to the expression of negro ideas was also inspired by a poem of Dunbar's. This was *Danse Nègre*, which was afterwards to be incorporated into what is one of the most important compositions of our times, partly because of its own musical quality, but more because it represents the successful entering of the highest field of creative music by the negro—the *African Suite*. His rhythms were deliberately drawn from the folk-music of his people; and *Danse Nègre* has a general resemblance to its source, but is in its fulfilment upon a much more advanced plane, as is natural to the composer who is familiar with all the resources of modern harmony and the modern orchestra.

The *African Suite,* the appearance of which was the unique event in music in the last generation, was published in 1898. It consists of four numbers, *Introduction, A Negro Love Song, Valse,* and *Danse Nègre,* and is scored for full orchestra. In this final form of *Danse Nègre* it differs from its first, which was that of a quintet for strings, the original manuscript of which is in the possession of Mr. Henry W. Down. The suite exhibits in miniature many of the characteristics of Coleridge-Taylor's work as a whole. The opening *Allegro con marcia* has a curious pedal, which continues intermittently for several bars *piano,* while the motto theme has a peculiar phrase of five notes which is thrice repeated, each time a note lower, in the four bars which make up the theme; but while we have the economy of material which this promises, we have also his irresistible love of transitions shown almost immediately, although not so pronouncedly as in later works. It exhibits, too, his sudden *fortes* and *pianos,* and his striking use of *accelerando* and *diminuendo.* The *Negro Love Song* is a revelation of melodic charm and strange, changing harmony; the *Valse* is especially noteworthy for its

R

rhythmical novelty, and its successive lightness, grace, dignity, and sonority; while the longest and final work, *Danse Nègre,* combines the weird rushing barbarity expressed by Dunbar's lines, with a delicate melodious middle movement, which, after a swift transition, is repeated before the loud, swift final phrases, in a manner strikingly his own. It is rather remarkable that this suite, which is a microcosm of his methods, and which is worthy of comparison with the *Peer Gynt Suite* in its strange and peculiar beauty, is not heard far more frequently at concerts than is the case. Successive hearings of the work do not falsify the impression of *The Times* critic, although we feel that the composer would not have subscribed to the criticism of Dvořák :

"An *African Suite,* with its deeply poetical 'Negro Love Song,' is worth a good many *New World* symphonies, for it has the genuine national or racial ring about it, not the imperfectly remembered mannerisms of the English comic song as seen through the medium of the American coloured race."

The idea of doing for negro music (to quote his own words) "what Brahms has done for Hungarian folk-music, Dvořák for the Bohemian, and Grieg for the Norwegian," came early into his mind. In common with Dvořák he held that great racial music is to be found in germ in the folk-songs of a people. Classical forms from sonata to symphony are highly civilised, and therefore largely artificial developments, and the new race, imagining such there be, that begins its higher musical expression with these, is of necessity unoriginal and imitative merely. The elements of all that differentiates it from the well-defined schools of other races are to be found in the simple, everyday utterances of the people nearest to their mother earth. Like that composer, therefore, he turned to the folk-music of his race, and found valuable material to his hand in the Jubilee Songs which had been collected in the 'seventies by Theo. F. Seward, and which were published as an appendix to the Rev. G. D. Pike's "Story of the Jubilee Singers."

Amongst the Jubilee Singers who visited England in 1875 was Frederick J. Loudin. He came again to England in the late 'nineties with a new generation of Fisk Jubilee Singers, who revived the tradition of the old choir in London and in the larger British towns. Coleridge-Taylor speaks of him as "the late world-renowned and deeply-lamented Frederick J. Loudin, manager of the famous Jubilee Singers, through whom I first learned to appreciate the beautiful folk-music of my race, and who did much to make it known the world over." Coleridge-Taylor attended some of the Jubilee concerts, and was deeply affected by the singing; the airs, indeed, struck a chord responsive in him; but in particular it was the quality of the voices that impressed him. The traditional reedy singing voice, which it is admitted was conspicuous in himself in later years, was absent, and the purity of the tenor tones and the deep forward tones of the bass, united with the power of using them to convey the whole range of emotion, were marked characteristics. Thereafter negro themes occur frequently in his work. After the *African Suite,* which is negro in intention rather than in its direct use of negro themes, the most important early work in which such a theme was used deliberately was the *Overture* to the *Song of Hiawatha.* This is built up upon the Jubilee song, *Nobody knows the trouble I see, Lord!* A curious choice, as we have noted in an earlier chapter, and one which removes the resultant work in character from the pagan Indian cantatas to which it is ostensibly the introduction. It is very undesirable, however, to press the importance of the originating theme too far. The hymn is of the most primitive character and very limited in range; the *Overture,* on the other hand, is the work of the highly conscious, fully equipped artist, who has at his disposal and employs every modern medium. It is doubtful whether or not the slaves who sang the hymn at their camp revival meetings would recognise their old favourite in its highly civilised form. Be that as it may, his employment of the theme at the moment when his reputation was at its highest point is significant of his attitude.

Most people, reasoning after knowing, found in Coleridge-Taylor's personal appearance the unmistakable features of his race. Indeed, I cannot remember myself at any time as having regarded him as otherwise than negroid. The short, rather undersized figure, with its long swinging arms, and short, rapid-striding legs was never more than thin, but it did not lack breadth when one regarded it carefully; but all these were thrown out of proportion by his large massive head. Looked at in full-face, the negro ancestry predominated in broad nostrils overset by faint high semicircular eyebrows, full lips, flashing teeth, and perhaps more than these in the thick frizzy silken hair that was as unlike European hair as it could be. A second glance, however, showed a huge, broad forehead, denoting unusual brain capacity, a forehead unruffled by any visible line of thought or care. Seen in profile, the intellectual predominated almost entirely in the face, and the broader features were unapparent. Even in intense moments this appearance of calm did not desert his forehead. His emotions expressed themselves more in quick movements of his head and flashings of his eyes. In spite of his so well-defined features, many who met him for the first time were unable to place him racially; he had been mistaken for a member of almost every foreign race under the sun, he told Mr. A. T. Johnson. During the Russo-Japanese War Coleridge-Taylor was travelling through the hopfields of Kent in a railway carriage alone with a clergyman. The latter watched him with considerable interest and that hesitancy of manner which sometimes betrays a desire for conversation. At last he screwed up courage.

"The hops are very beautiful here," he remarked.

"They are," agreed Coleridge-Taylor, "the soil seems perfectly adapted to them."

"And," inquired the clergyman, after a pause, "do you grow hops in this fashion in Japan?"

A similar incident, and one of quite a different kind in which his race was not mistaken, but which is still germane to the matter we are considering, he tells himself in a playful letter to Mr. Julien Henry, written on August 18, 1912:

"Three years ago I went to Hastings (2s. 6d. half-day trip). Everybody was most kind and interested. I found out soon afterwards that 'Uncle Tom's Cabin' was in the town. I got out by the next train. Last Thursday, at the same town, there was similar interest in my doings. I wondered why. It was the 'Maoris—straight from the hot springs of New Zealand.' And I must say I do look like a Maori—fine, handsome fellows as you know they are."

I have said enough to show how retiring was his nature; but, do what he would, his distinctive appearance and his celebrity made him a centre of interest wherever he went. The inquisitive stare followed him always, and caused him no little annoyance; but even this might be amusing. One evening, after he had conducted a successful performance of *Hiawatha* at the Albert Hall, he and his wife were awaiting their train at Victoria Station. A middle-aged gentleman, fashionably dressed, took up a position in front of Coleridge-Taylor and regarded him fixedly and intently.

"Why does that man stare, I wonder," said Coleridge-Taylor irritably, and, after a moment or two, "Very well; if he stares let us stare in return."

He therefore glared as intently at the offender. A few minutes passed, and the latter developed signs of embarrassment. Raising his hat, he advanced.

"Mr. Coleridge-Taylor, I believe?" he asked.

"Yes," said Coleridge-Taylor, shortly.

"Oh," rejoined the stranger, "I only want to thank you so much. I have just come with my family from the Albert Hall, and I thought I really *must* tell you how much I have enjoyed your *Hiawatha*."

This mild explanation of a well-meaning impertinence embarrassed Coleridge-Taylor as much as the stranger had been by his return staring; and they parted amiably.

While in retrospect these incidents caused him more amusement than irritation, more unpleasant experiences were not infrequent. Especially did they take the form of boys calling after him in the street. It was not unusual for young hooligans to cry "Blackie" after him as he passed along, quickly and nervously avoiding them. Beyond the quickened step, for long he gave no indication of the pain and annoyance this could cause him, but that it hurt him those who knew him were well aware. It was, therefore, with satisfaction that they saw in later years a more assertive manner and a determination to resent these insults. I feel gleeful when I remember the practical shape he once gave to this feeling. A big lad greeted him with the usual "Blackie." Without a moment's hesitation, Coleridge-Taylor seized him by the scruff of the neck, and administered to the shrieking young coward a salutary and satisfactory thrashing with his walking stick. But the event affected him severely; the pallor and exhaustion which followed this summary infliction of punishment caused his friends, while they approved of it, to wish that he could have dispensed with the necessity for it. The fighting spirit which it betrayed, however, grew with time, as I shall show.

His symphonic poem *Toussaint l'Ouverture*, written in 1901, is again directly the outcome of his racial sympathies. As I have already remarked, the music was designed to interpret and illustrate the character and tragedy of one of the most striking personalities that the negro race has given to the world. This composition was never mentioned by Coleridge-Taylor in my hearing, nor have I been able to discover, if, like so many of his similar compositions, it has original themes or themes derived from negro folk-song. It is a subjective study of Toussaint l'Ouverture's character, his warlike prowess, and his strong family affections. The first theme and its accessories illustrate his sterner virtues, the second his gentler qualities. In a third and fourth theme these two facets of the character recur in order. The work, which is for full orchestra, and has not been transcribed in piano score, was produced by the Queen's Hall Orchestra under the conductorship of Sir (then Mr.) Henry Wood on October 26, and was repeated on December 1.

I have already dealt fully with the Samuel Coleridge-Taylor Society, in the founding of which his race laid special claim to him, a claim in which I have also described his ready acquiescence. It was natural, when he was asked to contribute something original to the Washington Festival in 1904, that he should choose a subject closely linked with the mutual race of himself and the Coleridge-Taylor Society. The descendants of slaves could not but be interested in Longfellow's "Songs of Slavery," from which Coleridge-Taylor drew the words of his *Five Choral Ballads,* three of which were presented at Washington. His treatment of these songs is of the simplest; his own idiomatic phrasings and repetitions with slight harmonic variations are present, but there is that remarkable restraint in his use of material and in his orchestration which only the master-hand shows. The numbers are : I. *Beside the Ungathered Rice He Lay,* in which the four voices of the chorus are used to depict the negro who, sleeping in the rice fields, dreams he is riding in freedom by the Niger, and ends "a useless fetter that the soul had broken and flung away." In modest compass the music conveys a wide range of feeling from dreamful quiet, through dramatic fugue, to the tragedy of death. II. *She Dwells by Great Kenhawa's Side* is set in two versions, in which the treatment differs widely. The first is a trio for two sopranos and one contralto, with a free orchestral accompaniment; the second is for four voices, or a solo quartet, with a different accompaniment. The ballad tells in appropriate fashion the daily round of the sweet schoolmistress working in the village school, who

> " . . . was rich and gave up all
> To break the iron bands
> Of those who waited in her hall,
> And laboured in her lands."

III. *Loud He Sang the Song of David* is a strong description, in short syncopated phrases, in a wild 2-2 time, with a smoother variation in 6-4 time, of the slave singing at midnight. IV. *The Quadroon Girl* has for its subject the sale of a quadroon girl to a slaver by her planter father. The simple tragedy is told by the baritone, who, in a large, broad melody brings out with much drama the growing intensity of the situation while the planter is considering the slaver's bid for his quadroon daughter, to the point of his acquiescence in the nefarious bargain. The background of the broad lagoon, with the ship riding at anchor awaiting the rising moon and the evening wind, and the land with its light winds laden with odours of orange-flowers and of spice, are well suggested; and the poignancy of the story is emphasised by the choral background, a wailing "Ah," given in sustained harmonies by the female voices. It is the most haunting of the *Ballads*. V. *The Slave in the Dismal Swamp* is a realistic setting, for four voices, of the well-known story of the aged hunted slave who, as he cowers in the dark fens, hears the bloodhound's distant bay, and realises in his anguish that the creatures of the earth and air are free, and on him alone is the curse of Cain.

It was in connection with his first visit to America that he received an invitation from the Oliver Ditson Company, music publishers of Boston, to arrange an album of negro

folk-songs for the piano.   After some consideration he consented, and the result was his *Negro Melodies Transcribed
for the Piano,* published in 1905, in which he attempted to
show the main currents of native negro music, and which
was, according to Dr. Booker T. Washington, who contributed a prefatory appreciation, "the most complete expression of Mr. Coleridge-Taylor's native bent and power."
"Using," continues Dr. Washington, "some of the native
songs of Africa and the West Indies with songs that came
into being in America during the slavery regime, he has in
handling these melodies preserved their distinctive traits
and individuality, at the same time giving them an art form
fully imbued with their essential spirit.   It is especially
gratifying that at this time, when interest in the plantation
songs seems to be dying out with the generation that gave
them birth, when the negro song is in too many minds
associated with ' rag ' music and the more reprehensible
' coon ' song, that the most cultivated musician of his race,
a man of the highest æsthetic ideals, should seek to give
permanence to the folk-songs of his people by giving them
a new interpretation and an added dignity." In passing, it
may be remarked that while in America in 1904 Coleridge-
Taylor expressed in no measured terms his contempt for
the mongrel product known as "rag-time," in which the
most vulgar elements of white and negro music are combined; a music which has no more relation to that of the
native negro than vodka has to champagne. Of the twenty-
four melodies, four are drawn from South-East Africa, two
from South Africa, one each from West Africa and the
West Indies, and the remainder from America.   The
method he adopted, Coleridge-Taylor describes in his pre-
face as almost without exception that of the *Tema con varia-
zioni,* the actual melody being given at the beginning of
each number as a motto, and upon this a series of variations is built.   It is interesting to learn that he found a
great deal of figurative meaning in these melodies, as one
does not regard allusiveness as a very obvious quality of

the primitive mind. Even more interesting are his comparative remarks. "There is a great distinction between the African and the American negro melodies. The African would seem to be more martial and free in character, whereas the American are more personal and tender, though notable exceptions to this can be found on either side. One of the most striking points regarding the music is, in the author's opinion, its likeness to that of the Caucasian race. The native music of India, China, and Japan, and in fact all non-European music, is to our more cultivated ears most unsatisfactory in its monotony and shapelessness. The music of Africa (I am not thinking of American negro music, which may or may not have felt some white influence) is a great and noteworthy exception. Primitive as it is, it nevertheless has all the elements of the European folk-song, and it is remarkable that no alterations have had to be made before treating the melodies. This is even so with the example from West Africa—a highly original number. One conclusion may safely be drawn from this—the negro is really and truly a most musical personality. What culture may do for the race in this respect has yet to be determined, but the underlying musical nature cannot for a moment be questioned."

As was appropriate, the *Twenty-four Negro Melodies* were published in America. To this fact, however, must be attributed their small vogue in England, where they are so little known that music-sellers have reported of them that they "cannot be traced." This is unfortunate, as, from the particular angle from which we are now considering Coleridge-Taylor, they are amongst his most characteristic work. The composer sent a copy of this work to his old professor, who acknowledged it as follows :

> 50 HOLLAND STREET,
> KENSINGTON, W.
> *May* 16, 1905.

MY DEAR COLERIDGE-TAYLOR,—It is very good of you to send me the Melodies. They look most characteristic and interesting. I wish you would send a copy to Percy Grainger (26 Coulson Street, Sloane Square, S.W.), who is greatly interested in folk-songs. By the way, one of the tunes, "The Angels changed my Name," is an Irish tune, and also I think "The Pilgrim's Song." Like some of the negro tunes Dvořák got hold of, these have reached the American negroes through the Irish Americans. A curious instance of the transmigration of folk-songs.—Yours very sincerely,

C. V. STANFORD.

Amongst the papers that he preserved I find various cuttings he had taken from London newspapers, dealing with the questions of Ethiopianism, which had been raised largely in connection with the turbulence of Dinizulu, the son of Cetewayo, in Natal. A correspondence upon the iniquities of the negro ran in the newspapers at about this time, and one letter accusing the negro of a perennial disposition to commit outrages upon white women, drew an effective rejoinder from Coleridge-Taylor. Its substance was that evil may certainly exist in the negro race, but that no impartial evidence is forthcoming that it is greater there than in the white races; and he reminded his readers of the words of Du Bois to the white men of the Southern American States: "O Southern Gentlemen! If you deplore their (the negroes') presence here, they ask, Who brought us? When you cry, Deliver us from the vision of intermarriage, they answer that legal marriage is infinitely better than systematic concubinage and prostitution. And if in just fury you accuse their vagabonds of violating women, they also in fury quite as just may reply : The rape which your gentlemen have done against helpless black women in defiance of your own laws is written on the foreheads of two millions of mulattoes, and written in ineffaceable blood."

He returned to the negro melodies for the theme of a work which he considered better, "stronger and more modern altogether" than *Hiawatha*. This was his *Symphonic Variations on an African Air,* which formed the first item on the programme of the Philharmonic Society on June 14, 1906, and the air is "I'm troubled in mind," another Jubilee song.   Although, as Coleridge-Taylor said in explaining the work, the tune is well-known in America in connection with the plantation hymn, there is reason to believe that it consists in large part of a much older native negro melody.   In the form in which it reached the composer, it is one of the most pathetic numbers in Seward's collection.   Those who listen to Coleridge-Taylor's work, with its great range of pathos, strength, and at times almost weird beauty, may care to be reminded that the original tune was taken from the lips of a slave in Nashville, who first heard it from her father.   After the aged slave had been flogged he always sat upon a log beside his cabin, and, with tears streaming down his cheeks, sang this song with so much pathos that few could listen without sympathy.   The original tune is as follows :

and at the outset, without alteration of note or time, but with a simple transposition, Coleridge-Taylor uses this tune, and upon it builds a series of variations of progressive complexity and beauty.   Between the pianissimo opening, where the motto is given out by the horns, to the whirlwind close, there are fifteen changes of key, and several more of tempo.   The effects are very largely orchestral, and the *Variations* suffer necessarily in transcription for the pianoforte, where the insistence upon the theme is perhaps too apparent.   In any case, this characteristic of economy in the use of theme and abundance in the treatment of its accessories is a striking feature of the work.

Amongst the *Negro Melodies* was the *Bamboula,* a West Indian dance, and this formed the ground-work of an orchestral rhapsody which he wrote in the early spring of 1910, and which he conducted at the Litchfield County Choral Union at Norfolk, Connecticut, on his third and last visit to America. The following particulars of the origin of the composition are from the pen of Mr. Carl Stoeckel :

"I saw Coleridge-Taylor in London in September, 1909, and arranged with him to come over and conduct his 'Indian Music' at our recent concert. As I was talking with him, the thought came to me what he might do in a musical way in his mature manhood, as compared with the 'Indian Music' of his student period. We could not use a choral work, so I proposed that he compose a work for full orchestra, using as a basis some African and American air, such a work to require not over fifteen minutes in rendition, to be brilliant in character, and suitable for a 'closing piece' for our concert. There was not the slightest condition about all this; it was only a suggestion on my part—the only stipulation being for an orchestral work not to exceed fifteen minutes. Coleridge-Taylor accepted the commission, and evidently thought well of the proposition, for in the spring he wrote : 'The orchestral piece is finished. It is a rhapsody dance on matter contained in my *Bamboula,* a West Indian melody. Of course it is very much amplified and enlarged and, in fact, quite different, but the actual four bars of the motto remain the same. I should say it will take ten to twelve minutes in performance. It is very brilliant in character, as you will see by the subject, which is taken from my collection of twenty-four negro melodies. The work is scored for full orchestra, and is dedicated to Mr. and Mrs. Stoeckel.' Coleridge-Taylor brought the score and parts with him when he came to America in May ; the work was corrected on the steamship, and tried for first rehearsal at Carnegie Hall, New York, May 27 ; second rehearsal at Norfolk,

June 2; first concert rendition under the composer the same evening. The composer was much impressed by the ability of our players to give such a fine rendition after only two rehearsals. The *Bamboula* seemed to hit the fancy of the musicians present as 'the best thing in an orchestral way yet done by the composer.' "

One of the most charming works of his later life, his *Fairy Ballads,* is a setting of six lyrics by Miss Kathleen Easmon, a young West African girl. For the amusement of some child friends Miss Easmon had written little verses, enshrining pretty conceits. These her mother showed to Mrs. Coleridge-Taylor, who in turn showed them to her husband. He took the copy without expressing any intention in regard to them; and a short while later Miss Easmon was delighted to learn that he had clothed them in his most characteristic style in some of the most charming of recent music. The *Fairy Ballads,* which were published in 1909, have proved very popular; *Big Lady Moon* and *Sweet Baby Butterfly* are already well known, and the remaining four songs deserve equal popularity, especially the exquisite *Alone with Mother.* Given a skilled accompanist, they are peculiarly adapted to the singing of little children, and I have never heard them sung better than by the composer's own little daughter, Gwendolen.

The last considerable work produced during his lifetime, the *Violin Concerto,* was first built upon negro tunes. I am indebted to Mr. Carl Stoeckel for an account of the occasion of its origin during Coleridge-Taylor's visit to conduct *Bamboula* at the Norfolk Music Festival. "After supper," writes Mr. Stoeckel, "my wife went into the library, and Coleridge-Taylor and I went into another room to have a smoke. She began playing on the piano, and suddenly Coleridge-Taylor dropped his cigarette, jumped to his feet, and said, 'What is that lovely melody?' It was an African slave song called 'Keep Me From Sinking Down, Good Lord,' which has never been in the books, as it was taken from the lips of a slave directly after the war by a teacher who went south and who gave it to my late father-in-law, Robbins Battell.* Coleridge-Taylor went into the library and asked my wife to play it again, which she did, singing the melody at the same time. He said, ' Do let me take it down. I will use it sometime.' For several days some of the violin passages in the *Bamboula* rhapsody had been running in my head, and the thought came to me that perhaps Coleridge-Taylor might be induced to write a violin concerto, using this African melody in the adagio movements. I proposed the matter to him then and there. He said that he was delighted with the idea, and would undertake it. He was, of course, to take his own time and to receive an honorarium therefor. In due season the manuscript of the violin concerto reached me. I took it at once to Madam Maud Powell, as the work was dedicated to her, and she was to give the first rendition. My original suggestion to Coleridge-Taylor was that the concerto should be founded on three African melodies characteristic of our so-called Southern negro airs. When we went over the concerto, we found that the second movement was based on an African melody, but not on ' Keep Me From Sinking Down,' which Coleridge-Taylor had found that he could not use, and he had substituted ' Many Thousands Gone ' for this movement. In the third movement he had used ' Yankee Doodle ' quite frequently, which, of course, is not strictly an African melody. We agreed that the second movement of the concerto was a beautiful piece of music, but both the first and the third movements seemed to us rather sketchy and unsatisfactory. While I was considering what to write about this work to Coleridge-Taylor, I received a letter from him, requesting me to throw it into the fire; and saying that he had written an entirely new and original work, all the melodies being his own, and that it was a hundred times better than the first composi-

* My courteous correspondent is in error at this point. The hymn appears as No. 21 in Seward's collection, in the Appendix to the " Story of the Jubilee Singers." London : Hodder and Stoughton, 1875.

tion. I returned his first composition to him at once, as it seemed a pity to lose the second movement; and a few weeks later the score of the second concerto arrived.   It was tried and found highly satisfactory. Its first rendition was at the Norfolk Festival of 1912, being played by Madam M. Powell, under the Directorship of Mr. Arthur Mees. After the first concerto arrived, which we did not use, and which did not contain the air ' Keep Me From Sinking Down,' I wrote to Coleridge-Taylor, and suggested that he should make a separate arrangement of this air either for violin or 'cello. He responded with promptness, and sent along with the second concerto an arrangement of the air for violin and orchestra. This was played as an encore by Madam M. Powell at the time of the rendition of the concerto."

Early in February, 1912, at Purley, a barrister addressed a debating society, presided over by a clergyman, upon, " The Negro Problem in North America."   The newspaper report which reached Coleridge-Taylor was afterwards admitted to be insufficient, but it contained such sublime ineptitudes as, "The black man was even nearer the ape than the white to the black; his skull was peculiar, and there was an odour from him unlike anything else on earth; the race had never done anything to improve itself; the result of the freedom of the slave had brought about a state of things worse than before the war," and much other arrant nonsense. Coleridge-Taylor was extremely angry; angrier than the obviously *ex parte* statements of a speaker who did not realise how brutal was the biological generalisation which closed the avenues of hope to one hundred millions of his fellow men, would seem to warrant.   He replied :

To the Editor of the [*Croydon*] *" Guardian."*

Sir,—I hear that the next subject for discussion at the " Purley Circle " is to be " God and His great mistake in creating Black Men," with Jack Johnson in the chair.

This meeting will be almost as interesting as the last meeting, at which (as I gather from your report) a clergyman-chairman actually thanked a lecturer for expressing not only un-Christian but unmanly sentiments about the race in question. Doubtless the " Purley Circle " is working up for a lynching in the near future. I hope I shall be a mere spectator and not the victim! Shame on the lecturer, and a thousand times on the clergyman! And yet there was a vast amount of humour in some of the things that were said at that meeting. The smell of the negro, for instance. All uncivilised people smell for a very obvious reason—they do not wash. But what about the smell of the lecturer's own ancestors who ran about half naked some centuries ago? Was it that of a June rose? I wonder!

It is amazing that grown-up, and presumably educated, people can listen to such primitive and ignorant nonsense-mongers, who are men without vision, utterly incapable of penetrating beneath the surface of things.

No one realises more than I that the coloured people have not yet taken their place in the scheme of things, but to say that they never will is arrogant rubbish, and an insult to the God in Whom they profess to believe. Why, I personally know hundreds of men and women of negro blood who have already made their mark in the great world, and this is only the beginning. I might suggest that the " Purley Circle " engage someone to lecture on one Alexandre Dumas, a rather well-known author, I fancy, who had more than a drop of negro blood in him. Who is there who has not read and loved his Dumas? And what about Poushkin, the poet? And Du Bois, whose " Souls of Black Folk " was hailed by James Payn as the greatest book that had come out of the United States for fifty years? I mention these three because not only are they distinguished men, but men of colossal genius. And will the lecturer refer to a chapter in H. G. Wells's " Future of America," called " The Tragedy of Colour "?—this, because Wells is undoubtedly possessed of the heaven-born gift of insight to a greater degree than any other living Englishman—not even excluding G. B. S.

The fact is that there is an appalling amount of ignorance
S

amongst English people regarding the negro and his doings. If the Purley lecturer (I forget his name, and am away from home, the Birmingham people having engaged me to direct something that has come out of my ill-formed skull)—I say, if he is right, then let us at once and for ever stop the humbug of missions to darkest Africa, and let the clergy stop calling their congregations "dear brethren," at any rate whenever a black man happens to be in the church. Let us change our prayer books, our Bibles, and everything pertaining to Christianity, and be honest.

Personally, I consider myself the equal of any white man who ever lived, and no one could ever change me in that respect; on the other hand, no man reverences worth more than I, irrespective of colour and creed. May I further remind the lecturer that really great people always see the best in others? It is the little man who looks for the worst—and finds it. It is a peculiar thing that almost without exception all distinguished white men have been favourably disposed towards their black brethren. No woman has ever been more courteous to me than a certain member of our own English Royal Family, and no man more so than President Roosevelt.

It was an arrogant "little" white man who dared to say to the great Dumas, "And I hear you actually have negro blood in you!" "Yes," said the witty writer; "my father was a mulatto, his father a negro, and his father a monkey. My ancestry began where yours ends!"

Somehow I always manage to remember that wonderful answer when I meet a certain type of white man (a type, thank goodness! as far removed from the best as the poles from each other), and the remembrance makes me feel quite happy—wickedly happy, in fact!—Yours, etc.,

S. COLERIDGE-TAYLOR.

MIDLAND HOTEL, BIRMINGHAM.
February 15, 1912.

Other letters followed to the same newspaper:

SIR,—It seems that several of the London dailies honoured me by quoting the letter I wrote to *The Guardian* last week.

May I ask you to be good enough to insert the " explanation," which appeared in *The Daily News* last Tuesday, and which I enclose? The "clergyman chairman" turned out to be the Vicar of Purley, from whom I have received a most courteous and explanatory letter on the subject. Hence my second letter to *The Daily News*.

As for the lecture itself, the less said the better. After reading a detailed account, I find that it was even more vindictive than your columns had led me to believe.

It may interest you to know that my original letter brought me a large number of sympathetic letters from all parts of the United Kingdom, and even Purley cried "No! no!" at the kindly suggestion of extermination.—Yours, etc.,

"ALDWICK," CROYDON.   S. COLERIDGE-TAYLOR.

February 22, 1912.

To the Editor of "The Daily News."

SIR,—In my letter to *The Croydon Guardian* on the subject of "Black and White," which you reprinted in your columns last Saturday, I referred to the clergyman who occupied the chair at the meeting in question.

Through a somewhat incomplete report, I was under the impression that he agreed with the lecturer.

I have learned since, however, that this was very far from being the case.

It is, therefore, with more than ordinary pleasure that I withdraw my remarks about this gentleman, who publicly sided with the negro during the debate which followed.

May I add that my letter on the subject was not written with the slightest idea of inciting discussion, but simply because I felt that the one-sided ideas expressed at Croydon are not those of the best white people of England and America—nor, for that matter, of any other country.

"ALDWICK," CROYDON.   S. COLERIDGE-TAYLOR.

February 19, 1912.

In the issue of *The Croydon Guardian* in which these last two letters appeared was published an answer to his first letter, signed M. E. B., in which the writer, although sympathetic to Coleridge-Taylor as "an exception-ally gifted half-caste gentleman," ventured to remind him that he was the son of a white woman, and that some usu-ally inherit their gifts from their mothers. Moreover, he thought that Dumas was of creole, not of West African, descent, adduced arguments about the odour of the average full-blooded negro, and included the statement with regard to lynching that, "white men and white women who have lived in countries where there is a predominance in numbers of the black race, are agreed that these ghastly occurrences are the only protection for the white woman from the black man." Coleridge-Taylor replied :

To the Editor of "The Guardian."

SIR,—I should not venture to trespass on your space for a third (and last) time were it not for the fact that two statements made by one of your correspondents call for correction.

First of all, Dumas was not a creole. The dark side of him was West Indian, and the dark West Indians hailed from Africa. Therefore, Dumas' own summing up of his nationality was correct.

Secondly, there is no reason for adopting an aggressive tone when discussing the coloured people of America. It must be remembered that they did not go to that country of their own accord; on the contrary, it was very much "by desire " of their white brothers.

A careful study of conditions between black and white in America during the past hundred years will throw a lurid and unexpected light on the subject. It is obvious, therefore, that had not the white Americans made the great mistake (shall we call it?) of forcing the blacks to pay them a long visit, there would be to-day no colour question at all in America.

As for South Africa, after all, the blacks were born there, and Africa is their own country in many ways. White people who go there must expect " occasionally " to meet a half-clothed native. And if these people will persist in employing

these native men as "chambermaids," there is sure to be a little trouble now and again. I wonder there is not more.
—Yours, etc.,

S. COLERIDGE-TAYLOR.

" ALDWICK," CROYDON.

March 1, 1912.

Two projects of 1912 had direct reference to his race. The first was that of an operetta in a single act, for which Mr. Lyell Johnson proposed to furnish the libretto. It was to have a West African scenic setting, and its subject was to be the intermarriage of white and black people. Coleridge-Taylor met Mr. Johnson several times for the discussion of the scheme, and the scenario was sketched, but death intervened before any great progress was made, and, so far as it has been possible to ascertain, Coleridge-Taylor did not make any notes for it, musical or otherwise. A more ambitious proposal that found favour with him was an opera with a similar background, which was to be produced in collaboration with Mr. Reginald R. Buckley, whose drama, *Arthur of Britain,* is known to lovers of contemporary poetry, and to music-lovers through its musical treatment by Mr. Randell Broughton. Mr. Buckley permits me to quote his own account of it :

" Mr. Kennerley Rumford wrote a letter to the Press in which he stated that the only way to popularise British opera was to write it around a ' star.' As you probably know, I am intimately connected with the Glastonbury Festival scheme, and am not unknown as a poet. But I wanted to write an ' opera,' and wrote to Coleridge-Taylor, whom I did not know. We dined together, and he, too, desired to do something at once worthy of his genius yet capable of popularity. I planned out the main lines of a West African drama, with strong Imperial interest, also with scope for native music, which he said laughingly would appeal to the ' savage ' in him. He did not shirk the colour question either. Indeed, he charmed me with his simple poetic spirit, and I felt that he would be a friend.

"I then wrote to Mr. Kennerley Rumford asking for an interview, and telling him that I had found a composer who would be capable of writing a work such as he needed, with a special view to Madame Clara Butt and himself. The Rumfords replied courteously from Berlin. Just before they returned I received a letter from Coleridge-Taylor saying he wanted to see me, and was very keen on the work. Within three days I heard the sad news of his death.

"I then went up to see Mr. Kennerley Rumford and explained who my composer was, and that the whole thing was so bound up with Coleridge-Taylor that I did not see my way clear.

"Our plan was to write and compose lyrically as in *A Tale of Old Japan,* but with a West African setting, and on a big scale. He took the liveliest interest in my *Arthur of Britain,* and our plans for producing it, and was quite free from the narrow spirit of many composers. He wanted popularity as much as I did, but we agreed that such a result can only be arrived at by simple and straightforward means. We intended to tell a story, full of African colour, yet not without a wide human appeal. And in this we were thwarted.

"We met two or three times at Cramers to plan it out."

In July, 1912, Mr. Duse Mohamed started *The African Times and Orient Review,* to advocate the cause of the coloured races in this country. Amongst the opinions on the venture published in the first issue was one from Coleridge-Taylor :

"I certainly think that the issue of a newspaper such as *The African Times and Orient Review* will be a most interesting event.

"Whether it will or will not be appreciated by the British public is, however, a point on which I am not so certain.

"There is, of course, a large section of the British people interested in the coloured races; but it is, generally speaking, a commercial interest only. Some of these may possibly be interested in the aims and desires of the coloured peoples; but, taking them on a whole, I fancy one accomplished fact carries far more weight than a thousand aims and desires, regrettable though it may be.

" It seems that the different sections of the whites are not interested in the aims of each other (excepting, perhaps, financially), and I doubt if more than a few will be inclined to study the aspirations of those of another race.

"Therefore it is imperative that this venture be heartily supported by the coloured people themselves, so that it shall be absolutely independent of the whites as regards circulation. Such independence will probably speak to the average Britisher far more than anything else, and will ultimately arouse his attention and interest—even to his support.

" That some medium for promoting a better understanding between Orient and Occident is wanted goes without saying; and as *The African Times and Orient Review* is setting out to become such a medium, it should be welcomed by all thoughtful and unprejudiced people as something which fulfils a long-felt want."

After the launching of the journal he writes again :

" ALDWICK," CROYDON.
August 28.

MY DEAR MR. MOHAMED,—I feel I must say how much I congratulate you on the second issue of *The African Times.*

You must remember you asked us all to give opinions before a single copy was published, otherwise I don't think any fear as to its future would have been expressed.

Also—may I suggest?—please do not publish such opinions as that of the " Welshman." Of course, you want all sides, but his was so uninteresting, and so rambling. Moreover, he is not a Welshman who has seen much, evidently. I know the Welsh so well, and I should say they are the least prejudiced amongst white peoples.

I have only just finished my *Hiawatha* Ballet. I've been a year working on it, but I think I've got it right now.

I shall do my level best to secure you subscribers, by mentioning and showing my copies.

Kindest regards.—Yours sincerely,

S. COLERIDGE-TAYLOR.

I have only just returned to town, or should have written earlier.

Thus, almost to his last hour, Coleridge-Taylor was occupied with the welfare of his race; and his contribution to humanity takes its significance from his blood. Other and greater musicians have lived, but he was the first of his race to reach recognition as a world musician. In the interval between the negro folk-songs and his work lie only the works of one negro composer of consideration, W. Marion Cook, whose talents, however, reach mainly in the direction of musical comedy, which in modern days has not been rich in permanent music. Both he and Coleridge-Taylor's friend, Harry T. Burleigh, have written songs, which, according to Professor B. G. Brawley, "satisfy the highest standards of art, as well as those that are merely popular music." But to neither does criticism award a place even approaching that held by Coleridge-Taylor, the greatness of whose style is only equalled by the many and advanced forms in which it revealed itself. One such man is a complete answer to all the biologists who generalise on the limitations of the negro genius:

> *Nations unborn shall hear his forests moan;*
> *Ages unscanned shall hear his winds lament,*
> *Hear the strange grief that deepened through his own*
> *The vast cry of a buried continent.*
>
> *Through him, his race a moment lifted up*
> *Forests of hands to Beauty as in prayer;*
> *Touched through his lips the sacramental Cup,*
> *And then sank back—benumbed in our bleak air.*

True as they are, the beautiful lines of the poet speak for to-day and for the past, but Coleridge-Taylor's work is prophetic as well.   He has shown that the "buried continent" is capable of producing the highest in at least one art.   The immediate moral of his life is modestly expressed in a letter I have received from the leader of his people, Dr. Booker T. Washington :

"I had the pleasure of meeting Coleridge-Taylor in Boston on one of his visits to America, and I have watched with interest the growing appreciation of his music among members of my race since that time.   The great value from my point of view of men like Coleridge-Taylor and others who have achieved conspicuous success is that their lives and work set the standard for the rest of us a little higher.   Aside from what he contributed through his musical composition to the common property of the world, Coleridge-Taylor performed a distinct service by demonstrating to the coloured people the possibilities of their race."

And in any future discussion of his possibilities, the negro may take heart in remembering that in the perfecting within itself of the race physically, morally, and intellectually, in an unswerving devotion to the higher human ideals, in a determination to stand upon its own achievements, lies the justification of the race.   In the songs of a Paul Lawrence Dunbar, the eloquence of a Du Bois, the practical contributions to social welfare of a Booker Washington, in the colour dreams of a Henry Ossowa Tanner, in the world-embracing genius of a Dumas or a Poushkin, and perhaps even more than in these, in the melodies of a Coleridge-Taylor, which thrill the heart-strings of mankind irrespective of creed, caste, or colour; in these lies the ultimate triumph of the oppressed people.   More and more as the race produces examples of the highest human genius and achievement, more and more will the race be lifted to the level of those who until now have been regarded as "more advanced."

CHAPTER XIII

1911-1912—"A TALE OF OLD JAPAN"—LAST WORKS—
THE VALLEY OF THE SHADOW

ALL the qualities which marked Coleridge-Taylor's work as conductor and teacher at Trinity College and other places of which I have written, were brought to bear in their most intense form on his work at the Guildhall School of Music. His career there was too brief to have become a matter of actual celebrity; but such was its efficiency that, since his death, the Principal, Mr. Landon Ronald, tells me he has had the greatest difficulty in filling his place; and more than one of his pupils is a cordial witness to the devotion to himself personally which he created unconsciously in those he taught. Some notion of the spirit in which he conceived his academic duties may be gauged from his action when Sullivan's *Yeoman of the Guard* was put in rehearsal for one of the Guildhall School concerts. The work was unfamiliar, and he had never seen it presented. He heard that the D'Oyley Carte Opera Company was performing it at Newport in Monmouthshire; and that very day, after a busy morning and afternoon at home and at the school, he took train from Paddington and reached Newport at eight. The theatre was crowded, but a chair was found for him near the stage, and he said that he enjoyed the performance thoroughly except for some of the orchestral playing. An hour before midnight he caught the return train for Paddington, reaching there at 3.30 a.m., and the journey, he said, "gave me plenty of time to study the score." He got home at 6.30 a.m., and was at the first rehearsal at the school the same morning. Genius has often this capacity for taking pains, but the human organism has limits of strength, and there is no doubt that this and similar trials of his strength were the actual if not the apparent cause of his death.

Early this year he learned for the first time with great interest that the metre of *Hiawatha* was not the invention of Longfellow, as he had supposed, but had a much more ancient origin in the natural and national epic of Finland, *The Kalevala.* He borrowed the work from the public library, and it was hoped that he would find new inspiration in it; but nothing more than an interest in the form of the work resulted.

It does not seem credible that Coleridge-Taylor's life could at any time have been more energetic than it was on the average. He was one of those extraordinary men to whom inactivity is really an affliction, in spite of his already-mentioned assurance that he was "a naturally lazy man." Yet 1911 was breathless in its activity. Let me repeat that he was conducting the Handel Society and the Blackheath Society; that he was teaching at Trinity College, at the Crystal Palace School of Music, and at the Guildhall School; that he was engrossed in rehearsals at and writing for His Majesty's Theatre; and yet, in spite of all these regular engagements, he found time to write *A Tale of Old Japan,* the greater part of *The Forest of Wild Thyme,* and the *Violin Concerto,* as well as a number of songs and other smaller works. He was a cardinal example of his implication when writing of Hurlstone, that the gifted composer is usually "remarkably prolific in composition." Ordinary mortals, however, who imagine that sustained art-work requires leisure, repose, retirement, may indeed wonder at this man's powers of creation. Useless as it is to speculate upon what he might have achieved had these comfortable conditions been granted him, one cannot help the speculation; but with the feeling that even with them it seems impossible that a man could have accomplished more than he did. In a playful way, but never seriously, he envied those men who made greater material success in music than came to him. Such a note he struck in writing to Mr. Read concerning a well-known conductor. "I ran into S—— just returning to H——, where he now lives. He looked fine—astrakan and all—and he goes first, bless you. He routed me out of my humble third and made me go as far as his place in the superior class. Lord, I wish I could conduct!" His attitude in general, however, was one of simple admiration and gratitude for the work of other men, and the one criticism that may be made of it is that it was sometimes too generous.

His choral works received many performances this year. *Kubla Khan* was heard at Woking in January; *Endymion's Dream* received a magnificent rendering at Evanstan, Illinois, in the same month, and another in February at the Birmingham Festival, where it was a companion work with Elgar's *Caractacus*; and he conducted the Handel Society on February 28 in *The Bon Bon Suite*.

He had a brief rest from composition in April, when Mr. Johnson found him in the state of having nothing to do. His schools ahd his societies were in vacation, the first version of the *Violin Concerto* was finished and sent off to Mr. Stoeckel in America, and he had completed *A Tale of Old Japan*. Apart from these larger works, he set in April Alfred Noyes's fine *Hymn to Peace* as a vigorous unison song for chorus singing, and a cycle of lyrics from the pen of Marguerite Radclyffe-Hall.

The principal event of the first half of the year was the production of *Othello* at His Majesty's Theatre on April 11, which was perhaps the most splendid spectacular presentation of the tragedy in the history of the stage. The music was mostly of the entr'acte variety, there being little incidental music. Pageantry rather than tragedy is the opening theme of the overture, the tragedy to come is scarcely foreshadowed, and throughout it was observed that the tender character of Desdemona rather than the jealousy of the Moor or the malignity of Iago is the predominating atmosphere. The bright rhythmic dance between the second and third acts, the children's chorus to which reference has been made, and a really exquisite setting of *The Willow Song,* are the most notable contributions Coleridge-Taylor made to the performance. Five of these numbers, *The Dance, Children's Intermezzo, Funeral March, The Willow Song,* and the *Military March* he afterwards worked into a most effective orchestral suite, and *The Willow Song* is published separately with the words, to be a delight for all who love a really inspired interpretation of Desdemona's simple and poignantly pathetic death-song.

The coronation festivities in May gave important hearings to several of his works. At the command performance at Drury Lane the music included his *Nero Suite*; and a little elation was not inexcusable when, at the Royal Concert at the Albert Hall, he learned that the only composers represented by more than one work were Wagner and Coleridge-Taylor, a fact upon which the Berlin newspapers commented.

Quite recently he had read for the first time the poems of Herrick, and one appealed to him so insistently that he set it immediately. This was the song, or rather scena, *The Guest,* which was not published until after his death.

During June he was busy, he told Mr. Julien Henry, revising proofs of *A Tale of Old Japan,* adding to his note a postscript : "Horatio Parker has just won $10,000 prize for the best American opera—what a fine country !" At the end of the month he conducted a classical concert at Brighton, and a few days later the South African Concert, at the Festival of Empire then being held at the Crystal Palace.

This month he visited Madame Tussaud's; he told his experience to Mr. Johnson : " I saw what looked like a girl selling programmes, and I took out sixpence and offered it to her. She seemed a long time taking it, so I said, ' One will be enough, thank you '; and it wasn't till somebody behind me burst out laughing that I found out my mistake." In the Chamber of Horrors, where he and his wife appeared to be the only visitors, he heard a subdued cry, which seemed first to proceed from one of the characters. Investigation discovered that a would-be visitor, a lady of ample dimensions, had managed to fill the turnstile so completely that she could not move. It required some effort on the part of Coleridge-Taylor and the official to extricate her.

In May he contemplated spending his summer vacation in Brittany at Duclair on the Seine, a place recommended by Miss Petherick, of whom he inquires: "Was it cheap, and quiet, and suitable for *us*, do you think?" But in July the prospect was banished. It was past the middle of the month when he was still rehearsing *The Yeoman of the Guard* at the Guildhall for the concert at the end of the term; and early in August he was adjudicating at an eisteddfod in South Wales. Further, Sir Herbert Tree commissioned him this month to provide music for Israel Zangwill's new drama, *The God of War*, which was billed for the first week in September; and to the astonishment of his friends, he mortgaged himself still more heavily by accepting, at the suggestion of Mr. Landon Ronald, the conductorship of the Stock Exchange Orchestral Society. He writes to Mr. Read: "I don't know where we're going for holidays this year; but, in any case, I shall try to run down for a day to see you if you are in Eastbourne during August."

A letter, written during August by the musical critic of *The Standard,* and addressed to Mr. Bernard Victor, who had made a protest, should be inserted here.

August 31, 1911.

Dear Sir,—I beg to acknowledge, somewhat belated, however, your letter of the 11th instant.

If among the many British composers I was forced to omit from my Promenade articles was Mr. Coleridge-Taylor, I assure you it was from no indifference to the high place he has earned among musicians of our time.

No one could be more alive than myself to the power and originality of Mr. Coleridge-Taylor's best work, and there is little doubt that his gifts will be duly recognised in the near future.

Whether his own ease and fluency of expression are not being undermined through lack of self-confidence, and by undue " intellectuality " in the management of the orchestra, is not for me to discuss here.

On one point you may rest perfectly assured, namely, that the young composer's race and blood, far from detracting from his progress in this country, give him a distinction as a " representative " composer that he would perhaps not otherwise enjoy.

Thanking you for your letter.—I am, yours faithfully,

LIONEL BINGHAM

(*Music Critic*).

The publication and production of *A Tale of Old Japan* are matters second only in importance in the record of Coleridge-Taylor to the appearance of *The Song of Hiawatha*. It was accepted for production by the London Choral Society, and put into rehearsal early in the autumn. The work has achieved so great a popularity since that it seems almost a work of supererogation to give any details of it. The poet has told in a ballad metre, and in verse that often reaches excellence, the story of O Kimi San, the niece of Yoichi Tenko, the painter who "dwelt by the purple sea" and taught pupils in his school. To him a brilliant scholar, Sawara, came and learned from him the secrets of his craft, and then far excelled them by his own native genius, and also became the lover of Kimi. Having learned all that Tenko could teach, Sawara departed, lightly pledging himself to Kimi, and "far away his growing fame lit the clouds," but Kimi and Tenko were forgotten, although Kimi remembered too well. After an attempt of Tenko to marry her to a rich young merchant, Kimi runs away from home and reaches a neighbouring island, where eventually she is found by Sawara, who in the interval has wedded. An intense love passage ends with the death of Kimi in his arms. It is an old and familiar story, but in this form it had simplicity, colour, romance, and tragedy. Coleridge-Taylor himself explained the sources of its appeal to him. "I think the names attracted me first. Think of ' Yoichi Tenko the painter '—the opening line—then of ' Little O Kimi San ' and ' Sawara, lissom as a cherry spray.' Then, as I read on, the beauty of the poetry and imagery held me, and I *had* to express it musically." The work is laid out for four solo voices and chorus. The method is dramatic, almost operatic, although the poem is narrative in form. Yoichi Tenko and the principal narrator parts are taken by the baritone, Sawara by the tenor, Kimi by the soprano, and the contralto has narrative parts. The work is short in its kind, and has several exquisite moments; instance may be made of the delicate and unusual introduction, which is almost ethereal in its lightness, the splendour of the chorus, "Peonies, peonies, crowned the May," the effective voice combinations in the quartet, "He could paint her tree and flower," the valuable use of the "And the ebbing sea-wave sighed," after the lovers' plighting, the flowing loveliness of the chorus, "Moon and flower and butterfly," and the harmonious treatment of Kimi's prayer. The orchestration is picturesque and pictorial, as is the use of the bells to represent Sawara "riding on a milk-white mule," the blatant brass to represent "the rich young merchant" who woos Kimi with his bags of gold; and there is a beautiful and pathetic use of the theme of Kimi's prayer for Sawara as the accompaniment in the scene where "Sawara the great painter," returning to Tenko "in royal rich array," confesses that he actually has forgotten Kimi. The work is like light through a prism, full of various beauty.

Mr. Arthur Fagge, the conductor of the London Choral Society, persuaded the composer not to attend the rehearsals until the study of the work was well advanced. Then, he tells me, "the pleasantest recollection I have of

Coleridge-Taylor was when he stood by the piano in the Memorial Hall, where we rehearsed, when the work was ready. He beamed; he had nothing to suggest; he thought the results could not be improved." At the suggestion of Mr. Fagge, however, he raised the contralto solo, "Far Away His Growing Fame," several notes, as it was in danger of being smothered by the accompaniment; another instance of his grateful willingness to accept suggestions.

The year before he had told Julien Henry that he had written parts in this work specially for him, and he was disappointed when he learnt that his friend had not been chosen to sing them at the first performance of the work. "The people selected," he wrote to Mr. Henry, *"I don't even know,* and except Miss Martyn, I've never heard any of them." He consoles him, "The work may be a frightful frost, and then look at all your trouble! This I mean really seriously, and it is only *a very little* part too! In any case, please don't worry about it; it isn't worth it. If it should be a success, I shall have every right to dictate about my principals for further hearings." The terms on which the friends stood may be gathered from words he adds later in the letter: "Do write a letter with a funny story in it, and shut up the kind of growl you wrote me yesterday for always!"

The autumn was a crowded time. Apart from his engagements, he was engrossed in his work on the second version of the *Violin Concerto* for the Connecticut Musical Festival. He makes brief reference to this in another letter to Julien Henry:

" ALDWICK,"
St. Leonard's Road,
Croydon.
November 30, 1911.

MY DEAR HENRY,—Please forgive my long silence; but I've had to treat everyone so. It's been one continual rush.

Several times I've almost got to Clifton Gardens, but

T

there has always been something within an hour's time a good way off, so it was impossible.

I haven't been indoors at tea-time for five weeks.

I do hope you and Mrs. Henry and the kiddies are all well, especially Desmond.

It would have been so nice to have heard you in *Carmen*, but my Stock Exchange rehearsals are on Fridays, and on that particular one I *had* to go to the Guildhall concert out of respect to the orchestra and Ronald.

How are you on Thursday? Can you come and hear me do the Stock Exchange concert at Queen's Hall? Please let me know.

I would send you tickets for *A Tale of Old Japan,* but Fagge hasn't given me one yet. If you come on Thursday, it will be delightful, because there is a long interval.

I am writing to Godfrey to-day about the performance of *Hiawatha* at Bournemouth.

Even now I haven't heard any soloist in my new work except Miss Felissa, who is splendid.

If I can, I'll look in next Wednesday afternoon for a little while, but I cannot promise.

I have re-written every note of my fiddle Concerto for America—it is absolutely a different work; so now I feel free to breathe again.

With kindest regards from us both to you and yours.— Yours as always,

S. COLERIDGE-TAYLOR.

A month later he makes a similar reference in writing to Mr. Read. "Are you in Eastbourne all through the holidays?" he enquires. "I ask because I've entirely re-written my *Concerto,* retaining nothing but the opening subject (which was my own), and I should rather like you to see it—there is no fiddle part yet, but there will be soon, unless Novellos want to see the MS. I think you'll like it ten thousand times better than the other—those native melodies rather tied me down." The remark on native melodies, as I show elsewhere, is explained by the fact that the first version of the *Violin Concerto* was built upon negro melodies, and this was rejected because of the limitations they imposed.

On December 7 he made his first appearance as conductor of the Stock Exchange Orchestral and Choral Society, and next evening *A Tale of Old Japan* received its first performance at Queen's Hall. The principals were Miss Leah Felissa, Miss Effie Martyn, Mr. Maurice D'Oisly, and Mr. Dalton Baker, and Coleridge-Taylor had no reason to be other than gratified by their efforts. The performance was a success in almost every way—although the composer told me that he thought the tempo was too fast—and the effect on the public was instantaneous. He had come into his own again. The critics were unanimous in their praise with one exception, and that was the somewhat superior notice in *The Daily News*, which admitted that "it sounded quite inspired by contrast with the other works present," and went on stupidly, "It is pretty, simple music, full of colour and picturesqueness. The composer has achieved his aim, and that is something." His aim, it seemed, was often beyond the understanding of this critic, and in any case to have achieved it was to have written one of the most beautiful choral works in the whole range of British music, as the public was not slow to recognise.

Performances of this work soon became as numerous as those of *Hiawatha*; and it is interesting to know that of the three most popular choral works ever written by British composers, which are Sullivan's *The Golden Legend,* and Coleridge-Taylor's *Hiawatha* and his *A Tale of Old Japan,* the second far out-distanced the first, and the *Tale* also surpassed *The Golden Legend*. To have such a record for two works of high musical quality is a circumstance of some importance. With this new and energising success, with promises of performances in various parts of the country, and with his brain and heart full of new schemes of work the year closed happily.

Our memories of the early part of 1912 are of a confused medley of engagements of all kinds, work at all hours, no rest for any length of time, a general overworking of the human machine, the operations of a spirit,

> *" A fiery soul, which working out its way*
> *Fretted the pigmy-body to decay,*
> *And o'er informed the tenement of clay."*

He confided to me in the middle of the previous year that he contemplated writing a ballet.   In 1909 he had appeared at one of the London music halls with some dances of an oriental character, and the then happy results may have encouraged him to hope for success on a larger scale, or it may be that the warm reception of Elgar's *Masque of India* in recent days at the Coliseum had furnished the suggestion.   For his subject he returned to Longfellow's "Hiawatha," but the work now planned, although it was to include the scenes of his early trilogy, was musically unconnected with it. The scenes chosen were "Hiawatha's Wooing," "The Wedding Feast," "The Famine," "Hiawatha's Departure," and "The Reunion in the Land of the Hereafter," and they were to receive subsequent arrangement in an orchestral suite.   At this work he laboured assiduously, with what were, even for him, unusual pains to realise his conception, writing and re-writing no small part of it several times.   He introduced occasional brief choruses the words of which were his own.

This work, his various societies, and his teaching account for the greater part of the first few months of the year.   He revised, however, the second version of his *Violin Concerto,* in order that it might be well studied by Madame Maud Powell for the Norfolk Musical Festival in June; and he was sincerely of the opinion that this work surpassed any previous work he had written.   If possible, his letters are briefer than usual this year, but his faculty of praising warmly he still found time to express.   "I never heard anything like your singing on Saturday," he

writes to Julien Henry on February 12. "I've not heard
you from the front for a long time. It was simply great."
At the risk of being wearisome I touch again upon this
characteristic of the man; he did not seem to understand
the ordinary jealousy to which human nature is prone;
except in so far as his own work was concerned the cold,
analytical, critical habit of mind was absolutely foreign to
him. Another letter to Mr. Henry sounds this note again,
but there is also another, more sinister, note in it:

"ALDWICK,"
March 1.

MY DEAR HENRY,—I tried to write to you immediately after
I telegraphed. Tree wants Heaven knows what to be played
over to him on Monday morning, so I shall have to make
a day of it to-morrow to get something done, and the copyist
is coming to collect it on Sunday evening.

I had to give up yesterday's Guildhall rehearsal again
because of that "tired feeling"! Have you seen the
Bournemouth papers yet? I enclose you *The Norwood News*
notice of *Old Japan.*

Are you away on Tuesday? I'm afraid you are, or
otherwise I'd look in some time after 6.30.

You're sure to have a tremendous success to-morrow,
so it's no good wishing it.

With all kinds of nice things to you both from us both.
—Yours always, S. COLERIDGE-TAYLOR.

In spite of the premonitory signs of exhaustion, he
continued his work without regard for possible consequences, as his next letter to Mr. Read, written more than
three weeks later, shows:

"ALDWICK,"
8 ST. LEONARD'S ROAD,
CROYDON.
March 27.

MY DEAR READ,—I must apologise for not answering your
other letter long before now.

The *Concerto* (in its new form) is in the hands of Maud

Powell, but I shall have it by the end of this month to score, and as I am probably coming to spend a few days at Eastbourne during Easter, I shall be able to let you have a look at it.

I am afraid I've been doing too much conducting lately (sometimes nine rehearsals a week), and have had to knock off a bit, so really I don't think I should consider any proposal to conduct again at Eastbourne.

Tree has just asked me to do the music for *Othello*,* and this has delayed my *Hiawatha* ballet for some time.

Of course, I shall be delighted to meet your sister again —either on Tuesday, when I am rehearsing the chorus, or on the concert day, Wednesday—will you tell her this?

We had a wonderful performance of *Old Japan* at Birmingham. The orchestra was really magnificent. By the way, the London Choral is repeating the performance at Queen's Hall, on April 18. I am anxious for you to hear it.

I hope you all like your new home as well as the other.

With all kindest regards to you and Mr. and Mrs. Cooper from us both.—Yours always, S. COLERIDGE-TAYLOR.

The concluding concert of the Lent term at the Guildhall School was a performance of another Gilbert-Sullivan opera; and he was delighted to receive on the day after it a letter from a member of his profession whose high position in music gave it a special value :

20 MUSWELL HILL, N.
March 31, 1912.

DEAR MR. COLERIDGE-TAYLOR,—Having attended yesterday at the performance of *The Gondoliers* at the Guildhall School of Music, and seen and heard you conduct, I feel I must write a few words of hearty and sincere congratulations on what I consider was your complete success. It is by no means every musician, nor every gifted composer, who can control a body of the amateur class, however good and reliable they may be; but you seemed to have them and the orchestra

---

* This seems to have been a slip of the pen ; he probably intended to write *The God of War*.

so entirely in your hand that the result was quite remarkable, and stamped you as cut out to make a career as a "conductor." It was a most creditable and enjoyable performance all round, and you were the pivot round which the whole well-balanced machine revolved. Once again I congratulate you, and remain your sincere friend,

FRANCESCO BERGER.

The summer term brought no relief. Mr. Landon Ronald was absent through ill-health from the Guildhall School, and an increasing amount of work fell to Coleridge-Taylor in consequence. Other work demanded his attention urgently, and it was only by rising at six in the morning and by retiring at midnight that he could compass it. I have selected a few letters written during the next two months which convey better than mere description his interests at this time :

"ALDWICK,"
ST. LEONARD'S ROAD,
CROYDON.
May 20.

MY DEAR READ,—I want to make use of you, and am therefore writing.

It is most possible that Wood is going to do my *Concerto* at one of the Proms., as well as my *Othello Suite* at Earl's Court.

Unfortunately, he will not hear of anyone playing the *Concerto* except Catterall—who, I hear, is excellent. But Catterall lives right up in Cheshire, and I have to get a copyright "performance" before *June* 4 to save performing rights. I've told Catterall, if he can come up before June 4, to do it for me; but he seems to think he cannot, in which case could you do it? *Would* you do it, rather? As you know, it is only a farce; only a half-dozen people need be present, and you need only play a few bars from each movement, *but it must be advertised* on one bill. I'll come to Eastbourne if you like, or would you rather Croydon?

Of course, you needn't *practice* it; it only need be read

through, but the "audience" will, of course, be personal friends. If you can do this, please let me know your best day—not Mondays nor Saturdays.

Kindest regards to you and Mrs. Cooper from us all.—Yours always,

S. COLERIDGE-TAYLOR.

The last concert that he conducted at the Blackheath, Brockley, and Lewisham Society was on May 4. Miss Montgomery writes : "We gave a really remarkable performance of his immortal *Hiawatha,* little dreaming how soon its creator was to claim *his* immortality. The Blackheath Concert Hall was literally packed with people, and choir and orchestra numbered over three hundred. It was the last time he conducted, and I am filled with thankfulness to remember the splendid ovation he received. During the slight pause between *The Wedding Feast* and *The Death of Minnehaha,* the trombones discovered that their parts were missing, and what might have proved a serious *contretemps* was averted by Mr. Coleridge-Taylor at once handing them his own score and conducting the rest of the performance without one. It was characteristic of him that the first thing he did after the performance was to congratulate the three trombonists on the way they read from the full score."

After one of the Blackheath rehearsals it was raining heavily, and a car was placed at his disposal to take him to the railway station. The car had not gone far when it overtook some members of the orchestra who were plodding to the station under umbrellas. He stopped the car immediately, saying : "I can't ride in this unless my friends come too." A small matter, perhaps, but very like the man.

On June 1 he writes to Miss Petherick from Leamington Spa, where he had been conducting and adjudicating at a musical festival, to apologise for not having written to her since the Blackheath concert : "I have been on the move almost ever since." The *Concerto* "copyright" performance is the subject of the next two letters to Mr. Read.

REGENT HOTEL,

ROYAL LEAMINGTON SPA.

Friday, May 30.

MY DEAR READ,—Thanks so much for yours. I have arranged for Tuesday, at 7.30.

What about a run thro'? Do you want such rehearsal, or shall we treat "it" as "it"?

I really think it unnecessary myself, and unless I hear from you I shall meet you at the hall just before 7.30.

Kindest regards. Great haste.—Yours always,

S. COLERIDGE-TAYLOR.

Please answer by return *here* by Saturday afternoon.

"ALDWICK."

June 2.

MY DEAR READ,—I didn't arrive home till midnight, to find your letter awaiting me.

No; not evening dress—only just as if you were accidentally in Croydon, and thought you would like to run through it! Only six people will be present! I cannot play a note of it myself, but that doesn't matter.

I heard some wonderful fiddle playing at Kennington Competitive Festival during the week.

You'll let me know, please, when you will arrive on Tuesday?

Kindest regards.—Yours very sincerely,

S. COLERIDGE-TAYLOR.

To Mr. Julien Henry.   "ALDWICK."

May 31.

MY DEAR HENRY,—I wish to goodness I'd known earlier. Here I am all alone till eleven or twelve with a beastly cold. Being reduced to such an extremity, I might have suggested that you should come down to a meal—you're an awfully good stop-gap when there's none better! But I am not sure that you're back in town again—are you?

I mistook your days last week, and never found out till

I 'phoned, and heard from Mrs. Henry that you were singing *that* night.

To make sure, book the 31st June for me, will you, please? Unless it thunders, I shall expect you then.

Hang your painted house! What price our roses in the side patch! Yah!

Kindest regards and things to you and Mrs. Henry from us both.—Yours always, S. COLERIDGE-TAYLOR.

CROYDON.
Sunday, June 2.

MY DEAR HENRY,—I arrived home at midnight yesterday, having been to Rhyl, North Wales, and also to Leamington all the week and more—hence the silence, which please forgive.

What do you *wish* to sing? Anything you like will suit me. If you feel inclined to do an *a* and *b*, I think "Sons of the Sea " is a good second song.

I feel so sorry about that Monday, but did I really say I was coming for sure?—or did you make it up?

The Leamington affair was splendid—singers were not much; the instrumentalists, on the other hand, were wonderfully fine—better than ever I've heard.

I don't know how it is, but I've not a grain of humour in me to-night. When it breaks out again I'll write further.

You'll send me a card about the songs?

Kindest regards from us both to you both.—Yours always,

S. COLERIDGE-TAYLOR.

To Mr. A. T. Johnson. " ALDWICK."
June 5.

DEAR MR. JOHNSON,—I had a cable from America, reading : " Great success—congratulations," which referred to my new *Violin Concerto* and *A Tale of Old Japan,* I presume performed on Tuesday.

I shouldn't have troubled you with this, but as on Tuesday evening at the Croydon Public Hall, quietly and before a special guinea (!) audience, we had a performance of the *Concerto* (for retaining performing rights).

We played it through twice. Mr. Willie Read came specially from Eastbourne to do it, and I played the orchestral parts on the piano.

I was going to invite you, but thought you'd probably be bored to death with my bad pianoforte playing!

Kindest regards.—Yours very sincerely,

S. COLERIDGE-TAYLOR.

To Mr. W. J. Read. "ALDWICK."

Sunday, June 9.

MY DEAR READ,—I ought to have written earlier to thank you for so kindly coming last Tuesday to play my *Concerto.* I was really amazed at your extraordinary power of interpretation, especially at such short notice. Everyone present was equally delighted.

You'll be pleased to know that, from a cable I received yesterday, the *Concerto* was a great success in America. I shall doubtless have details later.

I am sending you a bill and a ticket to-morrow, as you requested; and will you please let me know if you had enough to eat before you went, and also what your expenses were, however small?

I shall run down to Eastbourne one weekday or Sunday this month just for the sake of it, and will let you know in case you are free.

Kindest regards, and renewed thanks from both of us, and best of remembrances to Mrs. Cooper.—Yours very sincerely,

S. COLERIDGE-TAYLOR.

To Mr. Julien Henry. "ALDWICK."

Sunday, June 17.

MY DEAR HENRY,—Many apologies for not writing before. I've had to get all my next week's work in somehow in two days, and, as Ronald is away, I am at the Guildhall a great deal.

I do hope you'll have to go to Walsall; but how was it that *you* knew the date before I did? I only heard this morning. They give me two, and I've settled on March 20.

May I come to see you on Tuesday night after my opera

rehearsal—about 9.30? I'll only stay a few minutes. It is the only time I've got. Wednesday I go to Brighton again for the symphony concert.

My holiday is knocked on the head, as Tree has asked me to write music for Zangwill's new play, to be produced September 1.

I say, *do* come and do an "act" in our front garden one evening, will you? We'll have Japanese lanterns, etc., and I'll promise you an excellent and most appreciative audience —and incidental music (veiled) from my shed.

But I always knew you could act.

If you're out on Tuesday, please just say so on a post-card. Otherwise I shall turn up.

This makes my eighteenth letter—hence the writing. Have you seen *T. P.'s Magazine** for June?

Kindest regards from everyone to everyone.—Yours always,

S. COLERIDGE-TAYLOR.

On July 15 he wrote to Mr. Read for the last time :

> "ALDWICK,"
> ST. LEONARD'S ROAD,
> CROYDON.
> *July* 15.

MY DEAR READ,—I don't know what you'll think of me. I've simply been working against time.

You may expect to see me one day next week, as Mrs. Coleridge-Taylor is going to stay with her sister for a few days.—Kindest regards and great haste,

S. COLERIDGE-TAYLOR.

Two letters written to his former pupil, Miss Edith Carr, during this brief stay at Eastbourne, are specially interesting :

> CLIFTON HOTEL,
> EASTBOURNE,
> *Monday.*

MY DEAR MISS CARR,—I am writing to make good my sins of omission !

* An interview with himself appeared in this issue.

Will you not send me your song so that I may glance over it? I'll return it in a day or two.

And will you ask your mother to accept my thanks for a most delightful evening? It was ever so nice—the only blur was my incessant talk about myself.

And I want both you and Mrs. Carr to believe me when I tell you that my " outlook " on life is just as wholesome and beautiful as it was when I first knew you years ago.

I love the best in music, pictures and literature a thousand times more than I did when I was twenty.

I mention this because I had an idea on Friday that both you and your mother doubted this, and I hate to think of anyone (much less you two) being shaken in their belief of me.

Why didn't you offer to sing the other evening—ought I to have asked, and is your voice just as " inspired " as ever?

As you have such an excellent memory, perhaps you'll remember that was my criticism after I heard you sing for the first time !

With very kind regards to you and Mrs. Carr.—Believe me, yours always,

S. COLERIDGE-TAYLOR.

CLIFTON HOTEL,
EASTBOURNE.
Thursday.

MY DEAR MISS CARR,—I am returning your MS., and you will see I have made one or two suggestions which may or may not improve it—it is really quite charming, though not very original !

Please don't trouble to write, as I leave here to-day, and don't know where I shall be for the next day or two.

I wish you could have heard our really magnificent performance of the *New World Symphony* here.

Kindest regards to you and Mrs. Carr.—Yours in great haste,

S. COLERIDGE-TAYLOR.

On his return he made arrangements for the publication of the *Violin Concerto,* which were opened with a letter to

Mr. Charles A. Lucas, of Messrs. Metzler and Co., who eventually published the work :

" ALDWICK,"
ST. LEONARD'S ROAD,
CROYDON.
August 14.

DEAR MR. LUCAS,—Is it any use my coming to discuss my new *Violin Concerto* with you, with an idea of Metzlers publishing it?

It has recently been performed by Maud Powell in America, and she has five performances booked already for next season, including the New York Philharmonic and also Chicago—Thomas Orchestra.

Wood does it here at Queen's Hall on October 8, and I conduct it twice in Germany, at Berlin and Dresden.

If you like, I could bring some of the correspondence I have had on the matter.

I could, if you thought favourably of it, hand you the full score and a large set of parts in MS., and a fèe of £6 is to be paid to me for each of the American performances, part of which would, of course, go to you in the event of your doing it.

But I do not wish any performing fee to be charged in England, as I am sure it will hurt rather than help.

The work is not very long and not very difficult.

If you would let me know your best time, I could come any time Friday or Saturday.   I leave town on Saturday evening.

I hope the *Othello* Suite will go well.   Have copies been to the Ostend and Dieppe Orchestras, both of which have done things of mine?—Yours very truly,

S. COLERIDGE-TAYLOR.

His last letter to Mr. Julien Henry mentions the occasions on which he was mistaken for Uncle Tom, and for a Maori.   This paragraph I omit.

August 18.

My dear Henry,—It was so nice to hear from you. You see, we haven't yet gone away, but we are expecting to be off to-morrow or Thursday.

I've been too busy to go before, and the weather hasn't made me anxious!

I am trying to fix you in for Scarborough—*Tale of Japan* —if the committee can afford to engage me to go up to conduct. It hasn't quite been settled yet.

Godfrey's date is January 28, I think, or 18th; has he definitely settled with you about this yet? If not, please let me know.

Yes! thanks very much. I am to conduct my *Violin Concerto* for a Miss Whitman in Berlin and Dresden in November next, and Maud Powell has been requested to play it at the New York Philharmonic Concerts, and at Chicago, also November. Metzlers, and not Novellos, are doing it, because the latter insisted on the performing fee business. . . .

You say you got your house for the price of a song. What is exactly your idea of a song's worth? And that reminds me: I'm sending *Thou art Risen, my Beloved* for you to warble —you remember you liked it in MS. I hope you'll do ditto now its in print; and with our united kind regards, and when did you say you would be in London? because your letter is God knows where!

Best of everything from all of us to all of you.—Yours,

S. Coleridge-Taylor.

It had been a sunless year; a year of gloomy days when for weeks the sunlight was a rare visitant; a year of lowering clouds, keen winds, and cold rains; a year when summer seemed to have lost its place in the order of the seasons; when the reaped but ungathered hay rotted in brown and blackening heaps in cheerless fields; and upon Coleridge-Taylor its effect was singularly depressing. In a marked measure he was sensitive to weather influences; and the long continued absence of fair days lowered his vitality and reduced his buoyancy. As the summer drew on he would occasionally call upon Mr. Adolf Schmid, and stand shivering in the latter's office at His Majesty's Theatre. "I want sun," he would say; and to his wife he said : "If these rains do not stop I shall go mad."

August brought still unsettled weather, with a sprinkling of endurable days. As we have seen, his *Violin Concerto* was finished, and the arrangements made for its first performance by Sir Henry Wood at Queen's Hall in the coming October; the *Hiawatha Ballet* was finished, although as yet unscored; and he had done all that was possible at that time of his setting of Alfred Noyes' *Forest of Wild Thyme*. "I have never felt so free of work in my life," he said. A few weeks ahead was the prospect of holidays at Hastings; he had taken a small furnished house near the sea, and he looked forward to going there with that child-like enthusiasm which never deserted him.

It was at this time that his son, Hiawatha, contracted influenza in a severe form. This not only postponed the visit to Hastings, but required the constant devotion of Mrs. Coleridge-Taylor to the sick child. Coleridge-Taylor made no complaint, but wandered out for long lonely walks into the beautiful lanes around Croydon. His wife noticed his restlessness, and suggested that, as it seemed impossible for him to exist without working, he should commence a small religious cantata, *The Christ*, the libretto of which had made some appeal to him. He laughed, "No, I will do that for next year," and continued to amuse himself by walking. One such walk struck him as especially pleasant, along the lanes to Beddington, and across the quiet leafy road in front of Bandon Hill Cemetery, and so back in a half-circle to Croydon. In these lanes he met the organist, Mr. H. L. Balfour, whose musical and personal qualities he greatly admired, and their conversation cheered him greatly. "I was thirsting for a talk with a real musician," he said on his return.

One morning his mood seemed graver than usual. "I have had a lovely dream," he told his wife.

He was, as are most imaginative men whose genius is of the creative sort, a dreamer of many dreams; and Mrs. Coleridge-Taylor attached no immediate significance to the remark.

"What, another lovely dream?" she replied. "What is it this time?"

"Oh," was the reply, "I dreamt I saw Hurlstone in Heaven. I was just entering. Of course, we couldn't shake hands, but we embraced each other three times. You know what that means," he added, "I am going to die."

On Wednesday, August 28, he spent the morning in walking, writing letters, and playing and singing *Thou art Risen, my Beloved,* "a song," says his wife, "that we heard all day long." Apparently he was well in health. Small signs had not been wanting, which in retrospect are significant, but which then seemed unimportant. For example, he suddenly refrained from smoking cigarettes and refused tea, two things to which in general he was devoted. "During mid-day lunch," Mrs. Coleridge-Taylor writes, "he read aloud from a humorous journal, and as I could not follow the drift of the subject I asked him to stop. I thought, perhaps, that he had a headache, although from the meal he ate (which he remarked was his favourite lunch) no one could say he was not in his usual perfect health." After lunch he said : "I'll go and buy you some flowers, Jess, and take Gwennie with me." The child had been his constant companion of late owing to her brother's illness. He returned very shortly, having walked to West Croydon and come back by tram, bringing some large yellow chrysanthemums. " Here they are, Jess; aren't they lovely? " he said gaily, putting his head into the room where his wife was, and showing her the blooms.

The next half-hour Mrs. Coleridge-Taylor spent arrang-

U

ing the flowers and preparing to receive a lady who was calling for a cartoon of himself which Coleridge-Taylor had promised to sign for her. His wife thought that the

A Page of the MS. of " Thou art Risen, my Beloved."

composer was in the music-shed or had gone for one of his walks. In those days he was continually passing in and out of the house, and his absence had nothing unusual about it. What he had done, however, was to walk up to West Croydon Station and to take a ticket for the Crystal Palace, meaning to see the spectacle, "China," then on view there. At the station sudden illness overcame him, and he fell. The station is often more or less deserted, and it seems that no one saw this happen, but his own later statement and the dust upon his clothes bore witness to fact. He revived sufficiently to struggle to his feet and to make his way across the station-yard and the street to a tram. Still, strange to say, no one recognised the plight he was in. He crawled into "Aldwick." Mrs. Coleridge-Taylor, he found, had visitors; he could hear their voices in the drawing-room. Without disturbing them, he found his way upstairs to his bedroom. He was too ill to undress, but his passion for tidyness caused him to remove his boots ere placing himself upon the bed. Here his wife found him a little later, and saw at once that he was unusually ill. His doctor was summoned, but was unable to come, and sent his partner, to whom Coleridge-Taylor remarked: "I generally get a bilious attack once a year. I'll be all right in the morning." The case did not appear to be serious. He passed a somewhat restless night, and in the morning complained of severe chest pains. His own doctor came at 11.30, but did not seem to apprehend any danger. As a matter of fact, at this stage the illness itself was not important except for the fatal circumstance that he had used up his reserves of strength.

Mrs. Coleridge-Taylor nursed her husband incessantly until Saturday evening, when she was advised that a professional nurse should be engaged. In the afternoon he said to his wife: "I wish we could bore a hole through to the 'little room' so that you could go through the parts which have just come from America." He had been worried very much by the delayed return of the part of the

Violin Concerto after its first performance. "I'll do better than that, Coleridge," his wife replied. "I'll bring the parcel in here." The checking of these parts was his last work. "I shall never forget," says Mrs. Coleridge-Taylor, "his look of relief and thankfulness when he knew that the parts were all right, and therefore ready for Sir Henry Wood's use in October."

Next morning the nurse asked that the doctor might be called in, as she was alarmed by symptoms the patient had exhibited during the night. Accordingly, Mrs. Coleridge-Taylor telephoned for him; Doctor Duncan, of Croydon, who accompanied him, immediately diagnosed the illness as acute pneumonia, and pronounced Coleridge-Taylor to be in a very critical condition. From that moment his wife scarcely left his side until the end, which came at ten minutes past six in the evening. From the Saturday he was aware that he was drawing near to the Valley of the Shadow. Courage did not desert him, except for a brief moment when the unrealised possibilities of his life came vividly before him, and he broke down sobbing: "I am too young to die; I am only thirty-seven!" But the despairing mood was of short duration, and he faced the end with calm, saying that he looked forward to meeting "such a crowd of musicians." One characteristic persisted in this last illness. When he was told that the doctor was entering, he called hurriedly for a comb, and although he was so weak as scarcely to be able to lift his arm, he tried feebly to bring his hair under control with it. At intervals he was semi-conscious, and murmured many things about his friends and music. One phrase that recurred was: "When I die the papers will call me a creole." It was a last tragic irony.

Sunday, the first of September, was a calm day, one of the few pleasant days in the miserable summer. Except that he seemed weaker, there was, in the morning, no appreciable change in Coleridge-Taylor's condition. His wife read to him Allan Raine's "A Welsh Singer," a work which he admired so much that he wished someone would write him an opera libretto of the story. Soon after midday he became restless, and new doubts about his work seemed to trouble him. Later his mind reverted to the *Violin Concerto*. Propped up by pillows, he seemed to imagine an orchestra before and an audience behind him. With complete absorption, and perhaps unconsciousness of his surroundings, he conducted the work, beating time with both arms, and smiling his approval here and there. The smile never left his face, and the performance was never completed on earth. Still smiling and conducting he sank back on his pillows, and in that supreme moment of devotion to his art, his beautiful spirit set out on its voyage to the Land of the Hereafter.

In his coffin were placed masses of his favourite violets, and his love-letters. The funeral service was held at St. Michael's Church, Croydon, on September 5, on one of the rare beautiful days of the year when a soft warm light stole through the high windows of the graceful church. Long before the service commenced the building was thronged with mourners from Croydon and from all parts of England. Mr. H. L. Balfour, the organist of the Royal Choral Society, was at the organ, and during the waiting he played selections from the dead musician's works, in particular the lovely choral movement in which Chibiabos, "the sweetest of all singers, the best of all musicians," is invoked in *Hiawatha's Wedding Feast*. The service was conducted by the Rev. Canon R. W. Hoare, and the choir sang the hymn "The Saints of God." Then Mr. W. J. Read played the beautiful slow movement from the as yet unpublished *Violin Concerto in G minor,* and this, its second public performance, will live long in the memories of those who mourned him, as will the almost too poignantly pathetic rendering of his Sorrow Song, *When I am Dead, My Dearest,* by Mr. Julien Henry, which followed it. The service closed with the funeral march from *The Death of Minnehaha,* played by Mr. Balfour. At Bandon Hill

Cemetery, about two miles west of Croydon, and not far from the pretty village of Beddington, he was laid to rest amidst every sign of affection and regret.

His grave is marked to-day by a headstone of Carrara marble, with rustic outline. On the stone is the draped figure of an angel with outstretched wings, whose foot rests on clouds, and above whom is a wreath of laurel. The inscription, which is from the pen of Mr. Alfred Noyes, is as follows:

IN

MEMORY OF

SAMUEL COLERIDGE-TAYLOR

WHO DIED ON

SEPTEMBER 1st, 1912

AT THE AGE OF 37

BEQUEATHING TO THE WORLD
A HERITAGE OF AN UNDYING BEAUTY
HIS MUSIC LIVES.

IT WAS HIS OWN, AND DRAWN FROM VITAL FOUNTAINS.
IT PULSED WITH HIS OWN LIFE
BUT NOW IT IS HIS IMMORTALITY.
HE LIVES WHILE MUSIC LIVES.

TOO YOUNG TO DIE—
HIS GREAT SIMPLICITY, HIS HAPPY COURAGE
IN AN ALIEN WORLD,
HIS GENTLENESS, MADE ALL THAT KNEW HIM LOVE HIM.

SLEEP, CROWNED WITH FAME, FEARLESS OF CHANGE OR TIME,
SLEEP, LIKE REMEMBERED MUSIC IN THE SOUL,
SILENT, IMMORTAL; WHILE OUR DISCORDS CLIMB
TO THAT GREAT CHORD WHICH SHALL RESOLVE THE WHOLE.

SILENT, WITH MOZART, ON THAT SOLEMN SHORE;
SECURE, WHERE NEITHER WAVES NOR HEARTS CAN BREAK;
SLEEP, TILL THE MASTER OF THE WORLD ONCE MORE
TOUCH THE REMEMBERED STRINGS AND BID THEE WAKE.

TOUCH THE REMEMBERED STRINGS AND BID THEE WAKE.

Then follows a stave with four bars of music set to the words:

THUS DEPARTED HIAWATHA, HIAWATHA, THE BELOVED.

IN
MEMORY OF
SAMUEL
COLERIDGE-TAYLOR
WHO DIED ON
SEPTEMBER 1ST 1912
AT THE AGE OF THIRTY SEVEN
BEQUEATHING TO THE WORLD
A HERITAGE
OF AN UNDYING BEAUTY
HIS MUSIC LIVES

IT WAS HIS OWN AND
DRAWN FROM VITAL FOUNTAINS
IT PULSED WITH HIS OWN LIFE
AND NOW IT IS HIS IMMORTALITY
HE LIVES WHILE MUSIC LIVES
TOO YOUNG TO DIE
HIS GREAT SIMPLICITY
HIS HAPPY COURAGE IN AN ALIEN WORLD
HIS GENTLENESS
MADE ALL THAT KNEW HIM LOVE HIM
SLEEP CROWNED WITH FAME FEARLESS OF
CHANGE OR TIME
SLEEP LIKE REMEMBERED MUSIC IN THE SOUL
SILENT IMMORTAL WHILE OUR DISCORDS CLIMB
TO THAT GREAT CHORD WHICH SHALL
RESOLVE THE WHOLE
SILENT WITH MOZART ON THAT SOLEMN
SHORE
SECURE WHERE NEITHER WAVES NOR HEARTS
CAN BREAK
SLEEP TILL THE MASTER OF THE WORLD
ONCE MORE
TOUCH THE REMEMBERED STRINGS
AND BID THEE WAKE
TOUCH THE REMEMBERED STRINGS AND BID THEE WAKE
ALFRED NOYES

The Coleridge-Taylor Memorial, Bandon Hill Cemetery

and on the bevelled edge is the line I added at Mrs. Coleridge-Taylor's request :

ERECTED BY HIS WIFE AND OTHER LOVERS OF THE MAN
AND HIS MUSIC.

Tragic, almost, is the thought of these brief thirty-seven years; but he had lived longer than many who attain to twice his age. His memory is fragrant amongst all who touched his hand or heard his voice; he gloried in and glorified his art, and through it gave the purest pleasure to men. I have never heard of any to whom by word or deed he ever gave a moment of unhappiness; and in the record of men of fame, who have done positive work and who have faced disappointment and jealousy, there is surely no fairer praise.

APPENDIX

THE COMPOSITIONS OF SAMUEL COLERIDGE-TAYLOR

BY J. H. SMITHER JACKSON

THE following comprises a complete list of the music of Coleridge-Taylor, both published and unpublished, so far as it has been possible to trace it. Owing to the composer's somewhat erratic use of opus numbers, certain blanks still remain, and in all probability they were never filled. In one or two instances vacant numbers have been utilised by giving them to compositions of a similar period of which the numbers had inadvertently been duplicated, but this has been done as little as possible. In 1909, with the publication of the *Ballade in C minor for Violin and Pianoforte*, Op. 73, Mr. Coleridge-Taylor apparently dropped the use of opus numbers altogether; but for the sake of keeping the record of his work in some semblance of order, I persuaded him early in 1912 to devote a little time with me to revising the numbers. The list, therefore, is authentic, and may be taken to represent his views on the subject.

Op. 1. *Quintet in G minor.* (MS.)
    Pianoforte, 2 Violins, Viola, and Violoncello.
Op. 2. *Nonet in F minor.*
    Pianoforte, Wind and Strings. (MS.)
Op. 3. *Suite de Pièces.* (Schott.)
    Violin and Organ or Pianoforte. No. 1. Pastorale.—No. 2. Cavatina.—No. 3. Barcarolle.—No. 4. Contemplation.
Op. 4. *Ballade in D minor.* (Novello.)
    Violin and Orchestra. Also arranged for Violin and Pianoforte.
Op. 5. *Fantasiestücke.*
    String Quartet for two Violins, Viola, and Violoncello. Prelude. Serenade. Humoreske. Minuet. Dance.
Op. 6. *Little Songs for Little Folks.* (Boosey.)
    Sea-Shells. A Rest by the Way. A Battle in the Snow. A Parting Wish. A Sweet Little Doll. Baby Land.

Op. 7. *Zara's Ear-rings.*
Rhapsody for Voice and Orchestra. (MS.) (Imperial Institute.)

Op. 8. *Symphony in A minor.*
Orchestra. (MS.) (St. James's Hall, Royal College of Music Concert, 6.3.96.)

Op. 9. *Two Romantic Pieces.* (Augener.)
Violin and Pianoforte. Lament. Merrymaking.

Op. 10. *Quintet in A.* (Breitkopf.)
Clarinet, two Violins, Viola, and Violoncello.

Op. 11. *Dream Lovers.* (Boosey.)
Operatic Romance for two Male and two Female Characters, Chorus, and Orchestra.

Op. 12. *Southern Love Songs.* (Augener.)
No. 1. My Love.—No. 2. Tears.—No. 3. Minguillo.—No. 4. If Thou Art Sleeping, Maiden. — No. 5. Oh! My Lonely Pillow.
No. 1 also published with Orchestral Accompaniment.

Op. 13. *Quartet in D minor.* (MS.)
Two Violins, Viola, and Violoncello.

Op. 14. *Legend from the " Concertstück."* (Augener.)
Violin and Orchestra. Also arranged for Violin and Pianoforte.

Op. 15. *Land of the Sun.* (Augener.)
Part-Song (S.A.T.B.).

Op. 16. *Hiawathan Sketches.* (Augener.)
Violin and Pianoforte. No. 1. A Tale.—No. 2. A Song.—No. 3. A Dance.

Op. 17. *African Romances.* (Augener.)
No. 1. An African Love Song.—No. 2. A Prayer.—No. 3. A Starry Night. — No. 4. Dawn. — No. 5. Ballad.—No. 6. Over the Hills.—No. 7. How Shall I Woo Thee?
Nos. 6 and 7 are also published separately. No. 6 is also published with Orchestral Accompaniment.

Op. 18. *Morning and Evening Service in F.* (Novello.)
Te Deum. Benedictus. Jubilate. Magnificat and Nunc Dimittis.

Op. 19. *Two Moorish Tone-Pictures.* (Augener.)
No. 1. Andalla.—No. 2. Zarifa.
Also published separately.

Op. 20. *Gipsy Suite.* (Augener.)
Violin and Pianoforte. No. 1. Lament and Tambourine.—No. 2. A Gipsy Song.—No. 3. A Gipsy Dance.—No. 4. Waltz.
No. 3 also arranged for Violoncello and Pianoforte.

Op. 21. *Part-Songs* (S.S.A.). (Augener.)
We Strew These Opiate Flowers. How They So Softly Rest.

Op. 22. *Four Characteristic Waltzes.* (Novello.)
Full or Small Orchestra. No. 1. Valse Bohémienne.—No. 2. Valse Rustique.—No. 3. Valse De La Reine.—No. 4. Valse Mauresque.

Also arranged for Military Band (by Dan Godfrey, Jun.), Pianoforte Solo, Quintet for Pianoforte and Strings, and Violin and Pianoforte.

Op. 23. *Valse-Caprice.* (Augener.)
Violin and Pianoforte.

Op. 24. *In Memoriam.* (Augener.)
Three Rhapsodies for Low Voices and Pianoforte. No. 1. Earth Fades! Heaven Breaks on Me.—No. 2. Substitution.—No. 3. Weep not, Beloved Friends.

Op. 25. Missing.

Op. 26. *The Gitanos.* (Augener.)
Cantata-Operetta for Soprano, two Mezzo-Soprano and two Contralto Soli, three-part Female Chorus, and Pianoforte.

Op. 27. Missing.

Op. 28. Missing.

Op. 29. *Three Songs.* (Augener.)
No. 1. Lucy.—No. 2. Mary.—No. 3. Jessy.

Op. 30. *Scenes from the " Song of Hiawatha."* (Novello.)
Cantata for Soprano, Tenor, and Baritone Soli, Chorus, and Orchestra.
No. 1. *Hiawatha's Wedding Feast.* (Op. 30, No. 1.)
For Tenor Solo, Chorus, and Orchestra. (Royal College of Music, 11.11.98.)
No. 2. *The Death of Minnehaha.* (Op. 30, No. 2.)
For Soprano and Baritone Soli, Chorus, and Orchestra. (North Staffordshire Musical Festival, Hanley, 26.10.99.)
No. 3. *Overture to the Song of Hiawatha.* (Op. 30, No. 3.)
Orchestra. Also arranged for Pianoforte Solo. (Norwich Musical Festival, 6.10.99.)
No. 4. *Hiawatha's Departure.* (Op. 30, No. 4.)
For Soprano, Tenor, and Baritone Soli, Chorus, and Orchestra. (Royal Choral Society, Royal Albert Hall, 22.3.00.)
Nos. 1, 2, and 4 are published separately. No. 3 is a separate work. No. 1 is also published with German words.
The following Songs are also published separately from above, with Orchestral or Pianoforte Accompaniments :—
a. Onaway! Awake, Beloved (from No. 1). *b.* Spring Had Come (from No. 4). *c.* Hiawatha's Vision (from No. 4).
b. and *c.* are also published with German words.

Op. 31. *Three Humoresques.* (Augener.)
Pianoforte. No. 1 in D. No. 2 in G minor. No. 3 in A.
Nos. 1 and 3 are also published separately.

Op. 32. Missing..

Op. 33. *Ballade in A minor.* (Novello.)
Orchestra. Also arranged for Pianoforte Solo. (Gloucester Musical Festival, 14.9.98.)

Op. 34. Missing.

Op. 35. *African Suite.* (Augener.)

Pianoforte. No. 1. Introduction.—No. 2. A Negro Love Song.—No. 3. A Valse.—No. 4. Danse Nègre.

Nos. 2 and 4 are also published separately. No. 4 is also arranged for Orchestra. Nos. 2 and 4 are also arranged for Violin and Pianoforte.

Op. 36. *Nourmahal's Song and Dance.* (Augener.)

Pianoforte Solo. No. 1. Nourmahal's Song.—No. 2. Nourmahal's Dance.

No. 1 is also published separately.

Op. 37. *Six Songs.* (Novello.)

No. 1. You'll Love Me Yet.—No. 2. Canoe Song.—No. 3. A Blood-red Ring Hung Round the Moon.—No. 4. Sweet Evenings Come and Go, Love.—No. 5. As the Moon's Soft Splendour.—No. 6. Eleänore.

Published separately. No. 6 is also published with Orchestral Accompaniment.

Op. 38. *Three Silhouettes.* (Ashdown.)

Pianoforte Solo. Valse. Tambourine. Lament.

Published separately.

Op. 39. *Romance in G.* (Novello.)

Violin and Orchestra. Also arranged for Violin and Pianoforte by Theophile Wendt.

Op. 40. *Solemn Prelude.* (Novello.)

Orchestra. Also arranged for Pianoforte Solo. (Worcester Musical Festival, 13.9.99.)

Op. 41. *Scenes from an Everyday Romance.* (Novello.)

Suite for Orchestra. No. 1 in E minor. No. 2 in G major. No. 3 in B minor. No. 4 in E minor. Also arranged for Pianoforte Solo. (Queen's Hall, Philharmonic Society's Concert, 24.5.00.)

Op. 42. *The Soul's Expression.* (Novello.)

Four Sonnets for Contralto Solo and Orchestra or Pianoforte. No. 1. The Soul's Expression.—No. 2. Tears.—No. 3. Grief. —No. 4. Comfort. (Hereford Musical Festival, 13.9.00.)

Op. 43. *The Blind Girl of Castél-Cuillé.* (Novello.)

Cantata for Soprano and Baritone Soli, Chorus and Orchestra. (Leeds Musical Festival, 9.10.01.)

Op. 44. *Idyll.* (Novello.)

Orchestra. Also arranged for Violin and Pianoforte.

Op. 45. *Six American Lyrics.* (Novello.)

Contralto or Baritone. No. 1. O Thou, Mine Other, Stronger Part.—No. 2. O Praise Me Not.—No. 3. Her Love.— No. 4. The Dark Eye Has Left Us. — No. 5. O Ship That Saileth.—No. 6. Beat, Beat, Drums.

Published separately. No. 6 is also published with Orchestral Accompaniment.

Op. 46. *Toussaint l' Ouverture.* (Novello.)
　　　Concert Overture for Orchestra. (Queen's Hall, 26.10.01.)

Op. 47. *Incidental Music to " Herod."* (Augener.)
　　　Orchestra.—No. 1. Processional.—No. 2. Breeze Scene.—No. 3.
　　　Dance.—No. 4. Finale. Also arranged for Pianoforte
　　　Solo and Pianoforte Duet.
　　　Nos. 2 and 3 are also published separately
　　　Song.—Sleep, Sleep, O King. (Enoch.)

Op. 47. No. 2. *Hemo Dance.* (Novello.)
　　　Scherzo for Orchestra. Also arranged for Violin and Piano-
　　　forte.

Op. 48. *Meg Blane.* (Novello.)
　　　A Rhapsody of the Sea, for Mezzo-Soprano Solo, Chorus, and
　　　Orchestra. (Sheffield Musical Festival, 3.10.02.)
　　　The Epilogue, " Lord, Hearken to Me," is also published sepa-
　　　rately.

Op. 49. *Incidental Music to " Ulysses."*
　　　Orchestra. (MS.)
　　　Two Songs for Tenor and one Part-Song for S.S.A. (Novello.)
　　　Published as under :—
　　　Songs.—Great is He Who Fused the Might (Drinking Song).
　　　O Set the Sails.
　　　Part-Song.—From the Green Heart of the Waters.

Op. 50. *Three Song-Poems.* (Enoch.)
　　　No. 1. Dreaming for Ever.—No. 2. The Young Indian Maid.—
　　　No. 3. Beauty and Song.
　　　Also published separately.

Op. 51. *Ethiopia Saluting the Colours.* (Augener.)
　　　Concert March for Orchestra. Also arranged for Pianoforte
　　　Solo and Pianoforte Duet, and for Organ Solo by Edmond-
　　　stoune Duncan. (Albani Commemoration Concert, Albert
　　　Hall).

Op. 52. *Four Novelletten.* (Novello.)
　　　String Orchestra, Tambourine, and Triangle. No. 1 in A.
　　　No. 2 in C. No. 3 in A minor. No. 4 in D. Also arranged
　　　for Violin and Pianoforte.

Op. 53. *The Atonement.* (Novello.)
　　　Sacred Cantata for Mezzo-Soprano, Contralto, Baritone and
　　　Tenor Soli, Chorus and Orchestra. (Hereford Musical
　　　Festival, 9.9.03.)

Op. 54 *Five Choral Ballads.* (Breitkopf.)
　　　For Baritone Solo, Chorus, and Orchestra. No. 1. Beside the
　　　Ungathered Rice He Lay (S.A.T.B.). — No. 2a. She
　　　Dwells by Great Kenhawa's Side (S.S.A.). — No. 2b. She
　　　Dwells by Great Kenhawa's Side (S.A.T.B.). — No. 3.
　　　Loud He Sang the Psalm of David (S.A.T.B.).—No. 4.

The Quadroon Girl (Baritone Solo and S.S.A.). — No. 5. In Dark Fens of the Dismal Swamp (S.A.T.B.). (Norwich Musical Festival, 1905.)

Each number is also published separately, and Nos. 1, 2*b*, and 3, and Nos. 4 and 5 also in two separate books.

Op. 55. *Moorish Dance.* (Augener.)
Pianoforte Solo.

Op. 56. *Cameos.* (Augener.)
Pianoforte Solo. No. 1 in F. No. 2 in D minor. No. 3 in G. No. 3 is also arranged for Full and Small Orchestra.

Op. 57. *Six Sorrow Songs.* (Augener.)
Oh, What Comes Over the Sea. When I am Dead, My Dearest. Oh, Roses for the Flush of Youth. She Sat and Sang Alway. Unmindful of the Roses. Too Late for Love.

Each number is also published separately. Unmindful of the Roses is also published with Orchestral Accompaniment.

Op. 58. *Four African Dances.* (Augener.)
Violin and Pianoforte. No. 1 in G minor. No. 2 in F. No. 3 in A. No. 4 in D minor.

Op. 59. *Twenty-four Negro Melodies.* (Oliver Ditson Co.)
Transcribed for Pianoforte Solo. No. 1. At the Dawn of Day. — No. 2. The Stones Are Very Hard. — No. 3. Take Nabandji. — No. 4. They Will Not Lend Me a Child.—No. 5. Song of Conquest. — No. 6. Warriors' Song. — No. 7. Oloba.—No. 8. The Bamboula.—No. 9. The Angels Changed My Name. — No. 10. Deep River. — No. 11. Didn't My Lord Deliver Daniel ? — No. 12. Don't Be Weary, Traveller.—No. 13. Going Up.—No. 14. I'm Troubled in Mind.—No. 15. I Was Way Down A-Yonder.—No. 16. Let Us Cheer the Weary Traveller. — No. 17. Many Thousand Gone. — No. 18. My Lord Delivered Daniel. — No. 19. Oh, He Raise a Poor Lazarus.—No. 20. Pilgrim's Song.—No. 21. Run, Mary, Run.—No. 22. Sometimes I Feel Like a Motherless Child.—No. 23. Steal Away.—No. 24. Wade in the Water.

Nos. 4, 11, 15, 18, and 22 are also transcribed for Violin, Violoncello, and Pianoforte (published) and for Orchestra (MS.).

No. 10 is also transcribed for Violin and Pianoforte by Maud Powell.

Op. 60. *Romance.* (Augener.)
Violin and Pianoforte.

Op. 61. *Kubla Khan.* (Novello.)
Rhapsody, for Mezzo-Soprano Solo, Chorus, and Orchestra (Queen's Hall, Handel Society, London, 1906.)

Op. 62. *Incidental Music to " Nero."* (Novello.)

Orchestra. Prelude, Intermezzo (Singing Girls' Chorus), Eastern Dance, First Entr'acte, Second Entr'acte (Poppæa), Processional March.

Suite of Four Pieces.

Prelude, Intermezzo, Eastern Dance, Finale (First Entr'acte).

Also arranged for Violin and Pianoforte: Eastern Dance, Intermezzo (Singing Girls' Chorus), Prelude, First Entr'acte, Second Entr'acte (Poppæa).

Also arranged for Pianoforte Solo: Eastern Dance, Intermezzo (Singing Girls' Chorus), Prelude, Processional March, First Entr'acte, Second Entr'acte. (Poppæa.)

Suite of Four Pieces. No. 1. Prelude.—No. 2. Intermezzo.—No. 3. Eastern Dance.—No. 4. Finale (First Entr'acte).

Op. 63. *Symphonic Variations on an African Air.* (Novello.)

Orchestra. Also arranged for Pianoforte. (Queen's Hall, Philharmonic Society's Concert, 14.6.06.)

Op. 64. *Scènes de Ballet.* (Augener.)

Pianoforte Solo. No. 1 in C. No. 2 in A. No. 3 in A flat. No. 4 in B flat.

Op. 65. *Endymion's Dream.* (Novello.)

One-Act Opera for Soprano and Tenor Soli, Chorus, and Orchestra. (Brighton Musical Festival, 4.2.10.)

Another version of "Who Calls?" (the Tenor Scena from above) is published separately.

Op. 66. *Forest Scenes.* (Augener.)

Five Characteristic Pieces. Pianoforte Solo. No. 1 in A minor. The Lone Forest Maiden.—No. 2 in E flat. The Phantom Lover Arrives.—No. 3 in E. The Phantom tells His Tale of Longing.—No. 4 in E. Erstwhile They Ride; The Forest Maiden Acknowledges Her Love.—No. 5 in C. Now Proudly They Journey Together Towards the Great City.

No. 3 is also published separately.

Op. 67. Part-Songs (S.A.T.B.) (Augener.)

All My Stars Forsake Me. Dead on the Sierras. The Feast of Almachara.

Op. 68. *Bon Bon Suite.* (Novello.)

Cantata for Baritone Solo, Chorus, and Orchestra. No. 1. The Magic Mirror.—No. 2. The Fairy Boat.—No. 3. To Rosa. — No. 4. Love and Hymen. — No. 5. The Watchman.—No. 6. Say, What Shall We Dance? (First Complete Performance, Brighton Musical Festival, 14.1.09.)

Op. 69. *Sea-drift.* (Novello.)

Rhapsody for Unaccompanied Eight-Part Chorus
(S.S.A.A.T.T.B.B.)

Op. 70. *Incidental Music to "Faust."* (Boosey.)

Orchestral Suite. Dance of Witches (Brocken Scene).

The Four Visions: No. 1. "Helen."—No. 2. "Cleopatra."—No. 3. "Messalina."—No. 4. "Margaret."

Dance and Chant (Devil's Kitchen Scene).
Also arranged for Pianoforte Solo.
Song.—A King there Lived in Thule.

Op. 71. *Valse Suite.* (Augener.)
Three Fours. Pianoforte Solo. No. 1 in A minor. No. 2 in A flat. No. 3 in G minor. No. 4 in D. No. 5 in E flat. No. 6 in C minor.

Op. 72. *Thelma.*
Grand Opera in Three Acts. (MS.)

OP. 73. *Ballade in C minor.* (Augener.)
Violin and Pianoforte.

Op. 74. *Scenes from an Imaginary Ballet.* (Schirmer.)
Suite for Pianoforte Solo. No. 1 in D. No. 2 in B flat. No. 3 in G. No. 4 in A flat. No. 5 in A minor. Each number is also published separately. Also arranged for Orchestra by Elliott Schenck. (Lafleur.)

Op. 75. *The Bamboula, Rhapsodic Dance.* (Hawkes.)
Orchestra. (Norfolk Musical Festival, Conn., U.S.A., 1911.)

Op. 76. *A Tale of Old Japan.* (Novello.)
Cantata for Soprano, Contralto, Tenor, and Baritone Soli Chorus, and Orchestra. (Queen's Hall, London Choral Society, 1911.)

Op. 77. *Petite Suite de Concert.* (Hawkes.)
Full or Small Orchestra. No. 1. La Caprice de Nanette.— No. 2. Demande et Réponse.—No. 3. Un Sonnet d'Amour.—No. 4. La Tarantel'e frétillante.
No. 2 is also arranged for Pianoforte Solo and Violin and Pianforte.

Op. 78. *Three Impromptus.* (Weekes.)
Organ. No. 1 in F. No. 2 in C. No. 3 in A minor. Also arranged for Pianoforte Solo by Purcell J. Mansfield.

Op. 79. *Incidental Music to " Othello."* (Metzler.)
Orchestral Suite. No. 1. Dance.—No. 2. Children's Intermezzo. —No. 3. Funeral March.—No. 4. The Willow Song.— No. 5. Military March. Also arranged for Pianoforte Solo.
Song.—The Willow Song.

Op. 80. *Concerto in G minor.* (Metzler.)
Violin and Orchestra. Also arranged for Violin and Pianoforte. Second Movement is also published separately for Violin and Orchestra, and Violin and Pianoforte, and for Organ Solo by J. Stuart Archer. (Norfolk Musical Festival, Conn., U.S.A., 1911.)

Op. 81. *Two Songs with Orchestral or Pianoforte Accompaniment.*
No. 1. Waiting (Boosey). No. 2. Red o' the Dawn. (Augener.)

Op. 82. *" Hiawatha " Ballet in Five Scenes.* (MS.)
Orchestra. No. 1. Hiawatha's Wooing. — No. 2. The Wedding Feast.—No. 3. The Famine.—No. 4. The Departure.—

No. 5. The Re-union in the Land of the Hereafter. Also arranged for Pianoforte Solo.

WORKS WITHOUT OPUS NUMBERS

ACCOMPANIMENTS TO POEMS. (MS.)

Clown and Columbine. The Parting Glass. St. Agnes' Eve. (Keats-Shelley Matinée, 1912.)

ANTHEMS

Break Forth Into Joy (Novello). By the Waters of Babylon (Novello). In Thee, O Lord, Have I Put My Trust (Novello). Lift Up Your Heads (Novello). Now Late on the Sabbath Day (Novello). O Ye That Love the Lord (Novello). The Lord is My Strength (Novello). What Thou Hast Given Me (Weekes.)

HYMN TUNE

Luconor, " Jesu, the very thought of Thee." (Methodist S.S. Hymnal.)

ORCHESTRA

Incidental Music to the " Forest of Wild Thyme."
  Part published, and remainder and Songs in MS.
  Published :
    Three Dream Dances. (Ascherberg.) Orchestra.
      No. 1 in D. No. 2 in F. No. 3 in G.
      Also arranged for Pianoforte Solo.
    Intermezzo. (Ascherberg.) Orchestra.
      Also arranged for Pianoforte Solo.
      Op. 74, Scenes from an Imaginary Ballet (Schirmer), forms part of this work.
From the Prairie, Rhapsody. (MS.) (Norfolk Musical Festival, Conn., U.S.A., 1914.)
      Also arranged for Pianoforte Solo.
Re-orchestration of the Accompaniments to Ernst's Violin Concerto in F minor. (MS.)

ORGAN

Arietta. (Novello.)
  (" The Village Organist," Book 16.)
Elegy. (Novello.)
  (" The Village Organist," Book 15.)
Melody. (Novello.)
  (" The Village Organist," Book 12.)
Album. (Augener.) *In the Press.* (Arranged by Dr. A. Eaglefield Hull.)

PART-SONGS

S.A.
  Beauty and Truth (Curwen). Drake's Drum (original form. Curwen). Fall on Me Like a Silent Dew (Curwen). Oh ! the Summer (Curwen). Viking Song (original form. Curwen).

APPENDIX

321

S.S.A.

Encinctured with a Twine of Leaves (Novello). A June Rose
Bloomed (Augener). The Pixies (Novello). What Can Lambkins
Do? (Novello).

T.T.B.B.

All Are Sleeping, Weary Heart (Curwen). Drake's Drum (arranged
by P. E. Fletcher. Curwen). Loud Sang the Spanish Cavalier (Curwen). O Mariners, Out of the Sunlight (Curwen). O, Who Will Worship the Great God Pan? (Curwen). Viking Song (arranged by P. E.
Fletcher. Curwen).

S.A.T.B.

By the Lone Seashore (Novello). The Evening Star (Novello). The
Lee-Shore (Novello). The Sea-Shell (Curwen). Song of Proserpine
(Novello). Summer is Gone (Curwen). Viking Song (arranged by
P. E. Fletcher. Curwen). Whispers of Summer (Novello).

Unison.

Prayer for Peace (Curwen).

PIANOFORTE SOLO

Papillon. (Augener.)

Two Impromptus. (Augener.) No. 1 in A. No. 2 in B minor. Published separately.

Two Oriental Valses. (Forsyth.)

No. 1. Haidée.—No. 2. Zuleika. Published separately.

Album of Melodies. (Edited, arranged and revised by A. Roloff.)
(Augener.)

Idyll. From the East. Serenade. Cameo. Minguillo. Zarifa.
In the Sierras. Reflection.

SONGS

Ah, Sweet, Thou Little Knowest! (Ricordi). A Birthday (Metzler.
Also published with Orchestral Accompaniment). Candle Lighting
Time (John Church). A Corn Song (Boosey. Also published with
Orchestral Accompaniment). The Easter Morn (Enoch. Also with
Violin, Violoncello, or Organ Obligato). Eulalie (Boosey). An Ex-
planation (Augener). The Links o' Love (John Church). Love's
Mirror (Augener). A Lovely Little Dream (Metzler. Also published
with Orchestral Accompaniment). Low Breathing Winds (Augener).
My Doll (Boosey). My Lady (Augener). O Mistress Mine (O.
Ditson). Once Only (O. Ditson). She Rested by the Broken Brook
(O. Ditson). The Shoshone's Adieu (Boosey. Also published with
Orchestral Accompaniment). Song of the Nubian Girl (Augener).

Five Fairy Ballads. (Boosey.)

Sweet Baby Butterfly. Alone with Mother. Big Lady Moon. The
Stars. Fairy Roses. (Each number is also published separately. Sweet Baby Butterfly and Big Lady Moon are also
published with Orchestral Accompaniment.)

V

Five-and-Twenty Sailormen (John Church). The Gift - Rose (O. Ditson). The Guest (Augener. Also published with Orchestral Accompaniment). If I Could Love Thee (Presser). A Lament (Ricordi). Life and Death (Augener. Also published with Orchestral Accompaniment). My Algonquin (Summy).

Songs of Sun and Shade.

No. 1. You Lay So Still in the Sunshine.—No. 2. Thou Hast Bewitched Me, Beloved.—No. 3. The Rainbow Child.—No. 4. Thou Art Risen, My Beloved. — No. 5. This is the Island of Gardens. (Boosey.) (Each number is also published separately. No. 4 is also published with Orchestral Accompaniment.)

Sons of the Sea (Novello. Also published with Orchestral Accompaniment). The Oasis (Augener). Our Idyll (Augener). A Summer Idyll (Enoch). Tell, O Tell Me (Augener). Thou Art (Presser). The Three Ravens (arranged. Boosey). The Vengeance (MS.). Viking Song (Curwen; arranged by Percy E. Fletcher). A Vision (Presser).

Duet for Soprano and Tenor. (Novello.)

Keep Those Eyes.

VIOLIN

Slow Movement on a Negro Melody. (No. 10 Deep River.) Violin and Pianoforte. (MS.)

Transcription of the "Allegretto Grazioso" from Dvořák's Symphony in G major. Op. 88. Violin and Pianoforte. (Novello.)

VIOLONCELLO

Variations for Violoncello and Pianoforte. (MS.)

INDEX

INDEX

Printed by Cassell & Company, Limited, La Belle Sauvage, London, E.C.
F. 15.1015